MW00632587

GREAT BASIN
WILDFLOWERS

A Guide to
Common Wildflowers of the High Deserts of
Nevada, Utah, and Oregon

LAIRD R. BLACKWELL

FALCON GUIDE®

GUILFORD, CONNECTICUT
HELENA, MONTANA
AN IMPRINT OF THE GLOBE PEQUOT PRESS

A FALCON GUIDE®

Text design: Nancy Freeborn
Map by Stephen Stringall © 2006 Morris Book Publishing, LLC.
Photo credits: All photos by Laird R. Blackwell unless otherwise indicated.

Library of Congress Cataloging-in-Publication Data
Blackwell, Laird R. (Laird Richard), 1945-
  Great Basin wildflowers : a guide to common wildflowers of the high deserts of Nevada, Utah, and
Oregon / Laird R. Blackwell. — 1st ed.
    p. cm.
  Includes bibliographical references and index.
  ISBN 0-7627-3805-7
  1. Wild flowers—Great Basin—Identification. 2. Wild flowers—Great Basin—Pictorial works.   I. Title.
QK141.B53 2005
582.130979—dc22

                                                                                    2005025100

Manufactured in China
First Edition/First Printing

The author and The Globe Pequot Press assume no liability for accidents happening to, or injuries sustained by, readers who engage in the activities described in this book. Neither the author nor the publisher in any way endorses the consumption or other uses of wild plants that are mentioned in this book, and they assume no liability for personal accident, illness, or death related to these activities.

TO THE WILDFLOWERS:

Their beauty can heal and their joy is contagious.

AND TO MELINDA,

my love and cherished wildflower.

Wheeler Peak (13,063') in Great Basin National Park

CONTENTS

ACKNOWLEDGMENTS

First and foremost I would like to acknowledge the wildflowers themselves for their generosity of spirit and unabashed enthusiasm. With the tumult and unpredictability of human events, there is something so reassuring and comforting about the return of the wildflowers every spring and summer. Their lavish beauty and unrestrained exuberance remind us of what truly matters in life, and their rapid and repeating life cycles help us to treasure both the moment and the larger context of continuity and meaning. These glorious floral creatures help us see life as Goethe so beautifully described it— as "formation, transformation, eternal soul's re-creation."

And, of course, I'd like to acknowledge my human companions and fellow voyagers— the many students, friends, and colleagues over the years who have shared their love of things wild and have done their best to nourish and protect them. Not only have they nurtured life in the wild, but they have deepened and enlarged the wild in my soul.

And lastly, to the wonderful folks at The Globe Pequot Press who give so much time and energy and expertise to work with authors to create beautiful testaments to nature's wonders. In particular, I would like to thank editor Erin Turner, with whom it was such a pleasure and a joy to work.

INTRODUCTION

About the Great Basin and Its Flora

The Great Basin is a term coined by the explorer John C. Fremont in the mid-1800s for that vast sink in the American West corralled between the Sierra Nevada Range of California to the west and the Wasatch Range (of the Rocky Mountains) to the east, and between the Mojave Desert to the south and the Snake River Plain of southern Idaho to the north. There are several slightly different ways to delineate the boundaries of this area (see Trimble's fascinating natural history of the Great Basin, *The Sagebrush Ocean,* for a detailed discussion), but for the purposes of this book we'll adopt the definition used by Mozingo in his *Shrubs of the Great Basin* (see map page 2). Our Great Basin, then, will include most of the northern two-thirds of Nevada (excluding the Jarbidge Mountains and the Tahoe Basin), a touch of eastern California (in the south the Mono Lake area, the Sweetwater Mountains, and the White Mountains, and in the north the Honey Lake/Eagle Lake area), a bit of southeastern Oregon (including Steens Mountain), and most of western Utah (excluding the extreme southwestern corner) up to the Wasatch Range.

This Great Basin, this protected sink between the mountains, is a vast and isolated place with miles between people and months between rains. With an overall annual average of 9 inches of precipitation (most of which is snow), this is an achingly dry place where summers bake, winters bite, and the winds just keep blowing. In many people's minds this is a place of desolate landscapes, of barren salt playas and endless sagebrush plains. Surely a book about the wildflowers of such a place would be notable only for its brevity and distinguished only by its monotony!

But let's not be so quick to dismiss this place and its flora. It turns out that the Great Basin, this "barren" and "inhospitable" land, boasts more than 2,000 species of wildflowers—a large and widespread flora exceeded by that of only a few areas in the Union. How is this possible? What secret does this land hold?

Part of the secret—but only a small part—is the Mojave Desert to the south. Some of its diverse desert flora reaches up into the southern parts of the Great Basin, especially in the lower elevations of the mostly arid White Mountains in the southwest corner of the Basin. There are also desert regions in the north parts of the Basin, notably the Black Rock Desert in Nevada, the Alford Desert in Oregon, and the Great Salt Lake Desert in Utah. Although these all have some of their own desert flora, none has anything approaching the

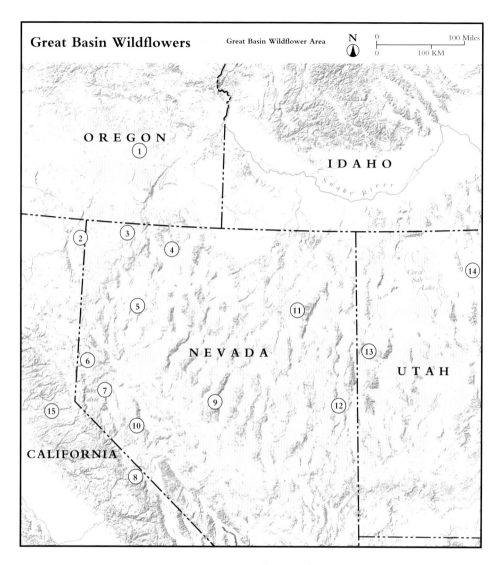

Great Basin Wildflowers

Great Basin Wildflower Area

N

0   100 Miles
0   100 KM

OREGON

IDAHO

Snake River

NEVADA

Great Salt Lake

UTAH

CALIFORNIA

Lake Tahoe

1   Steens Mountain
2   Goose Lake
3   Sheldon National Wildlife Refuge
4   Santa Rosa Range
5   Soldier Meadow
6   Peavine Mountain
7   Washoe Valley/Carson Valley
8   White Mountains

9   Toiyabe Range and Toquima Range
10 Wassuk Range
11 Ruby Mountains
12 Great Basin National Park
13 Deep Creek Range
14 Wasatch Range (Rocky Mountains)
15 Sierra Nevada Range

size or diversity of the flora of the Mojave Desert, so they add only a little to the flora of the Great Basin.

Most of the secret is in the mountains—the mountains within the Great Basin itself *and* the mountains just outside it. Yes, the Great Basin is an extensive sink, but it's a most unusual sink filled with range after range of mountains. To most people's surprise this area between the Sierra and the Rockies is the nation's most mountainous region with (depending on what is considered to be a "range") somewhere between 150 and 300 mountain ranges. Most of these ranges are north-south or northeast-southwest oriented and are 30 to 70 miles long and 10 or so miles wide—an armada of battleships neatly lined up and practically filling the Basin. Some of these ranges, mostly those along the western and eastern edges and in central Nevada, have peaks that rival in elevation the highest peaks in the Sierra and the Rockies. Although some of these ranges are as dry as the plains they rise above, many are not—many are lush "islands" in the sagebrush and shadscale "seas" with springs and melting snow, aspen groves and conifer forests, rushing streams and even lakes, and large and diverse montane floras. And some of the higher peaks, near their summits, even harbor an arctic/alpine flora more typical of the Far North and of the Sierra Nevada and the Rockies.

And this leads us to the other part of the secret of the mountains—the powerful influence of the floras of the Sierra/Cascades and the Rockies on the floras of the Great Basin mountains near them. In eastern California and western Nevada, the floras of the ranges just to the east of the Sierra Nevada—for example, the White Mountains (with White Mountain at 14,216 feet), the Sweetwater Mountains, the Virginia Range—the Pine Nut Mountains, the Wassuk Range, and Peavine Mountain (a desert outlier of the Carson Range)—show a considerable Sierra influence, especially in the higher elevations. For example, in the Sweetwater Mountains more than 90 percent of the montane alpine flora can also be found in the Sierra. Similarly, in western Utah and eastern Nevada, the floras of the Great Basin ranges that lie to the west of the Wasatch Range—for example, the Deep Creek Mountains, the Snake Range (with Wheeler Peak at 13,063 feet), the Schell Creek Range, and the Ruby Mountains (with magnificent Lamoille Canyon)—are strongly influenced by the Rocky Mountain flora. In southern Oregon, where there are few significant ranges between the Cascades to the west and the Rockies to the east, Steens Mountain (at nearly 10,000 feet) is an island rising above the Alford Desert and sagebrush plain. Its extremely rich flora have major components in common with both the Rockies and the Cascades.

So, though much of the Great Basin is indeed a "sagebrush ocean," there is considerably more to its flora than this—literally hundreds of "island" oases and the ever-present

Washoe Valley and Washoe Lake, just east of the Carson Range

influence of the massive Sierra Nevada Range and Rocky Mountains. And even those seemingly endless, homogeneous plains of sagebrush are not so floristically monotonous as they may first appear. A great diversity of wildflowers is tucked in between the shrubs, which can provide spectacular mosaics of color, especially in years of better-than-average winter and spring rain.

From desert plains to alpine tundra, from sand dunes and edges of salt playas to aspen groves and mountain streams, from sagebrush and shadscale "oceans" to pinyon-juniper woodlands and conifer forests, the Great Basin is blessed with diverse habitats and a rich and diverse flora. So, perhaps this wildflower guide to the Great Basin won't be so brief or monotonous after all. Instead, it just might be a glorious celebration of and tribute to the beautiful land and flowers of a truly fascinating region.

How to Use This Book

The main purpose of this book is to help you get to know some of the common and a few of the not-so-common wildflowers of the Great Basin—to help you find the flowers you seek, identify the flowers you find, and understand and appreciate a little of the flowers' lives. As interesting as identifying and naming are, I hope you also take the time to come to know these flowers as companions and fellow journeyers.

The book has several features that I hope will prove user friendly and helpful in accomplishing these goals.

1.) There are over 340 species of flowering plants identified (most herbs, a few shrubs), which are organized into sections by color (first blue, then red, yellow, white, and green or brown). Within each color section the flowers are sequenced alphabetically by family, and within family alphabetically by genus and species.

2.) For each plant there is one photograph of the entire plant or of the flower taken in the field; in some cases there is a second photograph showing special features. All the photographs were taken without filters (except UV), without artificial light, and without artificial backgrounds. No flowers were picked or damaged.

3.) In the narrative for each flower, there is a:

a. **Description** section, which presents key identifying characteristics, some information about the plant's life, and usually some subjective impressions.

b. **Flowering Season** section, which indicates the months you will find the flower in bloom somewhere in the Great Basin. Generally speaking, plants growing further south and/or at lower elevations will be in bloom toward the earlier part of the season, while plants growing further north and/or at higher elevations will be in bloom toward the later part of the season.

c. **Habitat/Range** section, which indicates the type of environment the plant typically inhabits (e.g., rocky, grassy meadows, streambanks), the plant's elevation range (in feet), and the plant's geographical distribution within the Great Basin (i.e., eastern California, southern Oregon, western Utah, western, northwestern, northeastern, eastern, and central Nevada). See the map on page 2 for the boundaries of the Nevada areas.

In addition, the "vegetation zone(s)" in which the plant typically occurs are also indicated. There are many ways to specify where a plant occurs, some much more technical and precise than others. I have chosen a very simple (and rough) way that will give you a general idea of what type of zone or "community" the plant can be expected in. The zones used here are (1) at the lowest elevations, the "desert shrub" (or shadscale); (2) at somewhat higher elevations with a little more precipitation, the "sagebrush steppe," sometimes including at its higher reaches pinyon-juniper woodlands; (3) at still higher elevations (in some places), the "montane" (which can be mixed conifer forest or mountain shrub), sometimes including at its higher reaches subalpine forest; and (4) at the highest elevations on some of the Great Basin's highest peaks above timberline, the "alpine" tundra. (See Cronquist et al., *Intermountain Flora,* Vol.1, for a much more detailed and precise delineation.)

In addition, one or two places in the Great Basin where the plant occurs are indicated, so you will have a more specific idea of where to look. These indicated places are, however, broad (e.g., Steens Mountain, Washoe Valley, the Ruby Mountains), so you will still have a challenge and an adventure to find the plant.

d. **Comments** section, which explains the meaning or derivation of the genus and species names. Sometimes the Latin names can reveal much about a plant's characteristics or human history.

4.) There are indexes in the back of the book for families (common names) and their genera, and for the common and scientific names of all the plants included in this book.

5.) There are plant lists (of the plants included in this book) for four special areas: (1) Steens Mountain in the north, (2) Peavine Mountain in the west, (3) the White Mountains in the south, and (4) Great Basin National Park in the east.

6.) There is a map in the Introduction delineating the Great Basin as defined in this book and delineating its major geographical divisions.

7.) In the introduction there is a brief discussion of 13 special genera (e.g., *Mimulus*) and types of flowers (e.g., "yellow sunflower") to help you understand that genus or type and to help you know what to look for to distinguish species within it and an illustrated glossary to further assist you.

There is a glossary in the back of the book that provides an explanation of some of the scientific terminology used here to describe flowers—terms such as *involucre, raceme,* and *umbel.* You can glance through this glossary before you begin the book to familiarize yourself with these terms or just turn to it while you're reading whenever you run in to an unfamiliar word.

Wildflower lovers seeking even more information about flora in the Great Basin and the intermountain West can turn to the references section at the end of this book.

Hopefully, you will find some or all of these features helpful in coming to better know the wildflowers of the Great Basin. These wonderful flowers are a familiar joy to some and will be a glorious surprise to others. In either case, enjoy, respect, and cherish them. Perhaps we'll meet on a trail someday, and we can share our delight.

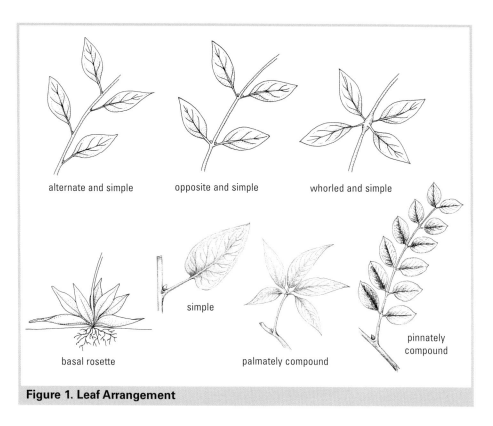

Figure 1. Leaf Arrangement

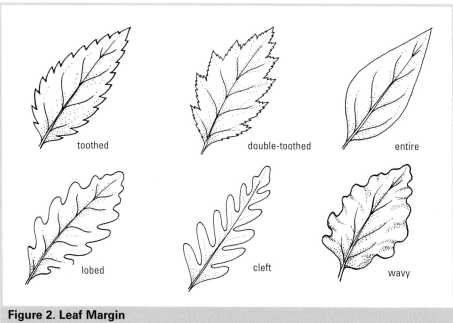

Figure 2. Leaf Margin

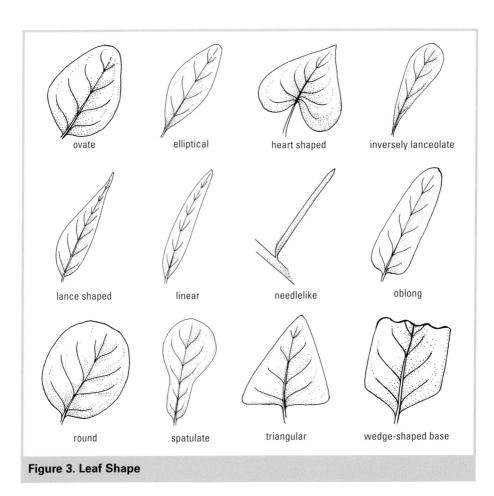

Figure 3. Leaf Shape

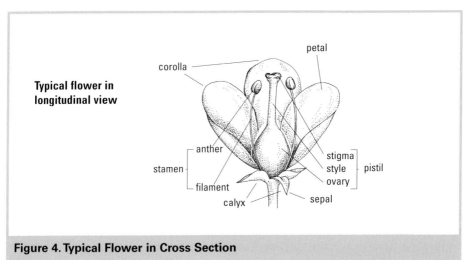

Figure 4. Typical Flower in Cross Section

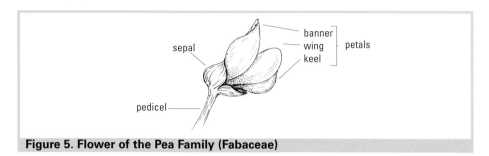

Figure 5. Flower of the Pea Family (Fabaceae)

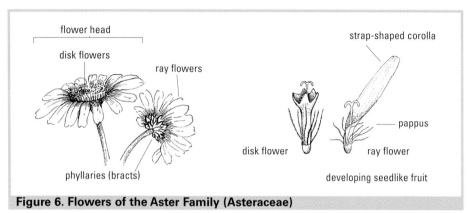

Figure 6. Flowers of the Aster Family (Asteraceae)

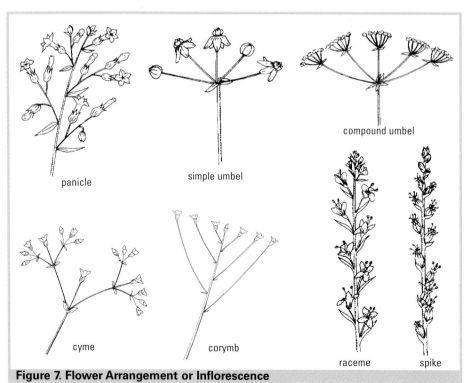

Figure 7. Flower Arrangement or Inflorescence

Lamoille Canyon in the Ruby Mountains

Featured Genera and Types

In this section of the introduction, you will find several featured genera and types of flowers that are especially well represented in the Great Basin and/or have particularly interesting Great Basin species. For each of these genera or types, I will describe its
characteristics, illustrate some of its most interesting Great Basin species, and explain
how to distinguish them. The page numbers for the species included in this book are indicated, so you can turn to the appropriate pages.

BUCKWHEAT *(Eriogonum* genus) see pages: 91, 158–63, 234–36.
The buckwheats may have several strikes against them in many wildflower seekers'
minds—their flowers are extremely small ($\frac{1}{8}$–$\frac{1}{4}$"); the plants typically grow in dry, rather
desolate habitats; they are extremely widespread and common; and there are scores of
species in the Great Basin, many of which are quite difficult to distinguish. However, there
is much to admire and appreciate in the buckwheats. Although in a few species the tiny
flowers are solitary (e.g., Spurry Buckwheat) or form small, few-flowered clusters, in most

species the tiny flowers cluster together to form large, showy umbels, heads, or cymes with whitish, bright yellow, or pink or red hues that can brighten up any landscape. And even an individual flower, if you take the time to examine it closely, will reveal intricate design and surprising color subtleties (e.g., colored stripes or shading).

Buckwheats have no true petals. Typically the 6 petal-like sepals are rather crepe-papery in texture, and the 9 stamens stick out a bit to create a rather fuzzy appearance.

The leaves of many species are mostly basal and are usually rather round or spoon shaped. In some species the plant stems are tall (e.g., Nude Buckwheat), while in others they reach only a few inches (e.g., Douglas Buckwheat). Several species occur near or above timberline and form dense mats or cushions (e.g., Oval-Leaf Buckwheat, King's Buckwheat).

Some species have stems that are swollen at the nodes, and almost all species with stem leaves have papery sheaths that enclose the base of the petiole at the node. Some buckwheats (e.g., Douglas Buckwheat) have a whorl of leaflike bracts around the stem, while others (e.g., Oval-Leaf Buckwheat) have no bracts at all.

CINQUEFOIL, AVENS, AND BUTTERCUP *(Potentilla, Geum,* and *Ranunculus* genera) see pages: 164–69.

Some of the brightest, shiniest yellow flowers around are the 5-petaled blossoms of cinquefoil *(Potentilla* genus), avens *(Geum* genus), and buttercup *(Ranunculus* genus). In all these flowers their sunny dispositions seem all the sunnier because of the dense clusters of yellow reproductive parts perched atop the bright, yellow petals. The density of reproductive parts is a characteristic of ancient families (residuals of using the wind for pollination); in this case the families are the Rose and the Buttercup.

Although many buttercups have a variable number of petals (usually more than 5), some have only 5 petals (or petal-like parts). This makes it more difficult to distinguish them from Rose Family members, which always have 5 petals. Many of these Buttercup species, however, have yellow sepals under the petals or no apparent sepals at all (so either the sepals have fallen off at blooming or the petal-like parts are actually sepals).

If you look under the 5 petal-like parts and find not only 5 green sepals, but also 5 tiny green bractlets between the sepals, you can be sure you're looking at either a *Potentilla* or a *Geum,* not a buttercup. When they are in seed, it's easy to distinguish these two green-sepaled genera, for *Geum* species have astonishing, Dr. Seuss-like seed clusters with beautiful, feathery styles. When they are in bloom, it's more difficult, but in the Great Basin there are only 3 species of *Geum,* each with distinctive leaves (large and broad in

Large-Leaf Avens, and deeply divided and rather lacy in Alpine Avens and Old Man's Whiskers). In distinguishing species of *Potentilla* from each other, the leaves again are the biggest help (whether they're palmately or pinnately compound, how many leaflets there are, and how toothed or lobed they are).

EVENING PRIMROSE *(Oenothera* and *Camissonia* genera) see pages: 151–54, 223–24, 226.

There is something deliciously mysterious about the evening primroses, as many species are night bloomers (opening at dusk and closing the following morning) and fill the night air with heavy, sweet perfume. To see these species in full bloom, you will need to be out near dusk or dawn, or perhaps on a brightly moonlit night with the moths.

And it's not just the sweet fragrance that attracts: Many of these flowers are spectacularly large (up to 5" across) and bright yellow or white. For an added touch of drama and poignancy, the blossoms have only a brief fling at life, blooming for only one night (or day). Many turn red-purple or crimson when they wither, so a plant or cluster of plants can present a strikingly beautiful, multicolored bouquet of fresh white or yellow and drying red—a dazzling reminder of mortality.

Oenothera and *Camissonia* species are quite similar in most regards but are easily distinguished by their stigmas—delicately divided into 4 narrow lobes in *Oenothera* and forming a dangling sphere in *Camissonia.* Also, most *Oenothera* species are truly *evening* primroses, opening at dusk, whereas most *Camissonia* species are actually day primroses, opening at dawn.

Although in some species, the spectacular flowers branch off tall plants (up to 6'), in many species the flowers lie on or nearly on the ground, a bit like water lilies floating on shallow ponds. For these ground-hugging flowers, the inferior ovaries don't have far to go to plant their seeds!

LOCOWEED, DAPPLEPOD, AND MILKVETCH *(Astragalus* genus) see pages: 69–73.

Worldwide, the Pea Family, the Orchid Family, and the Composite Family have the most species. Of the approximately 18,000 species in the Pea Family, the *Astragalus* genus is by far the largest with about 2,000 species, over 150 of which occur in the Great Basin. And what a beautiful and fascinating plant (in flower and in fruit) to be so profusely represented!

The flowers have the banner-wings-keel structure typical of the Pea Family, though unlike the lupines with their conspicuous, cupped wings, *Astragalus* species usually have

Fly Canyon in northwestern Nevada

less developed, less cupped wings that look more like praying hands. The most distinctive characteristics of the genus, however, are the pinnately compound leaves (often with 6 or more pairs of opposite leaflets below the one terminal one) and the intriguing, sometimes rather bizarre seedpods, which are frequently inflated and grooved and often curled or curved and mottled. These seedpods will be extremely helpful in distinguishing species, so for identification purposes you may want to visit the plant at least twice—once in flower and once in seed.

The flowers are relatively small (usually about ½"), but there are many of them, either branching off the usually up-curved stem or in a dense terminal umbel. The petals are usually some shade of pink or red-purple, frequently with darker streaks, especially on the upraised banner. The plants typically inhabit dry, sandy, or gravelly flats and slopes from the desert shrub and sagebrush steppe to above timberline.

As the name locoweed implies, many species are at least somewhat toxic, so you probably want to avoid eating these peas! The common names "locoweed," "dapplepod," and "milkvetch" are interchangeable, though for any particular species one of the names is usually more common.

LUPINE *(Lupinus* genus) see pages: 30–32, 209.

Although *Lupinus* (with about 20 Great Basin species) does not have anywhere near as many Great Basin (or worldwide) species as does its fellow pea genus *Astragalus* (with over 150 Great Basin species), lupines are actually more widely distributed in the Basin than locoweeds, for they occur not only on sandy or gravelly flats and slopes from the desert shrub and sagebrush steppe to above timberline, but they also can be found in wet meadows and along creeks and streams.

From dwarfed, ground-hugging plants (e.g., Brewer's Lupine) to robust plants over 4' tall in wet meadows (e.g., Large-Leaf Lupine), lupines offer their beautiful flowers as our companions practically anywhere we journey in the Great Basin.

Typical of members of the Pea Family, the flowers have specialized petals—banner, wings, and keel. In lupines the banner is large and erect, the wings are conspicuously cupped like the "hands of Allstate," and the keel is hidden inside the wings. Most Great Basin species have blue or blue-purple banners and wings, often with a splotch of white or yellow (turning to red-purple with age) at the base of the banner. There are some species with flowers that are usually white or yellow, but even these can sometimes be found in blue.

It's entertaining to watch bees operate the pollination mechanism—they land straddling the wings, their weight pushing the wings down and popping the keel with its hidden reproductive parts up to poke the bee.

Lupines are nitrogen fixing, so they are valuable components of any flora for the fertility of the soil. The peas in the pods have been used (e.g., by ancient Egyptians) for food, but you probably don't want to eat them as many species are at least mildly toxic.

MARIPOSA LILY *(Calochortus* genus) see pages: 82, 216–17.

Mariposa means "butterfly" and *Calochortus* means "beautiful grass." Both meanings give you a hint of the beauty of these flowers, which may indeed remind you of multicolored butterflies perched gracefully amid blades of grass.

As with almost all members of the Lily Family, the flower parts are in threes or multiples of threes. In most members of this family, the 3 sepals have modified to be identical or almost identical to the 3 petals (in color, shape, size, and texture), so all 6 of these perianth parts are given the same name—"tepals." However, in mariposa lilies, the sepals have modified only part way toward the petals and so are easily distinguishable—they are usually nearly the same color (though often a little greener), but are much narrower and are often thicker and tougher in texture.

Most Great Basin species of *Calochortus* are predominantly white, but some can be mostly pink or yellow, and one is bright orange or vermillion. Whatever their primary color, much of the beauty of these gorgeous flowers lies in their multicolored markings and colorful reproductive parts. At the base of each petal is a distinctive nectar gland above which can be found one or more vividly colored markings—spots, splotches, triangles, chevrons, or arches. Often the nectar gland is also fringed with colorful, slender hairs. The long, narrow, arrow-shaped anthers and the delicately three-parted stigma are often intensely colored as well.

The plants are relatively short (1–2') with only a few grasslike leaves that often wither early in the blooming, so the 1–3" wide flowers stand out all the more vividly, like butter-flies poised on a leafless branch.

MONKEYFLOWER *(Mimulus* genus) see pages: 98–99, 170–72.

Although the common and scientific names of the Snapdragon Family were derived from the genus *Scrophularia* with its oddly swollen, irregular, snapdragon flowers, in many ways the monkeyflowers are the prototype Snapdragon Family flowers. As the common name monkeyflower and the genus name *Mimulus* (i.e., little mime) suggest, these beautiful flow-ers with their well-developed petal lobes resemble (sort of) little faces. The 2-lipped flower tube characteristic of the family is clearly delineated by the 2 petals above the midline (the upper lip) and the 3 petals below it (the lower lip).

There are more than 20 species of monkeyflower that occur in the Great Basin, about half of which have bright yellow flowers and the other half of which have flowers some shade of red, pink, magenta, or purple. The plants range from ground hugging to 5' tall, while the flowers range from tiny (⅛–¼") to large (2" or more). Many species grow on dry, sandy, or gravelly flats and slopes, while several others like marshy meadows or streambanks.

All species of monkeyflower have a fascinating pollen-identifying mechanism that is most observable late in the season when the petals (and the attached male parts) have fallen off the plant, although you can see it anytime after the female has become receptive if you observe carefully. The stigma at the tip of the style is hinged and can fold closed. If anything (including an inquisitive flower lover) touches the open stigma, it will rapidly close. Then the magic begins! The stigma will reopen in a few minutes if any of the fol-lowing is true: (1) there was no pollen, (2) the pollen that touched the stigma was from a non-monkeyflower, (3) the pollen was from a different species of monkeyflower, or (4) the pollen was from the same species of monkeyflower but was from the same flower or

Steens Mountain with the Alford Desert to the east

another flower from the same plant. Only if the pollen was from the same species of mon-keyflower and was from a different plant will the stigma stay closed and will the pollen grain grow a thread down the style into the ovary to impregnate the ovules. So, if late in the season, you find a monkeyflower with no petals and an open stigma, you might try to find a plant of the same species in the vicinity with ripe male parts (though it may be too late to find any flowers with male parts still intact). With a pine needle and a gentle touch, you could do a "monkey" a real favor!

ONION *(Allium* genus) see pages: 78–81.
Although you may not always smell an onion before you see it, often you'll detect a faint pungency in the air and sometimes you'll be overwhelmed with a cloud of onion aroma well before you spot any plants. Don't settle for just the fragrance, though, for onion flow-ers are gorgeous in color and intricate in detail.

The individual flowers are small ($\frac{1}{4}$–$\frac{1}{2}$"), but they occur in large clusters atop the plant's stout, green stem. In addition to the onion odor and taste, the most noticeable characteristic is the umbel inflorescence—the many flowers at the end of an "umbrella spoke," all of which radiate out from the tip of the plant stem. Some species have long spokes, creating a large, rather loose umbel of flowers, while others have shorter spokes, creating a smaller, tighter umbel. In all of the more than 20 Great Basin species, however, the flower clusters are delightfully showy and exuberant, whether on a 1–2' plant or a 3" one.

The individual flowers are exquisite jewels: Their 6 tepals (3 petals and 3 sepals all looking alike) form delicate white, pink, or purple stars. Often the 6 radiating stamens are pressed down against the tepals, creating a beautiful star atop a star. The conspicuous superior ovary lies at the center of the flower a bit like a mysterious pearl cradled within an oyster. Often it is adorned with bumps or crests. This magnificent flower—this floral jewel—frequently sparkles with drops of nectar.

The long, basal, grasslike leaves are sometimes flat, sometimes cylindrical and fleshy, and often channeled. They usually wither early in the blooming, so the flowers may be on their own for much of their blossoming. Nibble a leaf or even a flower of an onion (*being certain of course that the plant is an onion,* for there are several *deadly* plants—e.g., Death Camas—that somewhat resemble onions) and you will experience true onionness. The most powerful taste is in the bulbs, but you wouldn't want to sacrifice the plant's future just for your pleasure!

PENSTEMON *(Penstemon* genus) see pages: 46–50, 103–5, 252.
The penstemons, like the monkeyflowers, are showy members of the Snapdragon Family with 2-lipped, tubular flowers that have 2 petal lobes above the midline and 3 petals below it. Whereas in monkeyflowers the face of the flower is the most conspicuous feature (being broader than the tube is long), in penstemons the tube is often the showiest feature, being longer than the face is broad. The face is still quite large and showy in many penstemons, however, often putting on a spectacular display of color variations, markings, hairs, and fascinating reproductive parts.

While there are about 20 species of monkeyflowers in the Great Basin, ranging from yellow to various shades of reds, purples, and pinks, there are many more *Penstemon* species (over 100), with an even wider color variation, from scarlet to pink to white to purple to blue. Worldwide there are about 250 *Penstemon* species.

Inside the flower tube the most noticeable features (other than the distinct nectar guides) are the male reproductive parts. Four of them arch up against the upper lip of the throat, each conspicuously displaying its 2 anther sacs (the filament attaches to the center

Goose Lake, northwest Great Basin

of the anther, so the 2 sacs project out in both directions from this attachment point). The most identifying feature of the *Penstemon* genus, however, is what *isn't* present. The fifth male part has the filament but no anther—it is infertile and is called a staminode. In many *Penstemon* species this staminode is beautifully bearded with long hairs (being bearded myself, perhaps I'm biased about the "beautiful" part).

In the Great Basin penstemons are our nearly constant companions, bringing their fascinating, showy, tubular flowers to the desert shrub, the sagebrush steppe, the high mountains, and even above timberline. They inhabit sandy or gravelly flats and slopes, washes, dunes, rock ledges and talus slopes, pinyon-juniper woodlands, dry openings in coniferous forests, grassy meadows, and alpine tundra. Practically the only habitat where you won't find them in the Great Basin is in very wet places—creekbanks, seeps, or marshy meadows.

PHACELIA *(Phacelia* genus) see pages: 35–36, 215–16.
The name *Phacelia* means cluster, which gives you a hint as to the look of these plants, though it will not prepare you for the amazingly crowded racemes of most *Phacelia*

species. In most species the relatively small (about ½") bowl-shaped flowers are jammed together in a coiled raceme, looking a bit like a curled-up caterpillar or a sea horse. Because there are so many flowers in such a tight inflorescence and because (as is typical of the Waterleaf Family) each flower has long-protruding reproductive parts and the plants are densely hairy, these caterpillars or sea horses are distinctively fuzzy looking.

To add to the allure of these intriguing plants, the flowers of most *Phacelia* species are blue (though some are white, off-white, or yellow). As suggested by the relative shortness of the blue section of this book, blue is a comparatively uncommon color for wildflowers. Only a few Great Basin genera (e.g., *Phacelia, Polemonium, Lupinus, Delphinium, Hackelia, Mertensia, Gentiana, Veronica, Downingia, Penstemon*) have predominantly blue-flowered species.

Although the leaves of phacelias can be simple and unlobed, the leaves of most species are either pinnately compound or deeply pinnately lobed or wavy on the edges.

Look for phacelias in dry habitats—sandy, gravelly, or rocky flats, slopes, forest clearings, or sagebrush plains. Not one of the Great Basin's over 40 species occurs in wet areas, though a few can be found in moist soil.

PHLOX *(Phlox* genus) see pages: 90, 229–33.
When you think of phlox, you may also think of flocks (of birds), for most *Phlox* species have dense clusters of flowers, sometimes so thick on the plant that they completely obscure the leaves, a bit like a tree with foliage that is almost completely hidden by scores of perching birds. The pinwheel-like flowers of all of the Great Basin's more than 10 species are either bright white, pastel pink, or purple, often starting white and turning pink or purple with age.

Although some species have plants 1–2' tall, the characteristic Great Basin phlox is a ground-hugging mat or cushion plant forming mounds of color on dry, sandy, or gravelly sagebrush plains or high mountain flats or ridges. Many of the species are quite similar in appearance, being distinguished primarily by the looseness or tightness of the mat or cushion and by the degree of stiffness of the narrow, needlelike leaves.

To see an austere rocky ridge or stony flat high above timberline adorned with mounds of phlox covered by "wall-to-wall" flowers is a stunning sight; getting down on your hands and knees and sticking your nose into the flowers is an exhilarating olfactory adventure!

WHITE "QUEEN-ANNE'S LACE" (many genera in the Carrot Family) see pages: 178–83. Although it's easy to determine that a plant is in the Carrot Family (also called Parsley Family) by its umbels (the flowers are at the end of "umbrella spokes") of tiny, 5-petaled flowers, it can be difficult to identify its species within that family. There are over 4,000 species in about 450 genera worldwide, with scores of species in over 20 genera in the Great Basin. Although a few species have yellow, red, or purple flowers, the vast majority have white or greenish white flowers, leading some flower seekers to just call them all "Queen-Anne's lace."

In a few species the flower heads are quite distinctive (e.g., the buttons in Ranger's Buttons), but to distinguish most genera and species, your best bet is to look at the leaves. They are usually pinnately divided, but in some genera the leaves are once divided into relatively large, serrate leaflets (e.g., *Cicuta*), while in other genera they are twice divided into lacy, fernlike leaflets (e.g., *Conium, Ligusticum*). In a few genera they are only faintly compound or are lobed rather than compound, either narrowly grasslike (e.g., *Perideridia*) or broadly maplelike (e.g., *Heracleum*).

Members of the Carrot Family are quite impressive even as they begin to bloom, for then you can see all the tightly packed rays and flowers of the umbels nearly explode out of the cocoonlike sheath where they have been cradled, waiting for this moment.

Many species in this family are familiar and important foods and herbs (e.g., Carrot, Parsley, Anise, Dill, Celery, Fennel), but leave the harvesting to the pros, for this family also contains some of the plant kingdom's most *deadly poisonous* members (e.g., Water Hemlock and Poison Hemlock).

YELLOW "SUNFLOWER" (many genera in the Composite Family) see pages: 111–35. When you think of sunflowers, you probably think of large, yellow flowers that resemble our childhood drawings of the sun—a central circle with radiating rays. There are so many similar species (from so many different genera) of these "sunflowers" that many people just give up on distinguishing them and call them all DYCs—"dang yellow composites."

The name "composite" is a good one, for it points out that these "sunflowers" are actually composites (i.e., flower heads) of many flowers—up to 150 to 200 in each flower head! The rays of the sun that appear to be petals are actually individual "ray flowers," each with a female reproductive part attached; the central button is actually comprised of scores (sometimes 100 or more) of tiny, tubular "disk flowers," each with a reproductive column (with male and female reproductive parts attached). You can see, then, that these composites are highly evolved, extremely efficient reproducers in which the successful pollination of only one of the many ray flowers or disk flowers is sufficient to reproduce the entire plant.

There are other composites with only disk flowers (e.g., thistles, pincushions, pussytoes) and still others with only ray flowers (e.g., dandelions); however, the most common arrangement for composites is to have both ray and disk flowers. Not all of these are yellow (e.g., daisies and asters are usually white, lavender, pink, or purple), but there are enough yellow species to cause identification despair. However, as you look through the yellow sunflowers in this book, you may begin to notice features that will help you begin to create order out of this chaos. Sometimes the leaves will help (e.g., opposite pairs of leaves in *Arnica,* very large and broad leaves in Mule Ears), sometimes the arrangement of rays (e.g., haphazard or scraggly in *Senecio)*, and sometimes the phyllaries under the rays (e.g., glandular in *Madia* and *Grindelia)*. The rays can be broad or narrow; entire, lobed, or fringed; square tipped, pointed, or rounded. The disk in the center can be flat or raised, round topped or square topped, yellow or brown or black. The phyllaries can be narrow or broad, appressed, spreading, or reflexed.

If you are sensitive to some of these features when you encounter one of these "DYCs," it just might move beyond a DYC to an FSF (familiar, sunny friend)!

BLUE AND PURPLE FLOWERS

This section includes flowers ranging from pale blue to deep indigo and from lavender to violet. Since lavender flowers grade into pink, you should check the Red and Pink section if you do not find the flower you're looking for here.

LAVA ASTER
Aster scopulorum
Composite Family (Asteraceae)

Description: With flower heads with an unusual color that will catch your attention and your delight from quite a distance, Lava Aster is one of the loveliest and most distinctive of the many species of Aster that occur in the Great Basin. It is a short plant (6–12" tall) with small (½"), narrow leaves, which are crowded on the lower ⅔ of the stem. The flower heads, however, are anything but small an inconspicuous. The 8–16 rays radiating from the yellow disk are a soft violet, creating a striking flower head up to 1½" across.

Flowering Season: May–June.

Habitat/Range: Dry, rocky slopes in the sagebrush steppe, 5,000–10,000', throughout the Great Basin, e.g., Fly Canyon, Steens Mountain.

Comments: *Aster* means "star." *Scopulorum* means "of the cliffs."

BACHELOR'S BUTTONS
Centaurea cyanus
Composite Family (Asteraceae)

Description: Along with its fellow alien, Blue Sailors *(Cichorium intybus)*, Bachelor's Buttons is one of the very few composites with blue flowers. Several species of asters and daisies are blue-purple or lavender, but Bachelor's Buttons is very definitely blue (occasionally white or pink). The showy flower heads are 1½–2" across, appearing to have 20–25 flaring, ruffled rays. It turns out that these "rays" are actually enlarged disk flowers (the flower heads have no true ray flowers), but they are no less showy for being disk flowers. The phyllaries under the flower heads are green with distinctive tips of tiny white or black teeth. Each tall (to 4') plant stem is topped by only one flower head.

Flowering Season: May–September.

Habitat/Range: Grassy fields, roadsides, disturbed places in the sagebrush steppe, to 6,500', throughout the Great Basin, e.g., Peavine Mountain.

Comments: *Centaurea* is from the Latin and is a reference to the centaur Chiron who was supposed to have discovered the medicinal uses of a plant in Greece that came to be called Centaury. *Cyanus* means "blue." Alien.

BLUE SAILORS
Cichorium intybus
Composite Family (Asteraceae)

Description: You almost welcome that barbwire fence when you see the gorgeous blue flower heads of Blue Sailors displayed against it along some Great Basin back road, for the fence provides a decorative and picturesque background for this exotic weed. The 1–3' ribbed stem bears many of these beautiful, windmill flower heads and numerous coarse, pinnately lobed leaves. Each 1½–2" wide flower head consists of 10–20 of the pale blue (sometimes pink) rays with the blunt, toothed tips. Completing this very unusual color scheme for a composite are the blue reproductive parts.

Flowering Season: July–September.

Habitat/Range: Dry fields, roadsides, disturbed places in the sagebrush steppe, to 6,000', throughout the Great Basin, e.g., Washoe Valley.

Comments: *Cichorium* is the ancient Arabic name. *Intybus* means "endive" in reference to the use of the leaves in salads. Alien.

HOARY TANSY-ASTER
Machaeranthera canescens
Composite Family (Asteraceae)

Description: Whether you find it on sandy flats in the desert shrub or on gravelly or rocky flats or ridges near timberline on the Great Basin's highest mountains, Hoary Tansy-Aster will brighten your day, for the 1–1½" flower heads present a gorgeous display of 8–25 intensely blue-purple rays radiating out of a bright yellow disk. The square-tipped phyllaries curl away from the involucre and are sticky to the touch. The long, narrow, toothed leaves are covered with fine, white hairs. There are several varieties of this species with somewhat different leaves and elevation ranges, but they all have the sticky, projecting phyllaries and the striking, purple rays.

Flowering Season: April–July.

Habitat/Range: Sandy, gravelly, or rocky flats and slopes in the desert shrub, the sagebrush steppe, and the montane, to 11,000', throughout the Great Basin, e.g., White Mountains, Steens Mountain.

Comments: *Machaeranthera* means "swordlike anthers." *Canescens* means "gray-hairy."

JESSICA'S STICKSEED
Hackelia micrantha
Borage Family (Boraginaceae)

Description: The stickseeds are certainly well named, as you will grudgingly acknowledge after returning from a late-summer or fall hike through a *Hackelia*-inhabited mountain meadow. Instead of spending all that time and energy trying to pick the prickly-sticky, round nutlets off your socks, you may just as well concede and plant your socks in your yard! It will save you a lot of effort and the flowers you might eventually get will certainly be beautiful. Jessica's Stickseed is a 1–4', much-branched plant that is loaded with deliciously blue, 5-petaled, ¼" pinwheel flowers. At the center of the blossom, around the throat, are 5 connected, slightly raised teeth. The nutlets are ringed with about 10 stalks, each tipped by tiny, hooked spines.

Flowering Season: May–August.

Habitat/Range: Grassy meadows, forest clearings in the montane, 6,000–10,000', throughout the Great Basin, e.g., Santa Rosa Range, Ruby Mountains.

Comments: Joseph Hackel was a 19th-century Czech botanist. *Micrantha* means "small flowered." Formerly known as *H. jessicae*.

MOUNTAIN BLUEBELLS
Mertensia ciliata
Borage Family (Boraginaceae)

Description: The clusters of nodding, 5-petaled, blue, tubular flowers of Mountain Bluebells are quite similar to those of other *Mertensia* species (e.g., Sagebrush Bluebells, *M. oblongifolia*). The flowers of all these species usually have a hint of pink (the flowers start pink in bud), the distal half of the flower tube is broader than the basal half, and the clapperlike style projects slightly from the corolla. Mountain Bluebells is distinguished by being a much taller plant than the other Great Basin bluebells, reaching up to 5'. The ovate leaves are large and broad with conspicuous veins.

Flowering Season: June–August.

Habitat/Range: Damp meadows, forest clearings in the montane, 6,500–10,000', in eastern California, western and northwestern Nevada, e.g., Charles Sheldon National Wildlife Refuge.

Comments: Karl Mertens *(M. oblongifolia)*. *Ciliata* means "having fine hairs" in reference to the hairs often found on the edges of the sepals.

SAGEBRUSH BLUEBELLS
Mertensia oblongifolia
Borage Family (Boraginaceae)

Description: There is such a soothing grace to the arching pedicels and the clusters of gently nodding blue bells of plants in the *Mertensia* genus. Although some species can be several feet tall, Sagebrush Bluebells rarely exceeds 1½', but this relatively short stem is dense with large, broad leaves that provide a lush background for the delicate, 5-petaled flowers. Each ½–1" flower is a narrow tube, which is slightly broader in its distal half. The flowers start pink in bud, so there usually is still a hint of pink in mature flowers.

Flowering Season: May–July.

Habitat/Range: Moist, brushy slopes in the sagebrush steppe and the montane, 6,500–11,000', throughout the Great Basin, e.g., Steens Mountain, Deep Creek Mountains.

Comments: Karl Mertens was a German botanist of the 18th and 19th centuries. *Oblongifolia* means "oblong leafed."

BACIGALUPI'S DOWNINGIA
Downingia bacigalupii
Bellflower Family (Campanulaceae)

Description: Whenever you see a downingia in the Great Basin, consider yourself blessed, for not only are they exceptionally beautiful, they are also quite uncommon. Even in California, where you can find several species in some profusion on the beds of dried vernal pools in the Central Valley, they are a treasure, for these vernal pool habitats are disappearing rapidly. In Bacigalupi's Downingia the 2 petals of the upper lip are solid blue-purple, while the lower lip (comprised of 3 petals) is blue-purple at the tip with a white patch at the base, upon which are superimposed 2 large yellow splotches. Probably the most striking feature of this dramatic flower is the long, deep purple, hooked anther tube, which looks a bit like a snooping periscope rising from the flower's depths. Bacigalupi's Downingia is unusual for its genera, for though it can be found in floodplains and on the floors of dried vernal pools, it will also be found among sagebrush and grass in open fields.

Flowering Season: May–June.

Habitat/Range: Floodplains, dried vernal pools, along creeks, among sagebrush and grass in damp fields in the sagebrush steppe, 4,500–6,500', in northern Nevada, southern Oregon, e.g., Sheldon National Wildlife Refuge, Steens Mountain.

Comments: A. J. Downing was a 19th-century American horticulturist. Rimo Bacigalupi was a 20th-century California botanist and curator of the Jepson Herbarium at the University of California, Berkeley.

PORTERELLA
Porterella carnosula
Bellflower Family (Campanulaceae)

Description: With its 2-lobed flower form (2 petals in the upper lip and 3 petals in the lower lip), its multicolored petals (blue-purple, white, and yellow), and its habitat (muddy pond edges and drying vernal pools), this gorgeous flower appears to be one of the uncommon Great Basin species of *Downingia*. It is indeed a close relative of that genus, also in the Bellflower Family, and it is also uncommon, but it has actually been placed in a separate genus all by itself. The differentiating characteristic is certainly a subtle one—*Porterella* flowers are at the tip of pedicels, while *Downingia* flowers are sessile (i.e., have no pedicel). This sounds like it would be an easily perceived difference, but to the nonbotanist it's not. Downingias appear to be at the tips of pedicels too, but it turns out that these are not pedicels but instead hypanthiums (i.e., structures derived from the fused lower portions of the sepals, petals, and stamens), so these pedicel-like structures are actually part of the flower rather than a flower stem. In any case, whether you come across a downingia or porterella, you are fortunate indeed and may find yourself on your hands and knees in gratitude and examination!

Flowering Season: May–July.

Habitat/Range: Muddy edges of ponds, dried vernal pool bottoms in the sagebrush steppe and the montane, 5,000–8,500', in western and northwestern Nevada, southern Oregon, e.g., Peavine Mountain, Charles Sheldon National Wildlife Refuge, Steens Mountain.

Comments: Thomas Porter was a 19th-century American botanist. *Carnosula* means "somewhat fleshy."

SILVER LUPINE
Lupinus argenteus
Pea Family (Fabaceae)

Description: Silver Lupine is an extremely variable and taxonomically difficult species, though in all its variations it is characterized by a rather silvery, satiny look due to the fine, silver hairs covering the leaves, stems, and sepals. It is a 1–3' (occasionally up to 5'), bushy, leafy perennial. The many leaves consist of 5–9, narrow, usually infolded, ½–2" leaflets. The 2–10" racemes of ½" flowers rise conspicuously above the leaves. Although these blooms are usually blue-purple, they can be lavender, pink, or even white. The white or yellow eye on the banner turns red-purple with age. To complete the silvery theme of this species, the back of the banner is often hairy and the pods are densely covered with silver hairs.

Flowering Season: April–July.

Habitat/Range: Dry slopes in the sagebrush steppe and the montane, 5,000–10,200', throughout the Great Basin, e.g., Peavine Mountain, Charles Sheldon National Wildlife Refuge.

Comments: *Lupinus (L. malocophyllus) Argentea* means "silvery" in reference to the silvery hairs over most of the plant.

BREWER'S LUPINE
Lupinus breweri
Pea Family (Fabaceae)

Description: If you are familiar with Large-Leaf Lupine *(L. polyphyllus)* of wet, mountain meadows that grows up to 5' tall or with Silver Lupine *(L. argenteus)* of dry, sagebrush slopes that forms 1–3' shrubs, you will easily recognize Brewer's Lupine as a lupine, but you may be surprised to find these familiar flowers on such a diminutive plant. Brewer's Lupine are only 1–8" tall, but despite their short stature, these plants can create their own lush (though miniature) gardens, for they often cover extensive areas of sandy or rocky hillsides with low, blue carpets. Although most lupines have a yellow or white patch on the banner petal, this (white) patch is larger on Brewer's Lupine than on most of its kin, taking up most of the front of the banner, so from a distance these plants have a rather blue and white checkerboard look to them. Since this plant inhabits dry areas, you won't be surprised to find that it is covered with thick, soft hairs.

Flowering Season: June–September.

Habitat/Range: Rocky ridges, sandy flats in the montane and the alpine, 7,000–12,000', in eastern California, western Nevada, e.g., Sweetwater Mountains, White Mountains. This species occurs mostly in the Sierra Nevada.

Comments: *Lupinus (L. malocophyllus).* William Brewer *(cardamine breweri).*

TORREY'S LUPINE
Lupinus lepidus
Pea Family (Fabaceae)

Description: Although Torrey's Lupine is in many ways a typical blue-flowered *Lupinus* species, it is easily identified even from a distance by its compact, symmetrically cylindrical spikes of flowers. These 2–4" racemes, tightly packed with scores of ½", dark blue, 5-petaled flowers, rise cleanly above the mostly basal leaves, creating the appearance of blue bottle brushes sticking up above a bed of leaves. Although the flowers are usually dark blue, they can tend toward violet or slightly pinkish. The leaves consist of 5–8 usually infolded, pointed leaflets. The leaves, stem, and sepals are covered with soft hairs. There are numerous varieties of *L. lepidus,* differing primarily in stature (from 2"–3' tall) and hairiness.

Flowering Season: June–August.

Habitat/Range: Sandy or gravelly flats, roadsides, forest openings in the montane, 6,000–9,000', throughout the Great Basin except for central Nevada, e.g., Sweetwater Mountains, Steens Mountain.

Comments: *Lupinus (L. malocophyllus). Lepidus* means "elegant, graceful."

NEVADA LUPINE
Lupinus nevadensis
Pea Family (Fabaceae)

Description: Nevada Lupine has a much busier look than most lupines, for the 2–7" inflorescences are thick with numerous flowers, which are not in neatly separated whorls, but rather fill every available space on the peduncles. And unlike some lupines with densely flowered inflorescences that rise well above the plant's leaves (e.g., Torrey's Lupine, *L. lepidus*), Nevada Lupine has its leaves well distributed along the plant stem, so the spikes of flowers and the leaves are intermingled. The leaves are comprised of 6–10 narrow, widely separated, pointed leaflets. The ½" flowers are blue with a white patch on the banner. The leaves, stems, sepals, and keel edge are covered with hairs.

Flowering Season: May–June.

Habitat/Range: Sandy or rocky valley floors and hillsides in the sagebrush steppe, to 7,000', in eastern California, western and northwestern Nevada, southern Oregon, e.g., Peavine Mountain, Charles Sheldon National Wildlife Refuge.

Comments: *Lupinus (L. malocophyllus). Nevadensis* means "of Nevada."

LARGE-LEAF LUPINE
Lupinus polyphyllus
Pea Family (Fabaceae)

Description: One of the largest, most densely flowered, and most showy of all the lupines, Large-Leaf Lupine can reach 5' tall. Its racemes (up to 18" long) are longer than some *Lupinus* species plants are tall! In wet meadows and along creeks, you will often find masses of these plants interwoven with other robust, brightly flowered plants (e.g., Paintbrush, Corn Lily, Senecio, Monkshood, Cow Parsnip, Shooting Star) to form a spectacular floral mosaic. Each ½–¾" blue flower has the typical yellow or white patch on the banner that turns red-purple with age, though the white is often much less pronounced than in many *Lupinus* species, so the flowers are more solid blue. This plant is not only thick with flowers, but also heavy with leaves, each of which is comprised of 5–17 broad leaflets. This species has numerous recognized varieties.

Flowering Season: May–August.

Habitat/Range: Wet meadows, streambanks in the montane, 6,500–10,000', in western Nevada, southern Oregon, western Utah, e.g., Steens Mountain, Deep Creek Mountains.

Comments: *Lupinus (L. malocophyllus). Polyphyllus* means "many-leaved." Also called Meadow Lupine.

EXPLORER'S GENTIAN
Gentiana calycosa
Gentian Family (Gentianaceae)

Description: In a genus of beautiful, usually blue flowers, Explorer's Gentian may be the most spectacular of them all. Each short stem bears several pairs of opposite, broadly oval leaves and 1–3 of the 2", vaselike flowers. The 5 deep blue, flaring petals are speckled with green spots and have white, green-spotted throats. Between the petals are small fringes. Contrasting with the blue of the petals are the black-purple sepals and the dark green leaves. Before the flowers open, the swirling, satiny sepals form a rich, floral torpedo. In bud or bloom Explorer's Gentian is a fascinating, sensual gift for any wildflower explorer.

Flowering Season: July–October.

Habitat/Range: Seeps about rocks, wet meadows in the montane, 7,000–10,500', in western and eastern Nevada, e.g., Ruby Mountains. This species occurs mostly in the Sierra Nevada and the Rockies.

Comments: *Gentiana (G. newberryi). Calycosa* means "full calyx."

ROTHROCK'S NAMA
Nama rothrockii
Waterleaf Family (Hydrophyllaceae)

Description: Coming across Rothrock's Nama on a rocky mountain slope or ledge is a true delight, as its large, spherical heads of blue or violet, 5-petaled flowers bring gorgeous flashes of color to this often rather austere environment. Since the plants spread by rhizomes, you will usually find extensive colonies of these low-growing (4–12") plants covering several square feet (or even yards) with their dramatic color. The leaves have their own appeal as well, for they are crinkly, serrated, deeply veined, and sticky-hairy—they catch your eye with their interesting shape and texture and stimulate your nose with their strong fragrance when they are crushed.

Flowering Season: June–August.

Habitat/Range: Dry, sandy or rocky flats and slopes, ledges in the montane, 7,500–10,000', in eastern California, western Nevada, e.g., Bodie Mountains, Wassuk Range.

Comments: *Nama* means "spring" or "stream." Joseph Rothrock was a 19th-century professor of botany at the University of Pennsylvania.

WASHOE PHACELIA
Phacelia curvipes
Waterleaf Family (Hydrophyllaceae)

Description: Almost all of the more than 50 species of *Phacelia* in the Great Basin have flowers that are some shade of blue-purple or blue. Washoe Phacelia is no exception, though its flowers shade more toward the violet. Though the plant is small and grows low to the ground, it probably won't be difficult to see, for its soft-hairy, 1–3", at least partly erect leaves and its ¼–½", bowl-shaped flowers are striking. The flowers are on short prostrate or up-curved pedicels and have a white throat, which dramatically highlights the 5 violet petal lobes. The leaves usually have 2 or more lateral lobes, giving them a bit of a mittenlike shape.

Flowering Season: April–June.

Habitat/Range: Dry, sandy or gravelly flats and slopes, washes, canyons, talus slopes in the sagebrush steppe, to 7,000', in eastern California, western and central Nevada, e.g., Virginia Range.

Comments: *Phacelia (P. heterophylla). Curvipes* means "with curved feet or stalks." Also called Dwarf Desert Phacelia.

DWARF PHACELIA
Phacelia humilis
Waterleaf Family (Hydrophyllaceae)

Description: Although Dwarf Phacelia, as its name suggests, is indeed a very "humble" plant (2–8" tall) with small (¼–½") flowers, it can be quite showy as its tight clusters of deep blue-purple flowers can carpet large areas nearly solid with color. As is typical of *Phacelia* species, the slender reproductive parts stick well out of the corolla, and the plant is covered with hairs (in this case, short and stiff), creating a fuzzy appearance. The white filaments bear tiny black or white anthers. The 1½" long, broad, deeply veined leaves seem especially large in comparison to the small, 5-petaled flowers and the prostrate plant.

Flowering Season: May–July.

Habitat/Range: Sandy flats, openings in the sagebrush steppe and the montane, 5,000–8,000', throughout the Great Basin except central and eastern Nevada, e.g., Santa Rosa Range, Steens Mountain.

Comments: *Phacelia (P. heterophylla). Humilis* means "low."

NARROW-LEAF PHACELIA
Phacelia linearis
Waterleaf Family (Hydrophyllaceae)

Description: With their beautiful, blue, bowl-shaped flowers, the many species of *Phacelia* that grace the Great Basin are a wonderful, treasured part of the area's flora. It's difficult to choose favorites, but Narrow-Leaf Phacelia will probably be one of them, for its clusters of ½" flowers are a striking blue-violet with darker purple midveins. The growth form of this plant is bit unusual for a phacelia, as the flowers tend to form small clusters, rather than dense, caterpillar-like coils. The main distinguishing feature, however, is the leaves. As the common and species names indicate, the leaves are narrow and unlobed (except for the 1–4 short, linear segments perpendicular to the main leaf lobe). The plant is covered with dense or sparse white hairs.

Flowering Season: April–July.

Habitat/Range: Dry, sandy, or rocky flats and slopes in the sagebrush steppe, to 6,000', in central and northwestern Nevada, southern Oregon, western Utah, e.g., Soldier Meadow.

Comments: *Phacelia (P. heterophylla). Linearis* means "linear, parallel sided" in reference to the leaves.

SILKY PHACELIA
Phacelia sericea
Waterleaf family (Hydrophyllaceae)

Description: Although having the clusters of fuzzy-looking, 5-petaled, bowl-shaped flowers typical of the *Phacelia* genus, Silky Phacelia is strikingly different from any of the other *Phacelia* species. The common name and the species name are well chosen, for the extremely long-protruding filaments (2–3 times longer than the corolla) along with the short, silver hairs on the sepals and stem create a distinctive silky appearance. The slender, purple filaments are tipped with tiny, yellow anthers. The 1–2' stems are rather stout and end with a long, slender raceme comprised of clusters of flowers. The pinnately lobed leaves are mostly basal, though there are some smaller ones along the plant stem.

Flowering Season: June–August.

Habitat/Range: Rocky slopes, forest openings in the montane, 6,000–11,000', throughout the Great Basin except western Nevada, e.g., Toiyabe Range, Steens Mountain.

Comments: *Phacelia (P. heterophylla). Sericea* means "silky" in reference to the plant's silky, silvery hairs and its very long-protruding stamens.

WILD IRIS
Iris missouriensis
Iris Family (Iridaceae)

Description: Although Wild Iris is common throughout most of the Great Basin, especially in fields where the competition has been over-grazed, it is nonetheless a joy to discover, for it is a spectacular plant with large (to 4" across), dazzling flowers. The most conspicuous of the flower parts are the outside ones—the 3 drooping, tonguelike sepals, which are blue or purple with a network of white or yellow veins. The 3 broad, erect, blue-purple petals are situated directly inside the sepals. The other 3 conspicu-ous, blue-purple structures, which are narrower than the petals and the sepals, are the pistils, which arch over the stamens and spring up to an erect position after picking up pollen. Each 1–2' stem bears only 1 or 2 flowers—any more and we could be drowned in a sea of blue! The grasslike leaves usually reach about as high as the flowers.

Flowering Season: May–July

Habitat/Range: Wet meadows, fields (especially overgrazed ones) in the sagebrush steppe and the montane, to 11,000', throughout the Great Basin, e.g., Washoe Valley, Ruby Mountains.

Comments: *Iris* means "rainbow" in reference to the multicolored flowers. *Missouriensis* means "of Missouri."

IDAHO BLUE-EYED GRASS
Sisyrinchium idahoense
Iris Family (Iridaceae)

Description: With their 6 deep blue-purple tepals with the even darker blue-purple veins and their bright yellow eye at the bottom of the flower tube, the ½–1" starlike flowers of Blue-Eyed Grass are a truly stunning sight. They are often as surprising as stunning, for the 4–16" plants with their grasslike leaves usually grow in damp or wet meadows thick with "real" grass, so you may not notice the plant at all until suddenly you see the striking flower—an island of intense purple floating in the green sea. You (and the insects) might expect the yellow eye in the center of the flower to be a nectar gland or a nectar guide, but you would be mistaken—it is only a patch of pigment designed to deceive insects into becoming pollinators.

Flowering Season: May–August

Habitat/Range: Creek banks, seeps, wet meadows in the sagebrush steppe and the montane, 5,000–10,000', throughout the Great Basin, e.g., Steens Mountain, Deep Creek Mountains.

Comments: *Sisyrinchium (S. douglasii). Idahoense* means "of Idaho."

SELF-HEAL
Prunella vulgaris
Mint Family (Lamiaceae)

Description: Although not native to America (it was introduced from Europe), Self-Heal is a welcome adopted child, for it is beautiful as well as a multipurpose healer (from heart ailments to inflammations and bruises). The gorgeous head of flowers is at the tip of a square, 4–20" stem, so it can be difficult to see among the thick grass that usually surrounds it. But when you find it, take some time to examine it closely—its form and colors are exquisite. The 5-petaled, ½" flowers emerge horizontally from a 1–2", pineconelike spike packed tightly with dark, red-purple or purple-tipped green, scalelike sepals. In sharp contrast to the dark background of the sepals are the delicately violet or pink flowers. The upper 2 petals form an awning over the protruding reproductive parts, while the lower 3 petals consist of 2 smooth wings and a larger, central, fringed bib—an ideal landing pad for the bees. There are several opposite pairs of serrated leaves along the stem, culminating in an opposite pair of bracts just below the flower head.

Flowering Season: May–September.

Habitat/Range: Moist, grassy meadows in partial shade in the montane, 5,700–7,000', in eastern Nevada, western Utah, e.g., Ruby Valley (just east of the Ruby Mountains). This species occurs mostly in the Sierra Nevada.

Comments: *Prunella* is a German word for "quinsy"—a disease that this plant was used to treat. *Vulgaris* means "common," though it isn't in the Great Basin. Alien.

PURPLE SAGE
Salvia dorrii
Mint Family (Lamiaceae)

Description: The flowers of Purple Sage have the typical mint structure, with 2-lipped, tubular flowers of rather odd shape. The upper lip consists of 2 "ears," while the lower lip is comprised of a long, tonguelike middle petal and 2 smaller, lateral petals. The pistil and the 2 stamens with yellow anthers are long and slender, looking rather like antennae sticking way out of the corolla. The flowers occur in whorls at intervals along the stem. Unlike many of the mints, Purple Sage is a shrub (up to 2½'). In some areas of the Great Basin, Purple Sage grows in huge masses, filling the air with its sweet fragrance and beckoning invitingly to those "riders of the Purple Sage."

Flowering Season: April–July.

Habitat/Range: Sandy or gravelly flats in the desert shrub, the sagebrush steppe, and the montane, to 9,600', throughout the Great Basin, e.g., Soldier Meadow.

Comments: *Salvia* comes from the Latin salveo, "I am well," and an herb, Salvia, used for healing, probably in reference to medicinal qualities. C. Herbert Dorr was a 19th-century plant collector in what was the Nevada Territory.

CAMAS LILY
Camassia quamash
Lily Family (Liliaceae)

Description: With the coming of the spring melt in midelevation meadows (often ringed, on slightly higher and drier ground, by sagebrush), the spectacular, deep purple blossoms of Camas Lily burst out of their buds. The plants often cover wide expanses of soggy meadows with "lakes" of color. Each 1–2' stem bears many of the 1–2" flowers with their 6 narrow, blue-purple tepals contrasting dramatically with the bright yellow anthers and the rich green ovary. In almost every field of Camas Lily blue you will find a touch of white—a few scattered albinos. Camas Lily fields in full bloom are one of the great gifts of spring—to the land and to color-starved flower lovers!

Flowering Season: May–June.

Habitat/Range: Moist or wet meadows in the sagebrush steppe, 4,500–6,500', in western and northern Nevada, southern Oregon, e.g., Steens Mountain.

Comments: *Camassia* means "sweet" in reference to the use of the bulbs by Native Americans as a major food source. *Quamash* also means "sweet."

BLUE FLAX
Linum lewisii
Flax Family (Linaceae)

Description: You will occasionally find a solitary Blue Flax plant, in which case it looks like a few fragments of blue sky fallen to earth, but usually you will discover solid fields of these glorious flowers, which might lead you to believe the entire sky fell. The sky—the mass of 5-petaled, 1–1½" flowers—can vary from deep azure to steely, silvery blue. Each flower is very short-lived and is easily blown off the plant, but each 1–2½' plant stem bears many flowers that extend the bloom across several weeks. Check the ground around these plants and you will usually find a sprinkling or covering of dried, dark blue petals—almost as beautiful a display as the flowers in bloom. The stems are tough and wiry; the leaves are linear. There are two types of flowers: one with long stamens and long pistils, and the other with short stamens and short pistils (this is called heterostyly). All of the flowers on any plant are of only one of these types. Since pollination can occur only between flowers of different types, pollination cannot occur between flowers on the same plant—an ingenious way to prevent self-pollination.

Flowering Season: May–August.

Habitat/Range: Sandy or gravelly flats and slopes, washes in the sagebrush steppe and the montane, 4,500–10,000', throughout the Great Basin, e.g., Peavine Mountain, Ruby Mountains.

Comments: *Linum* means "flax." Meriwether Lewis *(Lewisia pygmaea).*

NAKED BROOMRAPE
Orobanche uniflora
Broomrape Family (Orobanchaceae)

Description: With its 5-petaled, 2-lipped, long-tubular corolla, Naked Broomrape resembles a solitary penstemon flower. Despite its relatively large flower (½–1½" long) and gorgeous coloration, Naked Broomrape is easy to overlook because the flower branches horizontally off a tiny (1–2") stem (so it practically blooms right out of the ground) and it grows in moist places usually also inhabited by much taller, more robust plants. When you do find this wonderful flower, though, you will be grateful, for the glandular tube is a beautiful purple, pink, or yellow, often with veins and markings of other colors inside the tube. There are no leaves, as this plant survives by parasitizing its neighbors—usually sedums, saxifrages, or composites.

Flowering Season: May–July.

Habitat/Range: Moist, grassy meadows, seeps in rocks in the sagebrush steppe and the montane, to 10,000', throughout the Great Basin except central Nevada, e.g., Ruby Mountains.

Comments: *Orobanche (O. fasciculata). Uniflora* means "single flowered."

FEW-FLOWERED ERIASTRUM
Eriastrum sparsiflorum
Phlox Family (Polemoniaceae)

Description: With its pointed, needlelike leaves and branching growth form, Few-Flowered Eriastrum has a somewhat scraggly, bristly look. The slender stem, up to 1' tall, bears clusters of ¼" flowers, which tend to be somewhat hidden by the needlelike bracts under the flower heads that stick out well beyond the flowers. The pale blue or lavender flowers are regular (unlike those of some of the desert *Eriastrum* species), looking like tiny, symmetrical stars radiating out of their narrow flower tubes.

Flowering Season: May–August.

Habitat/Range: Dry, gravelly slopes and washes in the sagebrush steppe, to 7,500', throughout the Great Basin, e.g., White Mountains, Steens Mountain.

Comments: *Eriastrum* means "wooly star." *Sparsiflorum* means "few flowered." Also known as Great Basin Eriastrum.

GREAT POLEMONIUM
Polemonium occidentale
Phlox Family (Polemoniaceae)

Description: Great Polemonium is one of the loveliest and showiest residents of lush, wet areas in the mountains of the Great Basin. It has the gracefully beautiful, blue, 5-petaled, bowl-shaped flowers characteristic of the *Polemonium* genus, and it is by far the tallest (to 3') of any of the Great Basin *Polemonium* species. The sky-blue flowers have a white eye at the center from which protrude the long stamens with their large, yellow anthers and the even longer white pistil with its 2-branched stigma. Because the reproductive parts are so conspicuous, they are ideal for demonstrating the male-then-female sequence of ripening that is characteristic of almost all flowers and that helps reduce the chances of self-pollination—early in the blooming the anthers will be heavy with pollen and the pistil will be flat against the flower tube with closed stigma, while later the pistil will rise and the stigma will open to readiness, but by then the anthers will be shriveled and pollenless. So can be the frustrations of life! Great Polemonium has the pinnately compound leaves typical of all Jacob's ladders.

Flowering Season: June–August.

Habitat/Range: Wet meadows, creekbanks, seeps, and bogs in the montane, 7,000–11,000', throughout the Great Basin, e.g., Ruby Mountains.

Comments: *Polemonium* is probably after the Greek philosopher Polemon. *Occidentale* means "western." Also called Western Jacob's Ladder.

SHOWY POLEMONIUM
Polemonium pulcherrimum
Phlox Family (Polemoniaceae)

Description: Although not occurring as high in the mountains as its close relative Sky Pilot *(P. viscosum)*, Showy Polemonium will commonly be found on rocky ridges and stony flats up to and slightly above timberline. This plant, with its lovely, ½", blue or blue-purple flowers (with the yellow centers) and pinnately compound (ladderlike) leaves is easily recognizable as a species of *Polemonium* (i.e., Jacob's Ladder). It forms showy mounds about 1' tall that are dense with the tightly compound leaves and the colorful, 5-petaled flowers. Each leaf consists of 9–21 oval, ¼–½", overlapping leaflets that are sticky to the touch and a bit assaulting to the nose (with a skunklike odor). The protruding stamens with the white anthers add a bit more contrast to the striking blue and yellow of the corolla.

Flowering Season: June–August.

Habitat/Range: Talus slopes, rock crevices, rocky ridges in the montane and the alpine, 7,500–11,000', throughout the Great Basin, e.g., Toiyabe Range, Deep Creek Mountains.

Comments: *Polemonium (P. occidentale). Pulcherrimum* means "very beautiful."

SKY PILOT
Polemonium viscosum
Phlox Family (Polemoniaceae)

Description: As you struggle up toward the summit of some of the Great Basin's highest peaks (e.g., Wheeler Peak in Great Basin National Park), precariously picking your way across talus slopes and rock fields, you are likely to encounter one of the Great Basin's most beautiful flowers sheltering in the lee of a rock. Sky Pilot (a wonderfully evocative name, but potentially a confusing one too, for it is applied to several high-elevation *Polemonium* species of various parts of the American West) is a magnificent plant with spherical clusters of gorgeous, deep blue, 5-petaled, bowl-shaped flowers. The yellow or orange anthers at the tip of the purple filaments add a wonderful touch of contrast to the deep blue canvas of the petals. The long, narrow leaves are divided into many tiny segments, resulting in a leaf that looks a bit like a rat's tail. While the more romantically inclined might call this plant Sky Pilot, the more pragmatic call it Skunky Polemonium because of its strong, unpleasant odor.

Flowering Season: June–August.

Habitat/Range: Talus slopes, rock ledges in the montane and the alpine, 8,000–13,000', in central and eastern Nevada, southern Oregon, e.g., Steens Mountain, Great Basin National Park.

Comments: *Polemonium (P. occidentale). Viscosum* means "sticky." Also called Sticky Polemonium and Skunky Polemonium.

MONKSHOOD
Aconitum columbianum
Buttercup Family (Ranunculaceae)

Description: This spectacular, robust (to 6' tall) plant with the fascinating, dark blue flowers is the only species of *Aconitum* in the Great Basin. Noticing that its 1–2" flowers are highly irregular in structure, you would correctly expect that this plant has coevolved with a particular species of pollinator (in this case a bee). The cluster of many yellowish green reproductive parts is partly hidden within the deep blue, petal-like parts (actually sepals). The upper sepal forms the "monk's hood" (which looks like a duck's head in profile), the lateral 2 comprise the body, and the lower 2 comprise the legs. The 2 actual petals are small and are cradled within the sepals along with the reproductive parts. The leaves, especially those on the lower stem, are very large (to 7" long and 6" wide) and maplelike (i.e., palmately lobed).

Flowering Season: June–August.

Habitat/Range: Grassy meadows, streambanks, around trees in the montane, 6,000–10,000', throughout the Great Basin, e.g., Steens Mountain, Deep Creek Mountains.

Comments: *Aconitum* is the ancient Greek name. *Columbianum* means "of western North America."

ANDERSON'S LARKSPUR
Delphinium andersonii
Buttercup Family (Ranunculaceae)

Description: Anderson's Larkspur is a ½–2' plant with a stout, often reddish, generally hairless stem, which usually bears more than 10 of the blue, 1" flowers on ascending, ½–2½" pedicels. The ½–¾" nectar spur is often bent down at the tip. The large blue sepals are blunt at the tips. The lower 2 of the actual petals are dark purple and bilobed, while the upper 2 are white. The smooth, blue-green leaves are mostly basal and are palmately divided into many narrow segments that are further lobed. The few leaves further up the stem usually have only a few narrow segments.

Flowering Season: April–July.

Habitat/Range: Dry flats, canyons in the sagebrush steppe and the montane, 4,500–8,500', throughout the Great Basin, e.g., Peavine Mountain, Charles Sheldon National Wildlife Refuge.

Comments: *Delphinium* means "dolphin" in reference to the resemblance of the flower in bud to a swimming dolphin. C.L. Anderson *(Astragalus a.).*

GLAUCOUS LARKSPUR
Delphinium glaucum
Buttercup Family (Ranunculaceae)

Description: Very similar to Western Larkspur *(D. occidentale)* in being tall (to 6') and robust with 50 or more flowers, Glaucous Larkspur has even larger (to 2"), darker blue-purple flowers than its close relative. Since it grows in wet meadows and along streams (as opposed to Western Larkspur's damp meadows or rocky areas), it isn't surprising to find that it has larger (to 5" wide), palmately divided and lobed leaves. Although both species typically have more than 50 flowers, Glaucous Larkspur appears more flowery, since its flowers are in a more open raceme that is spread out along more of the stem. To see a dense stand of this lush, many-flowered, intensely blue-purple plant in a wet meadow or in a seep area is a truly exhilarating sight, especially since it is a rather late bloomer, reaching its peak after many of its neighbors have begun to wither.

Flowering Season: July–August.

Habitat/Range: Wet meadows, streambanks in the montane, 7,500–10,000', in northern and eastern Nevada, e.g., Ruby Mountains.

Comments: *Delphinium (D. andersonii). Glaucum* means "covered with a whitish film" in reference to the stem.

WESTERN LARKSPUR
Delphinium occidentale
Buttercup Family (Ranunculaceae)

Description: The two tallest species of larkspur in the Great Basin (reaching more than 3') are Glaucous Larkspur *(D. glaucum)* and Western Larkspur, both of which are robust plants with large, palmately divided and lobed leaves and a long raceme of scores of dark blue-purple flowers. These two species are quite similar and often hybridize, so intermediate plants are common. Western Larkspur tends to grow in damp rather than wet locations and tends to have a much tighter, more compact raceme. The 50 or so flowers branch out in all directions from the plant stem at about the same distance from the stem, creating an almost uniform cylinder of flowers.

Flowering Season: June–August.

Habitat/Range: Streambanks, moist areas on talus slopes, openings in aspen groves in the montane, 7,500–10,000', in northeastern and eastern Nevada, western Utah, e.g., Ruby Mountains, Deep Creek Mountains.

Comments: *Delphinium (D. anderonii). Occidentale* means "western."

SMALL-FLOWERED BLUE-EYED MARY
Collinsia parviflora
Snapdragon Family (Scrophulariaceae)

Description: One of the floral delights of spring that visits almost every part of the Great Basin, Small-Flowered Blue-Eyed Mary often carpets large patches of dry, open ground with a bluish haze. Although the plant stems can exceed 1', they often reach up only a few inches, so the many ¼" flowers practically hug the ground. Close examination of an individual flower reveals a wonderful, multicolored display with a small secret. The upper 2 erect petals are white (sometimes blue tipped), while the lower 2 are mostly blue (white at the base). Typical of Snapdragon Family members, there is a third lower petal (blue), but, atypically, it is folded into a narrow keel and is hidden between the other 2 lower petals. The stems, narrow leaves, and sepals can be smooth or can be sparsely glandular.

Flowering Season: April–July.

Habitat/Range: Dry or damp meadows, openings in the sagebrush steppe and the montane, 4,500–10,000', throughout the Great Basin, e.g., Charles Sheldon National Wildlife Refuge, Great Basin National Park.

Comments: Zaccheus Collins was a Philadelphia botanist at the turn of the 19th century. *Parviflora* means "small flowered."

ALPINE PENSTEMON
Penstemon davidsonii
Snapdragon Family (Scrophulariaceae)

Description: There are a few other *Penstemon* species with flowers as big or bigger, but the blooms of Alpine Penstemon look especially large because they grow on dwarfed (1–6"), alpine plants. In some cases, the spectacular, tubular flowers are actually longer than the plant stem is tall! The 5-petaled blossoms are blue-purple or pink-purple. The small, oval leaves often form extensive mats on rocky flats or ridges near timberline, so you will usually find the flowers in great masses. Frequently the blossoms reach up nearly vertically from the leaf mat like trumpets raised exuberantly to the heavens.

Flowering Season: July–August.

Habitat/Range: Talus slopes, rocky ridges, stony flats in the montane and the alpine, 7,000–11,500', in eastern California, northeastern Nevada, southern Oregon, e.g., Santa Rosa Range, Steens Mountain.

Comments: *Penstemon (P. deustus).* George Davidson was a 19th-century California plant collector. Also called Davidson's Penstemon.

SLENDER PENSTEMON
Penstemon gracilentus
Snapdragon Family (Scrophulariaceae)

Description: Although having the long, 2-lipped, tubular flowers characteristic of the *Penstemon* genus, Slender Penstemon has a very distinctive look. Not only are the 5-petaled, ½–¾" flowers very slender with barely flaring faces, but the 1–2½' stem is also very slender and bears only a few, loosely scattered flowers. The overall impression this plant makes is delicate and understated, very much in contrast to the robust and assertive impression of Showy Penstemon *(P. speciosus)*, with its dense clusters of large, broad flowers. The petals, sepals, and especially the pedicels are very noticeably glandular-sticky. The pairs of opposite leaves are very narrow.

Flowering Season: June–August.

Habitat/Range: Dry, brushy slopes, openings in the sagebrush steppe and the montane, to 9,500', in western and northwestern Nevada, e.g., Charles Sheldon National Wildlife Refuge.

Comments: *Penstemon (P. deustus). Gracilentus* means "slender and flexible."

GAY PENSTEMON
Penstemon laetus
Snapdragon Family (Scrophulariaceae)

Description: Gay Penstemon is a much-branched, ½–2½', woody-based plant with numerous horizontal or slightly ascending pedicels bearing the typical tubular penstemon flowers. Unlike Meadow Penstemon *(P. rydbergii)*, Gay Penstemon is more typical of its genus with individual flowers at the ends of relatively long pedicels that branch off the plant stem in only a few directions, rather than with clusters of flowers that whorl completely around the plant stem. As with many *Penstemon* species, the 5-petaled, 1" flowers have red-purple tubes with flaring, blue faces. The outside of the flower tubes, the sepals, and the pedicels are noticeably glandular-hairy. The 1–2" leaves are narrow and usually infolded. The hairless staminode reaches the mouth of the flower tube and is distinctly white.

Flowering Season: May–July.

Habitat/Range: Dry slopes and flats in the sagebrush steppe and the montane, to 10,000', in western and northern Nevada, e.g., Peavine Mountain.

Comments: *Penstemon (P. deustus). Laetus* means "vivid." Also called Mountain Blue Penstemon. Sometimes known as *P. roezlii*.

SMALL-FLOWERED PENSTEMON
Penstemon procerus
Snapdragon Family (Scrophulariaceae)

Description: Of the many blue-flowered *Penstemon* species in the Great Basin, Small-Flowered Penstemon can be distinguished by its clusters of relatively short (to 1½') flowering stems rising above a leafy (often mat-forming) base, its nonglandular, nonhairy inflorescences, its nontoothed leaves, and its 1–3 separated, somewhat chaotic whorls of short (to ½") flowers. The narrow flower tube is violet, the 5 lobes are blue-purple, and the throat is white. The staminode is hairless or has sparse, orange-yellow hairs at the tip.

Flowering Season: July–August.

Habitat/Range: Rocky slopes in the montane, 7,000–11,500', throughout the Great Basin, e.g., Steens Mountain, Great Basin National Park.

Comments: *Penstemon (P. deustus). Procerus* means "tall."

MEADOW PENSTEMON

Penstemon rydbergii
Snapdragon Family (Scrophulariaceae)

Description: Although Meadow Penstemon has the long-tubular, 2-lipped, 5-petaled flowers characteristic of the *Penstemon* genus, it is unusual for a penstemon in at least 3 noticeable ways: 1) its ½" long flowers occur in dense whorls all the way around the ½–2' stem; 2) it does not grow in dry places, but in moist meadows; and 3) it can create huge masses of plants of many square yards—from a distance a mass of Meadow Penstemon in a grassy meadow can appear to be a small pond! The small, flaring face is usually quite blue, while the long tube is more red-purple. The floor of the flower tube is covered with white or yellow hairs. The pairs of opposite leaves are narrow and sessile (i.e., they have no petioles, but attach directly to the plant stem).

Flowering Season: June–September.

Habitat/Range: Damp, grassy meadows, openings in the sagebrush steppe and the montane, to 11,000', throughout the Great Basin except eastern Nevada, e.g., Toiyabe Range.

Comments: *Penstemon (P. deustus)*. Per Axel Rydberg was a botanist at the New York Botanical Gardens at the turn of the 20th century. Also called Rydberg's Penstemon.

SHOWY PENSTEMON
Penstemon speciosus
Snapdragon Family (Scrophulariaceae)

Description: Although all *Penstemon* species are showy with their colorful, tubular flowers, Showy Penstemon is well named, for its 1–1¾" long flowers are among the largest of all penstemons, and its flowers are a rich, saturated, deep, sky blue. As with many species in this genus, the outside of the flower tube can be tinged with red-purple, but often it is as deep blue as the flaring flower face. Except for this occasional red-purple, the only thing tempering the pure blue of this amazing flower is the whitish markings on the inside of the throat. To further enhance the show, the 5-petaled flowers, which are spectacular individually, occur in 1-directional clusters, so the spectacle is multiplied and intensified. The 2"–2' plant stem has many narrow, 1–3", infolded leaves.

Flowering Season: May–July.

Habitat/Range: Dry slopes, rocky flats, and ridges in the sagebrush steppe and the montane, to 10,000', throughout the Great Basin, e.g., Virginia Range, Deep Creek Mountains.

Comments: *Penstemon (P. deustus). Speciosus* means "showy."

AMERICAN BROOKLIME
Veronica americana
Snapdragon Family (Scrophulariaceae)

Description: The flowers of American Brooklime may be quite small (¼"), but they occur in large numbers on the plant and they are a beautiful, perky blue color. The plant stem is stout and up to 2' long, but the plant usually is much closer to the ground as the stem is often decumbent. The long (to 2"), broadly oval, shiny leaves are thick on the plant, partly concealing some of the flowers, but most of the flowers are conspicuously displayed on opposite pairs of racemes that start in the leaf axils and outreach the leaves. Each 4-petaled, blue flower has a conspicuous green ovary and long, slender stamens. The broad upper petal has showy, red-purple marks at its base.

Flowering Season: May–September.

Habitat/Range: Creekbanks, shallow creeks, wet meadows in the sagebrush steppe and the montane, 5,000–10,000', throughout the Great Basin, e.g., Peavine Mountain, Great Basin National Park.

Comments: *Veronica* is probably after Saint Veronica, the woman who gave Jesus a cloth to wipe his face while on the way to Calvary, and so named because the markings on some species supposedly resemble those on her sacred handkerchief. *Americana* means "of America."

THYME-LEAF SPEEDWELL
Veronica serpyllifolia
Snapdragon Family (Scrophulariaceae)

Description: Thyme-Leaf Speedwell has the small (¼"), delicate, blue flowers characteristic of the *Veronica* genus, but it has a few features that (taken together) can distinguish it from its close relatives: 1) this 2–12" plant has a terminal raceme of flowers (as opposed to opposite pairs of racemes branching out of the leaf axils; 2) the tiny flowers tend to be pale blue or even white (as opposed to dark blue) with darker blue-purple markings; 3) the 2 stamens are as long as the petal lobes; and 4) the small leaves are relatively broad, closer to ovate than lanceolate. As in all veronicas, the upper petal is broader than the lower 3, being a result of the fusing of the 2 petals of the upper lip into 1 broad petal.

Flowering Season: May–August.

Habitat/Range: Creekbanks, wet meadows in the sagebrush steppe and the montane, 5,500–10,000', throughout the Great Basin, e.g., Peavine Mountain, Steens Mountain.

Comments: *Veronica (V. Americana). Serpyllifolia* means "creeping leaves" in reference to the often prostrate lower branches.

51

ALPINE VERONICA
Veronica wormskjoldii
Snapdragon Family (Scrophulariaceae)

Description: Alpine Veronica is very similar to its fellow *Veronica* species Thyme-Leaf Speedwell *(V. serpyllifolia)* with its beautiful, blue, veined, ¼" flowers in a terminal raceme and its opposite pairs of oval or elliptic leaves. As with all veronicas the upper petal (formed by the fusion of the 2 petals of the upper lip) is somewhat larger than the lower 3 petals, and there are only 2 stamens. Distinguishing Alpine Veronica from its close kin are its deep blue (not pale blue or white) flowers, its shorter stamens (not as long as the petals), and the long, silky hairs on the stems. The 1–1½" leaves can be narrow or broad.

Flowering Season: June–August.

Habitat/Range: Streambanks, moist meadows in the montane, 8,000–11,500', throughout the Great Basin, e.g., Ruby Mountains.

Comments: *Veronica (V. Americana).* Morton Wormskjold was a 19th-century Danish plant collector.

NORTHERN BOG VIOLET
Viola nephrophylla
Violet Family (Violaceae)

Description: Although several of the Great Basin's violets are not at all violet (being yellow or white), there are a few that are faithful to the name or are at least close to it. Northern Bog Violet is one of these—beautiful, deep blue-violet with darker purple veins. The base of the lower petals is white. The 1" flowers nod off the slender, 2–10" peduncle (the plant has no true stem). The leaves are probably exactly what you think of when you think of violets—broad (up to 2"), toothed, and heart shaped. Northern Bog Violet is quite similar to *V. adunca*, which occurs in similar habitats, but Bog Violet has more heart-shaped leaves and narrower petals (especially true of the middle petal of the lower lip).

Flowering Season: April–June.

Habitat/Range: Creekbanks, wet meadows, openings often with aspens in the montane, 6,000–8,000', throughout the Great Basin, e.g., Peavine Mountain, Ruby Mountains.

Comments: *Viola (V. macloskeyi). Nephrophylla* means "kidney-shaped leaves."

RED AND PINK FLOWERS

This section includes flowers that range in color from pale pink to deep rose to true red. Since these colors grade into shades of blue, orange, and even yellow, and since some plants produce flowers that range across the spectrum, you should check the sections for blue and purple flowers and orange and yellow flowers if you don't find the flower you are looking for here.

SPREADING DOGBANE
Apocynum androsaemifolium
Dogbane Family (Apocynaceae)

Description: With its low, much-branched stems, Spreading Dogbane can cover quite an area with its broad, dark green leaves and its delightful, 5-petaled, urn-shaped flowers. Because the ¼" flowers often vary from creamy white to pale pink to intense rose even in the same flower cluster, they may remind you of peppermint ice cream! Many flowers occur on each raceme, vividly displayed against the dark green background of the leaves, which occur in opposite pairs along the stem. The distinct veins on the leaves add one more appealing touch to the artistic design of this plant.

Flowering Season: June–August.

Habitat/Range: Dry slopes, roadbanks, brushy meadows in the montane, 5,500–11,000', throughout the Great Basin, e.g., Peavine Mountain, Deep Creek Mountains.

Comments: *Apocynum* means "away from the dog," apparently in reference to the use by some cultures of plants of this genus as dog poison. *Androsaemifolium* means "leaves like *Androsace*," a genus in the Primrose Family.

PURPLE MILKWEED
Asclepias cordifolia
Milkweed Family (Asclepiadaceae)

Description: Purple Milkweed is a very leafy plant, each thick stem bearing as many as 10 or even more pairs of 2–8" long and 1–4" wide, opposite, ovate or heart-shaped leaves. Although the pairs of leaves toward the tip of the stem are a bit smaller than those more toward the base, this difference is not great, so leafiness seems to be everywhere. But as the common name indicates, green is not the only color this plant boasts. Branching off the tips of the plant stems are several umbels of slender, purplish pedicels at the tips of which are the odd, reflexed-petal flowers typical of milkweeds. The 5 tonguelike petals are a deep red-purple, which contrasts vividly with the creamy white (or violet) horns that surmount them. These horns look a bit like kernels of corn or maybe small teeth. The buds resemble tiny, red-purple pumpkins.

Flowering Season: May–July.

Habitat/Range: Gravelly or sandy hillsides in the sagebrush steppe and the montane, to 8,500', in western Nevada, southern Oregon, e.g., Virginia Range.

Comments: *Asclepias (A. speciosa). Cordifolia* means "heart-shaped leaves."

SHOWY MILKWEED

Asclepias speciosa
Milkweed Family (Asclepiadaceae)

Description: Although Showy Milkweed is a weedy plant that is common along roadsides and in other disturbed areas, it is indeed showy with its intricate, two-toned flowers and interesting buds and fruits. The 2–6' plant bears rather spherical clusters of many of the 1–1½" flowers, each with 5 reflexed, tonguelike, pink or rose petals surmounted by 5 up-curving, white or pale pink horns that are about as long as the petals. In bud the spherical cluster of flowers resembles a bunch of pink, furry grapes. The 3" seedpods hold the silky-parachuted seeds we frequently see floating across Great Basin plains. Showy Milkweed is a very leafy plant with many opposite pairs of long (to 8"), broad, felty leaves. Stop the next time you spot these plants growing in some ditch along the road and check them out—you'll be rewarded with quite a stunning, colorful show of leaves, buds, blooms, and fruits!

Flowering Season: April–September.

Habitat/Range: Roadsides, ditches, grassy fields, disturbed places in the sagebrush steppe and the montane, to 8,500', throughout the Great Basin, e.g., Washoe Valley, Steens Mountain.

Comments: *Asclepias* is after Asklepios, the Greek god of healing. *Speciosa* means "showy."

WESTERN EUPATORIUM
Ageratina occidentale
Composite Family (Asteraceae)

Description: Bringing delightful color to late summer and fall landscapes with its lovely, soft, pink flower heads, Western Eupatorium cascades down rocky slopes, sometimes almost completely covering them. The ½–2½' stems are thick with broad, dark green, triangular leaves and pink flower heads. Out of the disk flowers protrude long, white styles. At a time of year when most flowers have dried and gone, it is a delight to come across Eupatorium in full bloom—delicate reminders of the flower season now almost over and sweet mementos (in your mind) to carry you over the winter.

Flowering Season: July–September.

Habitat/Range: Rocky slopes, ledges in the montane, 5,000–10,000', throughout the Great Basin, e.g., Steens Mountain, Ruby Mountains.

Comments: *Ageratina* means "resembling *Ageratum*," another genus in the Composite Family. *Occidentalis* means "western." Eupatorium comes from the Greek name Mithridates Eupator, King of Pontus about 115 BC, who is said to have discovered an antidote to a commonly used poison in one of the species. Formerly known as *Eupatorium occidentale*.

SPOTTED KNAPWEED
Centaurea maculosa
Composite Family (Asteraceae)

Description: Spotted Knapweed is a tall (to 5'), much-branched, weedy plant of roadsides and other disturbed places, but despite its invasive and rather scraggly nature, it has showy flower heads of beautiful, pink-purple, threadlike rays. The teardrop phyllaries form a narrowing vase from which the rays flare. As the species name indicates, the phyllaries have a conspicuous black tip. The leaves are pinnately lobed into narrow, fingerlike segments. The leaves and stems are covered with a thin, loose mat of white hairs.

Flowering Season: July–September.

Habitat/Range: Dry roadsides, disturbed places in the sagebrush steppe, to 6,500', northeastern and eastern Nevada, western Utah, e.g., just east of Great Basin National Park.

Comments: *Centaurea* is from the Latin and a reference to the centaur Chiron who was supposed to have discovered the medicinal uses of a plant in Greece that came to be called Centaury. *Maculosa* means "spotted" in reference to the black spots on the tips of the phyllaries.

EATON'S THISTLE
Cirsium eatonii
Composite Family (Asteraceae)

Description: Being used to tall, coarse thistles invading low-elevation fields and other disturbed areas, you many be surprised to discover Eaton's Thistle well away from human habitation on rocky slopes in the high mountains, even extending to above timberline. Although it has the spiny leaves and spiny involucre bracts typical of thistles, Eaton's Thistle is a delicate-looking plant, for its 1/2–2 1/2' stem is rather slender and is topped by broad flower heads of long, soft, lavender-purple disk flowers. The deeply lobed leaves are narrower than those of most thistles, and the 1/2–1", needlelike spines at the tip of each leaf lobe are almost as long as the leaf is wide!

Flowering Season: July–September.

Habitat/Range: Rocky flats and slopes in the montane and the alpine, 7,500–11,500', eastern Nevada, western Utah, e.g., Ruby Mountains.

Comments: *Cirsium (C. scariosum)*. Daniel Eaton was a 19th-century botany professor at Yale University.

COBWEB THISTLE
Cirsium occidentale
Composite Family (Asteraceae)

Description: Of the several tall, imposing, somewhat intimidating thistles of the Great Basin, Cobweb Thistle may be the most distinctive, for its stout, 5–10' stem, its 4–16" lobed leaves, and its spiny involucre bracts are all covered with a silvery gray, felty, cobwebby mat of hairs. So, although it does have photo-synthesizing leaves, there is little green to be seen on this haunting, ghostly plant. In some ways this makes the deep red flower heads all the more dramatic, as they are practically the only color other than cobwebby gray on the entire plant! The flower heads are 1½–3" wide and about the same height, so they appear squarish. The sharp-pointed involucre bracts (i.e., the phyllaries) are mostly spreading.

Flowering Season: May–July.

Habitat/Range: Dry or moist flats, disturbed places in the sagebrush steppe, 5,000–7,000', eastern California, western Nevada, southern Oregon, e.g., Peavine Mountain, White Mountains.

Comments: *Cirsium (C. scariosum). Occidentale* means "western." Also known as *C. pastoris* and called Snowy Thistle.

STEENS MOUNTAIN THISTLE
Cirsium peckii
Composite Family (Asteraceae)

Description: Steens Mountain Thistle is a stunning member of the mountain flora in southern Oregon, lining the trail up to the summit of Steens Mountain with its large, bright pink (or lavender) flower heads. Especially if you're up there when the sun is low in the sky and you can see this plant backlit, it can take your breath away. The stout, hairy, 1–4' stem has many deeply lobed and sharply spiked leaves that often cradle the flower heads, which are at the tips of short stems or rest directly in the leaf axils.

Flowering Season: June–August.

Habitat/Range: Dry slopes, rocky places in the sagebrush steppe and the montane, 6,500–9,700', very limited distribution in southern Oregon, e.g., Steens Mountain.

Comments: *Cirsium (C. scariosum).* Morton Peck was a 20th-century Willamette College biology professor who authored *A Manual of the Higher Plants of Oregon.*

BULL THISTLE
Cirsium vulgare
Composite Family (Asteraceae)

Description: One of the several tall (2–7'), coarse thistles in the Great Basin, Bull Thistle is probably the most common, seeming to invade almost every abandoned field and roadside. Despite its "*vulgare*-ness" and weedy nature, it does have its appealing attributes—many lovely, red-purple flower heads. The stout, winged (i.e., with raised ribs) stem is usually profusely branched in its upper half, each branch again branching. The resulting candelabra can bear scores of 2–3" long and wide flower heads, each crammed with 100 or more delicate, threadlike, red-purple disk flowers. The involucre bracts (i.e., phyllaries) are short and narrow and are more erect than spreading, so the flower cup is neater than in many thistles. The leaves are pinnately lobed into narrow segments that are tipped with fine spines.

Flowering Season: June–August.

Habitat/Range: Roadsides, dry flats, disturbed places in the sagebrush steppe, to 8,500', throughout the Great Basin, e.g., Peavine Mountain, Steens Mountain.

Comments: *Cirsium (C. scariosum). Vulgare* means "common."

WANDERING DAISY
Erigeron peregrinus
Composite Family (Asteraceae)

Description: We are fortunate that Wandering Daisy wanders across the American West (and even into eastern Asia), for it is a delightful plant with 1½–2", cheery flower heads. The 30–100 pink, lavender, or purple rays crowd joyfully around the central, bright yellow, domelike button crammed with over 100 disk flowers. The ½–1½' stems are branched above, each branch usually bearing a single flower head (though there can be up to 4). The phyllaries are rather messy (reflexed and spreading) and are distinctly glandular-sticky. The 2–8" leaves are oblanceolate or spoon shaped and mostly basal, though there are also a few clasping stem leaves.

Flowering Season: July–September.

Habitat/Range: Moist, grassy meadows, forest openings in the montane, 7,000–10,000', throughout the Great Basin, e.g., Steens Mountain, Ruby Mountains.

Comments: *Erigeron (E. filifolius). Peregrinus* means "wanderer" in reference to this plant's wide distribution, which extends beyond North America.

NARROW-LEAF STEPHANOMERIA
Stephanomeria tenuifolia
Composite Family (Asteraceae)

Description: With its 5 fringed "petals" and its few reproductive parts, Narrow-Leaf Stephanomeria is a bit deceptive as to its family affiliation. You probably wouldn't initially think of the Composite Family, but there are several clues that could lead you in this direction: (1) the "petals," though only 5, do have the squared tips and slight lobes that many composites have; (2) if you carefully inspect the flower structure, you will discover that each "petal" has a reproductive column attached; (3) the male parts are not immediately obvious and turn out to be bumps on the column under a delicately 2-parted female part (the stigma); (4) what appear to be sepals underneath are fingerlike and occur in more than 1 series; and (5) the seeds are transported by parachute-like pappi. Each of these signs, and certainly all of them together, point to the Composite Family, which means that the 5-"petaled" flowers are actually flower heads with 5 ray flowers and the "sepals" are actually phyllaries subtending an entire flower head. The much-branched, ½–2' plant bears threadlike leaves and several of the delicately pink flower heads.

Flowering Season: June–September.

Habitat/Range: Dry slopes, plains in the sagebrush steppe and the montane, 6,000–8,000', throughout the Great Basin, e.g., Charles Sheldon National Wildlife Refuge, White Mountains.

Comments: *Stephanomeria* means "wreath division." *Tenuifolia* means "narrow leaved."

HOLBOELL'S ROCK-CRESS
Arabis holboellii
Mustard Family (Brassicaceae)

Description: Of the numerous *Arabis* species in the Great Basin, *Arabis holboellii* is easy to distinguish, for unlike most species with small, delicate, 4-petaled flowers that are held upright or horizontal from the plant stem, the flowers of Holboell's Rock-Cress spend most of their blooming phase hanging down close to the stem on gracefully down-curving pedicels. Each ¼–½" pink or white flower flares out of a long, narrow calyx that conceals most of the flower tube. The narrow seedpods, which can be up to 3" long, also are distinctive, hanging down almost parallel to the ½–3' plant stem. The gray-green leaves are mostly in a basal cluster, but some plants also have numerous narrow, clasping stem leaves.

Flowering Season: April–August.

Habitat/Range: Gravelly or rocky flats and slopes in the sagebrush steppe and the montane, 5,500–12,000', throughout the Great Basin, e.g., Peavine Mountain, Santa Rosa Range.

Comments: *Arabis* means "of Arabia." Carl P. Holboell was a 19th-century Danish ornithologist.

ELEGANT ROCK-CRESS
Arabis sparsiflora
Mustard Family (Brassicaceae)

Description: Unlike its close relative Holboell's Rock-Cress *(A. holboellii)*, with its flowers and seedpods that hang down close to the plant stem, Elegant Rock-Cress has its 4-petaled flowers and seedpods held upright, horizontal, or arching. Though the 1½–2½' plant bears only a few of the ½" flowers, they are striking for their rich pink-purple color. The 2–4" seedpods are straight or curved. The clustered basal leaves are lancelike with smooth or shallowly toothed margins, while the many stem leaves are narrowly arrow shaped and clasp the stem. Although the plant can be glabrous, often you will find soft, white hairs scattered loosely on the stems, pedicels, sepals, and leaves.

Flowering Season: April–July.

Habitat/Range: Rocky slopes, thickets in the sagebrush steppe and the montane, 5,000–8,200', in western and northwestern Nevada, southern Oregon, e.g., Virginia Range, Steens Mountain.

Comments: *Arabis (A. holboellii)*. *Sparsiflora* means "sparsely flowered."

DAGGERPOD
Phoenicaulis cheiranthoides
Mustard Family (Brassicaceae)

Description: Before, during, and after its blooming, Daggerpod is a striking sight—its basal cluster of furry, 1–6", gray-green, tonguelike leaves brings a soft pastel to the sharp edges of its rock or cliff habitat. The ½–1" flowers reinforce the gentle theme, for their 4 pale rose or pink, rounded petals seem a perfect match for the bed of cotton-soft leaves. The fruits, however (as the common name suggests), provide quite a jolting contrast to all this benevolence, for they are ½–3", sharp-edged blades. When the plant is in seed, a loose cluster of these blades projects horizontally in all directions from the top half or so of the otherwise naked plant stem.

Flowering Season: April–August.

Habitat/Range: Gravelly or rocky slopes, talus, cliffs in the sagebrush steppe and the montane, 5,000–10,000', throughout the Great Basin except western Utah, e.g., Washoe Valley, Steens Mountain.

Comments: *Phoenicaulis* means "visible stem." *Cheiranthoides* means "resembling *Cheiranthes*," which was another genus in the Mustard Family (now incorporated into the genus *Erysimum*).

HEDGEHOG CACTUS
Echinocereus engelmanii
Cactus Family (Cactaceae)

Description: Although the large (to 3" wide), spectacular magenta flowers of Hedgehog Cactus bear some resemblance to those of Beavertails *(O. basilaris)*, Hedgehog Cactus, as the name suggests, is a much more dangerous-looking plant. Its 6–18" cucumber-like stems, which usually grow in clusters of 5–15, are covered with sharp-pointed silver or straw-colored spines. These rapiers occur in clusters of 10–18, each cluster consisting of 2 or a few long, up-curved, central spines and several shorter, lateral ones. The magnificent flowers are usually a darker red than the flowers of Beavertails and have distinct brown or black stripes on the outer perianth parts. Hedgehog Cactus flowers are also usually more closed (i.e., cuplike) than the flowers of Beavertails. At the center of the dense cluster of yellow stamens is the stigma, divided into several green, fingerlike lobes.

Flowering Season: April–May.

Habitat/Range: Sandy slopes, washes in the desert shrub and the sagebrush steppe, to 5,000', in eastern California, western and eastern Nevada, western Utah, e.g., White Mountains. This species occurs mostly in the Mojave Desert.

Comments: *Echinocereus* means "hedgehog candle." George Englemann was a 19th-century American botanist and friend of the renowned botanist Asa Gray *(Ligusticum grayi).*

BEAVERTAILS
Opuntia basilaris
Cactus Family (Cactaceae)

Description: One of the several stunning cactus species of the Mojave Desert that also occurs in the Great Basin, Beavertails is one of the first to bloom in the spring. Its large (to 3" across), intense magenta flowers bring dazzling color to the early spring desert shrub landscape. Each 1–1½' plant can consist of several pads (the broad, flat stems, which do leaf duty as well), from which sprout several of the gorgeous flowers. The pads are spineless, though the many eyespots are ringed with small, brownish bristles that can cause quite an irritation if touched. The many crinkly, satiny petals overlap, surrounding a dense cluster of crimson, white-tipped or yellow-tipped stamens. In the center is the solitary, disklike, white stigma.

Flowering Season: March–May.

Habitat/Range: Sandy or gravelly flats, washes, canyons in the desert shrub and the sagebrush steppe, to 6,000', in eastern California, western Nevada, e.g., White Mountains. This species occurs mostly in the Mojave Desert.

Comments: *Opuntia (O. polyacantha). Basilaris* means "basal, from the base."

PLAINS PRICKLY PEAR
Opuntia polyacantha
Cactus Family (Cactaceae)

Description: Although Plains Prickly Pear is described in the yellow section of this book *(O. polyacantha)*, it can also have intense rose or magenta flowers; and because its flowers, yellow or red, are so strikingly beautiful, I have made an exception and repeat this plant here in the red section. It can easily be distinguished from other red-flowered relatives by its spiny pads (not spineless as in Beavertails, *O. basilaris,* and not cucumber-like, cylindrical stems as in Hedgehog Cactus, *Echinocereus engelmanii*). As with its yellow-flowered siblings, the red-flowered Plains Prickly Pear is dazzling: The silky rose petals, the clumps of yellow-anthered stamens, and the green-lobed stigma light up the landscape like a brilliant smile lights up a face.

Flowering Season: May–June.

Habitat/Range: Sandy or gravelly flats, scrubby slopes, rock crevices in the desert shrub and the sagebrush steppe, to 8,000', throughout the Great Basin except northwestern Nevada and southern Oregon, e.g., Great Basin National Park.

Comments: *Opuntia* is probably derived from a Papago Indian word. *Polyacantha* (*O. polyacantha* in the yellow section).

PINK BEE PLANT
Cleome serrulata
Caper Family (Capparaceae)

Description: Pink Bee Plant can reach 3½' tall and often grows in large clusters. From a distance a "forest" of these plants looks like a soft, pink-purple haze floating delicately in the air. The scores of 1" flowers, each consisting of 4 narrow, widely separated, pale pink-purple petals and numerous long-protruding, threadlike stamens tipped with tiny, green anthers, appear feathery light. In fruit as much as the top 1½' of the stem bears the cylindrical, 1–2" seedpods. The lower part of the stem is thick with leaves, each consisting of 2–6 elliptic leaflets.

Flowering Season: June–September.

Habitat/Range: Dry flats, roadsides in the sagebrush steppe, 4,000–6,500', in northeastern and eastern Nevada, western Utah, e.g., Great Basin National Park.

Comments: *Cleome (C. lutea). Serrulata* means "sawlike."

MOSS CAMPION
Silene acaulis
Pink Family (Carophyllaceae)

Description: Moss Campion is the prototype alpine plant, forming dense, rounded cushions rising only a few inches above the rocky ground it contours, but often spreading for 2' or 3'. The tiny (⅛–¼") leaves become so tightly packed together that they form an almost impenetrable, smooth surface. You will usually see a few of the ¼–½", starlike, 5-petaled, pink flowers scattered over this leaf surface, but sometimes at peak blooming the entire mat of leaves can be hidden by solid blossoms. Just before the bloom, the cushion looks like a green mat punctuated by deep red torpedoes (the buds).

Flowering Season: June–August.

Habitat/Range: Rocky ridges, gravelly flats, tundra in the montane and the alpine, 9,500–13,000', eastern Nevada, western Utah, e.g., Great Basin National Park.

Comments: *Silene (S. douglasii). Acaulis* means "stemless."

SPINY HOPSAGE
Grayia spinosa
Goosefoot Family (Chenopodiaceae)

Description: Although Spiny Hopsage can be quite a showy plant, it may not be immediately apparent just what gives it its showy color. For most of the year, the most noticeable aspect of this 1–3', much-branched shrub is its many small, fleshy, elliptic leaves. The actual flowers are small and barely noticeable, mostly stamens in male plants and pistils in female ones (sometimes a plant has both male and female flowers). However, when the (female) plant goes to fruit, it "blossoms" with color, for the seeds become surrounded by 2 enlarged bracts that form a ½", winged structure that can be a rich rose or creamy yellowish color. These bracts are usually quite thick on the plant, creating a tapestry of color sometimes almost concealing the gray-green leaves beneath.

Flowering Season: March–June.

Habitat/Range: Dry flats and slopes in the desert shrub and the sagebrush steppe, to 7,000', throughout the Great Basin, e.g., Soldier Meadow, Great Basin National Park.

Comments: Asa Gray *(Ligusticum g.). Spinosa* means "spiny." Sometimes known as *Atriplex spinosa.*

RUSSIAN THISTLE
Salsola tragus
Goosefoot Family (Chenopodiaceae)

Description: Russian Thistle is a strange invader into the American West from the plains of southeastern Russia and western Siberia. It is a bushy plant with slender, 1–3' stems that vary from red to yellow-green, often with darker stripes. The young leaves are narrow and pointed, but drop off early to be replaced by short, awl-shaped, spiny ones. The small flowers are in the leaf axils and have no petals, but they do have 5 papery sepals that more or less unite into a veiny wing in fruit that is usually the same color as the stems (i.e., either red or yellow-green). As odd as this plant is alive, it may be even stranger in the fall when it dies and breaks away from its roots. Then the familiar tumbleweed with its sphere of interlaced, dried branches rolls across the steppe, scattering up to 50,000 seeds as it rolls! Despite its efficient method of seed dispersal, fortunately it is not an aggressive competitor and usually only succeeds in establishing itself in disturbed areas.

Flowering Season: March–October.

Habitat/Range: Dry, salty flats, disturbed places in the desert shrub and the sagebrush steppe, to 7,500', throughout the Great Basin, e.g., White Mountains, Soldier Meadow.

Comments: *Salsola* means "salted" in reference to its often saline habitat. *Tragus* is derived from a word meaning "goat." Also called Tumbleweed. Alien.

ROSY SEDUM
Sedum rosea
Stonecrop Family (Crassulaceae)

Description: It might surprise you to find such a lush, succulent plant in the rocks near and above timberline, but succulence is a wonderfully effective adaptation to such dry places—there's nothing like carrying your own water! The 2–12" stems of Rosy Sedum, with their masses of small, thick leaves, grow in such dense profusion that the plant appears to be a shrub (often several feet in diameter). Technically it's not, for it lacks woody stems. The 4-petaled flowers (unusual for a *Sedum*) are an intense wine-red color, forming round clusters at the tips of the stems.

Flowering Season: July–August.

Habitat/Range: Rocky slopes and ridges in the montane and the alpine, 8,500–13,500', in eastern California, eastern Nevada, western Utah, southern Oregon, e.g., Steens Mountain, Ruby Mountains.

Comments: *Sedum (S. debile) Rosea* means "rosy."

SWAMP LAUREL
Kalmia polifolia
Heath Family (Ericaceae)

Description: Coming across the delightful, ½",
pink or rose, shallow bowl-shaped flowers of
Swamp Laurel in a cold, boggy meadow high in
the mountains is a happy surprise—the flowers
seem so much warmer than the surroundings!
The flowers often are so thick on the 4–12" shrub
that they form a jumbly, overlapping ground cover
that almost conceals the small, rolled-under,
evergreen leaves. Each flower is an intricate
architectural wonder—the 10 filaments radiate
out against the bowl (the corolla) with their tiny,
black anthers tucked into pockets on the 5 petals.
These anthers are spring loaded, as any unsus-
pecting insect visitor will discover, for when the
insect trips the mechanism, the anthers spring
free of the pockets, pop up, and shake pollen over
the insect like a diner salting his appetizer.

Flowering Season: May–September.

Habitat/Range: Marshy meadows, creekbanks,
bogs in the montane, 6,500–10,000', eastern
Nevada, southern Oregon, e.g., Steens Mountain,
Ruby Mountains.

Comments: Peter Kalm was a student of Linnaeus
(the creator of binomial nomenclature) in the
1700s. *Polifolia* means "white leaved" in reference to the white hairs on the undersides of the
leaves. Also called Alpine Laurel.

ANDERSON'S MILKVETCH
Astragalus andersonii
Pea Family (Fabaceae)

Description: In a genus of so many similar
species, Anderson's Milkvetch is distinguished by
its lovely, pale pink or white flowers and its small
(¼–½"), narrow leaflets. The 2–8" stems can lie
flat or be erect. The stems, leaves, and reddish
sepals are covered with short, white or gray hairs.
Each 1–4" leaf consists of 9–21 leaflets. The
racemes are comprised of 12–26 flowers with
pedicels that curve up at first, then reflex later in
the blooming period. The seedpods are roundish,
stiffly papery, and hairy.

Flowering Season: April–July.

Habitat/Range: Sandy flats in the sagebrush
steppe, to 7,000', eastern California, western
Nevada, e.g., Sweetwater Mountains, Carson
Valley.

Comments: *Astragalus (A. lentiginosus).* C. L.
Anderson was a Nevada physician and naturalist
of the late 19th and early 20th centuries.

FRECKLED DAPPLE-POD
Astragalus lentiginosus
Pea Family (Fabaceae)

Description: Freckled Dapple-Pod is an extremely variable species (with almost 20 recognized varieties) that ranges across the Great Basin from desert shrub to gravelly ridges near timberline. The 5-petaled flowers can range from dark purple to light purple to cream to white, usually with conspicuous veins at the base of the banner. The silvery-hairy stems lift the raceme of 10–30 flowers well above the broad, silvery-hairy leaflets. Perhaps most distinctive of this dapple pod, in its numerous varieties, are the bladderlike, grooved, pointed seedpods that are usually greenish with reddish freckles.

Flowering Season: March–July.

Habitat/Range: Gravelly or sandy flats in the desert shrub, the sagebrush steppe, and the montane, to 11,000', throughout the Great Basin, e.g., Soldier Meadow, Great Basin National Park.

Comments: *Astragalus* means "dice," presumably in reference to the dried seeds rattling in the pods. *Lentiginosus* means "freckled" in reference to the mottling on the seedpods.

SHAGGY MILKVETCH
Astragalus malacus
Pea Family (Fabaceae)

Description: Shaggy Milkvetch is a very inviting plant, both for its delicate, red-purple flowers and for the soft, white hairs densely covering the leaves, stems, and sepals. The 4–16" stems tend to spread out, putting the leaves close to the ground and the flowers usually only a bit higher. The shaggy leaves consist of 7–21 elliptic leaflets that are often rather infolded. The raceme is crowded with 10–35 of the ½", red-purple, 5-petaled flowers with darker red-purple lines on the banner. The narrow, shaggy, red-mottled, slightly up-curved pods hang from the stems.

Flowering Season: April–June.

Habitat/Range: Dry flats and slopes in the sagebrush steppe, to 8,000' in eastern California, western Nevada, southern Oregon, e.g., Carson Valley, Charles Sheldon National Wildlife Refuge.

Comments: *Astragalus (A. lentiginosus). Malacus* means "soft" in reference to the dense, white hairs covering the plant.

NEWBERRY'S MILKVETCH
Astragalus newberryi
Pea Family (Fabaceae)

Description: Although the seedpods of Newberry's Milkvetch are quite striking, they don't monopolize all the attention as the pods of some *Astragalus* species do, for the 5-petaled flowers are also quite showy—large (1") and a beautiful pink-lavender with a conspicuous white splotch on the banner. This is a ground-hugging plant with flowers that barely rise above the leaves. There can be as many as 13 of the small, round leaflets, but often there are only 3 or 5. The leaves and stems are covered with appressed, silky hairs.

Flowering Season: April–July.

Habitat/Range: Rocky slopes, canyons in the sagebrush steppe and the montane, 4,500–8,000', throughout the Great Basin, e.g., Steens Mountain, Deep Creek Mountains.

Comments: *Astragalus (A. lentiginosus)*. John Newberry *(Gentiana newberryi)*.

PURSH'S MILKVETCH
Astragalus purshii
Pea Family (Fabaceae)

Description: There are so many *Astragalus* species in the Great Basin, many of which have numerous varieties, that it can be very difficult to distinguish them. Pursh's Milkvetch tends to be a prostrate plant (to 5" tall) with 3–17 small, roundish leaflets per leaf. Although many *Astragalus* species are hairy, Pursh's Milkvetch is unusual, for its stems and leaves are covered with fine, cottony, white hairs. The 5-petaled, ½" flowers can be white or cream colored, but are often a shiny pink-purple. The pods are quite distinctive, being short, almost round, and covered with cottony, white hairs. A plant in fruit with its cluster of cotton balls sitting on the ground under the pinnately compound leaves is quite striking and distinctive.

Flowering Season: April–June.

Habitat/Range: Dry flats and slopes in the sagebrush steppe and the montane, to 8,500', throughout the Great Basin, e.g., Peavine Mountain, Steens Mountain.

Comments: *Astragalus (A. lentiginosus).* Frederick T. Pursh *(Purshia stansburiana).*

WHITNEY'S LOCOWEED
Astragalus whitneyi
Pea Family (Fabaceae)

Description: Although you may find Whitney's Locoweed on dry slopes in mid-elevations, you can also come across it on dry, rocky, or gravelly terrain high in the mountains, even above timberline. The 5-petaled, pink-purple or white flowers with the darker lines on the banner, the 4–10" sprawling stems, and the 5–21 small, narrow, pinnate leaflets per leaf are not at all unusual for an *Astragalus* species, so how (other than its sometimes high elevation habitat) can you distinguish this locoweed (milkvetch) from its many Great Basin kin? If you're at all familiar with the *Astragalus* genus, you can probably guess—the seedpods. In a genus with many distinctive and fascinating seedpods (some smooth, some hairy, some straight, some curved,

many mottled), Whitney's Locoweed has astonishing ones—gold or yellow-green, red-splotched, inflated, papery bladders. Shake them in the fall, and they will rattle as the tiny seeds bounce off the papery pod walls.

Flowering Season: May–August.

Habitat/Range: Rocky flats, talus slopes in the sagebrush steppe, the montane, and the alpine, 5,000–12,000', throughout the Great Basin except western Utah, e.g., White Mountains, Steens Mountain.

Comments: *Astragalus (A. lentiginosus).* Josiah Whitney was the 19th-century geologist and explorer after whom Mt. Whitney was named.

73

NEVADA INDIGOBUSH
Psorothamnus polydenius
Pea Family (Fabaceae)

Description: Nevada Indigobush is a 2–5' shrub with gray or white stems, pinnately compound leaves, and colorful, ½", banner-wings-keel flowers. The 5-petaled flowers are not exactly indigo, rather a more reddish purple or rose (sometimes with a yellow spot on the banner). You'll have to get close to the plant to see its most distinctive feature—the small, red-orange glands dotting the stems and sepals. If you look at these spots under magnification, you can almost imagine you're looking at the skin of some exotic wild cat or even of some tropical fish!

Flowering Season: June–September.

Habitat/Range: Sandy or gravelly flats and slopes in the desert shrub and the sagebrush steppe, to 6,000', in eastern California, western and central Nevada, e.g., White Mountains. This species occurs mostly in the Mojave Desert.

Comments: *Psorothamnus* means "scabshrub" in reference to the glands that dot the plant. *Polydenius* means "many glands," also in reference to the intriguing red-orange glands.

ANDERSON CLOVER
Trifolium andersonii
Pea Family (Fabaceae)

Description: Anderson Clover is unusual for a clover in a couple of ways: First, although you can find it in the sagebrush steppe, it extends all the way to above timberline, so, it's not surprising that it's a tufted or matted plant; and second, it has 4 or 5 (not 3) palmately compound leaflets. As you would expect from a plant that extends above timberline, the leaflets, stems, and sepals are matted with silky hairs. The roundish flower heads are tightly packed with 12–20, red-purple or pink, 5-petaled, ½" flowers. Whether you come across this wonderful plant on some barren talus slope or ridge high above timberline or on a rocky flat at a much more modest elevation, it is a dramatic and beautiful encounter.

Flowering Season: May–August.

Habitat/Range: Dry hillsides, washes, rock ledges, talus slopes in the sagebrush steppe, the montane, and the alpine, 5,000–13,000', in eastern California, western Nevada, western Utah, e.g., Virginia Range, White Mountains.

Comments: *Trifolium* means "3-leafed," although this doesn't apply to *T. andersonii*. C.L. Anderson *(Astragalus a.).*

PEAVINE
Vicia americana
Pea Family (Fabaceae)

Description: Peavine has the distinction of
having a mountain named after it—Peavine
Mountain just northwest of Reno. Unlike the
mountain, this plant usually can't stand by itself,
so it clings onto its neighbors with its slender
tendrils. Each leaf stem has 4–8 opposite or
almost opposite pairs of ½–1½" elliptic, pointed
leaflets at the tip of each of which is a tiny
bristle. The stipules at the leaf axil are also
narrow and pointed. The flower stem bears 3–9
of the ½", pink-purple or lavender (with purple
veins), banner-wings-keel flowers. Since the plant
stems cling to other plants (grass, bushes, herbs),
these beautiful flowers are usually in among
other plants and flowers, appearing to have been
joyfully scattered like rose petals at a wedding.

Flowering Season: April–July.

Habitat/Range: Grassy meadows, thickets in the
sagebrush steppe and the montane, to 11,000',
throughout the Great Basin, e.g., Peavine
Mountain, Great Basin National Park.

Comments: *Vicia* is the ancient Latin name.
Americana means "of America."

FILAREE
Erodium cicutarium
Geranium Family (Geraniaceae)

Description: An invasive weed throughout the
Great Basin, Filaree can dominate disturbed flats
and fields with its prostrate, spreading stems. The
hairy, lacy leaves are deeply pinnately lobed into
tiny, pointed segments. Two or more of the ¼",
starlike, 5-petaled flowers cluster at the tips of
the stems. Despite the plant's weedy nature, the
flowers are quite beautiful—pink with darker red-
purple streaks and tiny, spherical, yellow-pollened
anthers. One of the reasons that this plant spreads
so effectively is its long-beaked seedpods that
peel back and launch to become rotating
helicopters that transport and bury the seeds.

Flowering Season: March–July.

Habitat/Range: Gravelly or sandy flats,
roadsides, disturbed places in the desert shrub
and the sagebrush steppe, to 6,500', throughout
the Great Basin, e.g., Washoe Valley, Great Basin
National Park.

Comments: *Erodium* means "heron" in reference to
the long-beaked fruits. *Cicutarium* means
"resembling *Cicuta*" in reference to the
resemblance of the pinnately lobed leaves to those
of the water hemlock genus in the Carrot Family.
Also called Heron's Bill and Stork's Bill. Alien.

PURPLE NAMA
Nama aretioides
Waterleaf Family (Hydrophyllaceae)

Description: Purple Nama has gorgeous red-purple (with white or yellow centers), funnel-shaped, 5-petaled flowers that hug the ground in showy patches above narrow, hairy leaves and prostrate stems. It's very similar to its close relative of the Mojave Desert, *Nama demissum* (Purple Mat), but tends to be less branched. How fortunate we are in the West to have a stunning, ground-covering, purple species of *Nama* whether we are in the desert or in the steppe, for they light up the ground with dazzling color that will catch your eye and your heart even from quite a distance away.

Flowering Season: May–June.

Habitat/Range: Sandy or gravelly flats, washes in the sagebrush steppe, to 6,500', in eastern California, western and central Nevada, southern Oregon, e.g., Virginia Range, Steens Mountain.

Comments: *Nama (N. rothrockii). Aretiodes* means "resembling the genus *Aretia.*"

GRASS WIDOWS
Sisyrinchium douglasii
Iris Family (Iridaceae)

Description: With its large (to 2" wide), intense magenta or red-purple flowers displayed against a background of dark green, grasslike leaves, Grass Widows is one of the most spectacular floral treasures of the Great Basin. The flowers have a yellow eye at their center from which project the long pistil with 3 stigmas and the not-quite-so-long stamens. The 6 magenta (sometimes white) tepals usually have darker red-purple veins. The 1–3 flowers are on short pedicels that are attached part way up the ½–1½' stems. The erect, grasslike leaves also reach higher than the flowers. Grass Widows blooms in early spring, often growing in large masses; later, flowerless, it blends in with the surrounding grass.

Flowering Season: April–June.

Habitat/Range: Damp, grassy meadows in the sagebrush steppe and the montane, to 7,000', in northeastern Nevada, southern Oregon, e.g., Santa Rosa Range, Steens Mountain.

Comments: *Sisyrinchium* is the ancient Greek name for an irislike plant. David Douglas *(Silene d.).*

HORSEMINT
Agastache urticifolia
Mint Family (Lamiaceae)

Description: Horsemint is a 3–5' plant with stems that end in 2–7", cylindrical flower spikes crammed with scores of ½" tubular flowers. Since the plants usually grow in great masses, you will usually encounter large clusters and sometimes even vast "forests" of these beautiful flower spikes. The pastel pink or white petals contrast dramatically with the red-purple sepals. As with all mints, the leaves are in opposite pairs. In horsemint, the leaves are broad, toothed, and triangular. Though they do smell minty when crushed, the fragrance is a bit harsher than that of its fellow mint and frequent companion Pennyroyal *(Monardella odoratissima)*.

Flowering Season: June–August.

Habitat/Range: Dry, brushy slopes, grassy meadows, among trees in the montane, 6,000–9,000', throughout the Great Basin, e.g., Santa Rosa Range, Ruby Mountains.

Comments: *Agastache* means "many spikes." *Urticifolia* means "nettle leaved" in reference to the similarity of the broad, triangular, veined leaves to those of Stinging Nettle *(Urtica dioica)*.

PENNYROYAL
Monardella odoratissima
Mint Family (Lamiaceae)

Description: One of the most fragrant plants of dry, sagebrush slopes, Pennyroyal can fill the air with clouds of sweet mint aroma. The leaves (dried or fresh) and even the flowers can be steeped (or even just swirled) to create a tasty tea, though it should be drunk in moderation, as more than a couple of cups can create quite an intestinal disturbance. The square, ½–2' plant stems have several opposite pairs of narrow leaves and are topped by ½–1", flat-topped flower heads that are crammed with scores of the tubular, 5-petaled flowers. The narrow, pointed petals and their protruding reproductive parts can vary from white to pale pink-purple to intense purple.

Flowering Season: June–August.

Habitat/Range: Dry, open slopes in the sagebrush steppe and the montane, 5,500–10,000', throughout the Great Basin, e.g., Santa Rosa Range, Ruby Mountains.

Comments: Nicholas Monardes was a 16th-century Spanish physician and botanist. *Odoratissima* means "very fragrant."

DARK RED ONION
Allium atrorubens
Lily Family (Liliaceae)

Description: Though Dark Red Onion is a relatively short plant (2–7"), it is nonetheless a showy one, for there can be up to 50 of the ½", shiny, red-purple flowers in each spherical umbel. The pedicels can be almost 1" long, so the umbel can be quite large. The 6 glistening tepals are sharply pointed and mostly solid red-purple. (There is a southern variety of *A. atrorubens* with flowers that are pale pink or white.) The stamens are a bit shorter than the tepals; the red anthers are held against the tepals early in the blooming and project up out of the corolla later. The 1 grasslike leaf is a bit longer than the stem, and its tip is tightly coiled when the leaf is fresh.

Flowering Season: April–June.

Habitat/Range: Dry, sandy or gravelly slopes and flats in the sagebrush steppe, 5,000–8,000', throughout the Great Basin except southern Oregon, e.g., Peavine Mountain, White Mountains.

Comments: *Allium (A. bisceptrum). Atrorubens* means "dark red."

ASPEN ONION
Allium bisceptrum
Lily Family (Liliaceae)

Description: Sometimes on dry, sagebrush slopes in the Great Basin, you'll come across a magical oasis where a spring, seep, or creek has created a lush sanctuary from the hot sun and scratchy shrubs. You find yourself in a secret garden of aspens—a canopy of shimmering, dark green leaves supported by pillars of glistening, silvery white trunks, and a floor of thick, green grass. It's a quiet and soothing place, as much a haven for you as for wildflowers. One of the floral treasures you're likely to find here is Aspen Onion—a 4–16" scape bearing a showy, 1–2" wide umbel of a few or many lovely, pink or rose-purple (sometimes white), star-shaped flowers. The 6 tepals are narrow and pointed; in bud they look a bit like floral teardrops. The umbel of flowers is subtended by two papery, ovate bracts. There are 2 or 3 tapering, channeled, grasslike leaves. If you look at the flower very carefully, you may notice the pair of fringed crests atop the ovary lobes that give this plant its species name.

Flowering Season: May–July.

Habitat/Range: Streambanks, wet meadows, often under aspens in the sagebrush steppe and the montane, to 10,300', throughout the Great Basin, e.g., Toiyabe Range, Steens Mountain.

Comments: *Allium* is the ancient Latin name for garlic. *Bisceptrum* means "2-crested" in reference to the pair of appendages on top of the ovary lobes. Also known as Twin-Crest Onion.

SIERRA ONION
Allium campanulatum
Lily Family (Liliaceae)

Description: Although the flowers of Sierra Onion are similar in shape and color to those of Aspen Onion *(A. bisceptrum),* there's no confusing these two species. First and foremost, Sierra Onion grows in dry, sandy or gravelly habitats—you won't ever find it in wet meadows under aspens where you will find Aspen Onion. So it isn't surprising, then, that Sierra Onion tends to be a shorter plant (2–12"). Despite its smaller stature, however, it is no less showy—its ½", slightly cupped flowers are a dazzling, intense red-purple or pink with a darker red-purple crescent arching above the whitish base of each tepal. You will often see droplets of silvery nectar glistening on the tepals. For much of the bloom, the rectangular, red-purple anthers nestle against the tips of the 6 tepals. The umbel of flowers is generally quite loose (the pedicels can be up to 4 times as long as the flowers, so the 5–45 flowers in each umbel are quite spread out). There are only 2 grasslike leaves, but you may not find them, for they usually wither by the time the flowers bloom.

Flowering Season: May–August.

Habitat/Range: Sandy or gravelly flats and slopes in the montane, 6,000–8,000', in western and northwestern Nevada, southern Oregon, e.g., Peavine Mountain, Steens Mountain.

Comments: *Allium (A. bisceptrum). Campanulatum* means "bell shaped" in reference to the slightly cupped flowers.

DWARF ONION
Allium parvum
Lily Family (Liliaceae)

Description: Onions are easily recognized by their umbels of small, 6-tepaled, star-shaped, rose or pink or white flowers and their 1 or 2 (occasionally more), long, grasslike leaves. A nibble on a leaf (or even a flower) will give you an unmistakable onion taste. *Be absolutely certain* that the flowers are in an umbel and you have identified the plant as an onion before you nibble—there are other 6-tepaled members of the Lily Family that are deadly poisonous, e.g., *Zigadenus* species. Whereas most Great Basin onions are at least 6" and often 1' or more tall, Dwarf Onion is only 1–2" tall, so its cluster of pink or rose (sometimes white) flowers lies practically on the ground. The pointed tepals have a dark rose-purple midrib. The tepals are usually somewhat cupped and are longer or as long as the reproductive parts, so the reproductive parts do not stick out of the corolla. The 2 or more leaves are 2–3 times as long as the scape (i.e., the plant stem).

Flowering Season: March–July.

Habitat/Range: Sandy or gravelly flats in the sagebrush steppe and the montane, to 9,500', throughout the Great Basin, e.g., Carson Valley, Steens Mountain.

Comments: *Allium (A. bisceptrum). Parvum* means "small."

FLAT-STEM ONION
Allium platycaule
Lily Family (Liliaceae)

Description: Although Flat-Stem Onion lies close to the ground (on a 1–6" stem), it can put on a spectacular show, for frequently many plants mass together to cover large areas of otherwise nearly bare, rocky, or sandy slopes and flats with their striking rose or pink-purple flowers. Each plant has 2 long, broad, flattened leaves above which rises the short stem, at the tip of which is a large, tightly clustered, ball-shaped head of 30–90 flowers. With so many flowers packed together of such an intense color, Flat-Stem Onion will catch your attention from quite a distance and will insist that you come closer to investigate! Unlike many onions, the 6 tepals of this onion are very narrow, almost threadlike.

Flowering Season: May–July.

Habitat/Range: Rocky or sandy slopes and flats in the sagebrush steppe and the montane, to 7,000', in northwestern Nevada, southern Oregon, e.g., Charles Sheldon National Wildlife Refuge.

Comments: *Allium (A. bisceptrum). Platycaule* means "broad stemmed."

SWAMP ONION
Allium validum
Lily Family (Liliaceae)

Description: You won't confuse Swamp Onion with any other *Allium* species—it is a tall (1–2½'), imposing plant with scapes (flower stems) that bear large, showy umbels of 15–30 intensely red-purple or rose flowers. To add to the show, these stunning plants often form large clusters or even massive "jungles" in marshy areas, dazzling your eye with bright color as they fill your nose with clouds of pungent onion fragrance. The flowers usually don't open as much as most onions, the 6 tepals staying mostly erect to form a vase for the long, black-anthered stamens. The color contrast of the deep green meadow, the bright red-purple tepals, and the conspicuous, jet-black anthers is almost as striking as the intense onion aroma! The several flat, grasslike leaves are usually shorter than the stout scape and remain fresh well into the blooming season.

Flowering Season: June–August.

Habitat/Range: Wet meadows, streambanks, marshes in the montane, 6,500–9,500', throughout Nevada, e.g., Ruby Mountains.

Comments: *Allium (A. bisceptrum). Validum* means "strong" in reference to the fragrance.

DESERT MARIPOSA LILY
Calochortus kennedyi
Lily Family (Liliaceae)

Description: In many species of *Calochortus*, the most striking features are the splotches, bands, spots, or stripes (or many of the above) of vividly contrasting colors. Although Desert Mariposa Lily does not have as many color contrasts as most species, it is nonetheless one of the most spectacular, for its 3 petals are a solid, flaming orange or vermillion that will catch your eye from a long way off. Close inspection, however, will reveal more color contrast than was initially apparent: A purplish black splotch at the base of each petal; long, narrow, purple anthers; and delicate, red-purple hairs tipped with yellow on the inside of the petals above the nectaries. The plants are usually low to the ground but will grow up through shrubs, lifting the flowers up to 2½'

high. Sometimes a plant will have only 1 of the 2–4" wide flowers; sometimes there will be a few in an umbel, which is subtended by 2 leaflike bracts. There are 2–4 grasslike, 4–8" leaves.

Flowering Season: April–June.

Habitat/Range: Dry hillsides and flats in the desert shrub and the sagebrush steppe, to 6,500', in eastern California, western Nevada, e.g., White Mountains. This species occurs mostly in the Mojave Desert.

Comments: *Calochortus (C. bruneaunis).* William Kennedy (ca. 1827–?) was a plant collector in the American West.

KELLEY'S TIGER LILY
Lilium kelleyanum
Lily Family (Liliaceae)

Description: The flowers of Kelley's Tiger Lily are 2–3" wide and long, brilliantly colored, and intriguingly shaped. The stout, 2–5' stem bears 2–5 whorls of narrow, 3–7", pointed leaves above which branch 1–25 of the gorgeous, nodding flowers, each on a long, sometimes snaking pedicel. The 6 tonguelike tepals, which are bright orange or yellowish with profuse red-purple spots, curve all the way back to touch or nearly touch the base of the flower tube. The cylindrical anthers and the thick pistil project considerably below the tepals. The long, snub-nosed buds hang from slender, arching pedicels. From a

distance or from close range, Kelley's Tiger Lily is a stunning sight, especially against a background of bright, blue sky.

Flowering Season: June–August.

Habitat/Range: Streambanks, wet meadows, willow thickets in the sagebrush steppe and the montane, 5,000–6,000', in western Nevada, e.g., Peavine Mountain. This species occurs mostly in the Sierra Nevada.

Comments: *Lilium* is the ancient Greek name. The species name is of uncertain origin.

CHECKERMALLOW
Sidalcea glaucescens
Mallow Family (Malvaceae)

Description: Although not as startling as the bright orange flowers of Desert Mallow *(Sphaeralcea ambigua),* the flowers of Checkermallow have their own more soothing beauty. The ½", bowl-shaped flowers have 5 soft pink or pink-purple petals with distinct white veins. The ½–2½' plants bear many of the flowers along the upper foot or so of the slender plant stems. The broad leaves are shallowly palmately lobed toward the base of the plant, usually becoming deeply lobed higher on the plant. Checkermallow is a wonderful flower to inspect carefully several times during its blooming—early the creamy, frothy male parts are evident surrounding the reproductive column, while only later do the delicate, scarlet threads of the female emerge from the column's tip.

Flowering Season: May–August.

Habitat/Range: Sandy slopes and flats, dry meadows in the sagebrush steppe and the montane, to 9,000', in western, northwestern, and central Nevada, e.g., Peavine Mountain, Toiyabe Range.

Comments: *Sidalcea* is a combination of two genera in the Mallow Family—*Sida* and *Alcea*. *Glaucescens* means "covered with a waxy, powdery film." Also called White-Veined Mallow.

BOG MALLOW
Sidalcea oregana
Mallow Family (Malvaceae)

Description: The flowers of Bog Mallow are easily identified as of the Mallow Family, for they have the typical 5 separate petals surrounding the central reproductive column, which bears both the frothy, white stamens and the scarlet, threadlike style. Bog Mallow is very similar to its close relative Checkermallow *(S. glaucescens)* with its shallow, bowl-shaped, pink flowers with the veins on the petals; however, it is a taller plant (1–5') with many flowers packed on its spike, and it grows in bogs and wet meadows instead of in dry areas.

Flowering Season: June–August.

Habitat/Range: Wet meadows, bogs, seeps in the sagebrush steppe and the montane, to 10,000', throughout the Great Basin, e.g., Charles Sheldon National Wildlife Refuge, Deep Creek Mountains.

Comments: *Sidalcea (S. glaucescens). Oregana* means "of Oregon."

DESERT MALLOW
Sphaeralcea ambigua
Mallow Family (Malvaceae)

Description: A complex species with several varieties, Desert Mallow in any of its forms is a spectacular plant with 1–1½", showy, bowl-shaped flowers with orange, apricot, pink, or red blossoms that contrast vividly with the gray-green leaves. The plant stem can be up to 3' tall, the upper foot or so dense with flowers clustered in the leaf axils. The 1–2" leaves are broad, shallowly or deeply palmately lobed, crinkled, and wavy or smooth-margined. The leaves and stems are covered with short, irritating hairs, so be careful about touching this plant. The 5 brilliant petals are distinctly veined and overlap to form a deep bowl, which houses the dense cluster of yellow-anthered stamens. The headlike stigmas are pink or purple.

Flowering Season: March–June.

Habitat/Range: Sandy or gravelly flats, roadsides in the desert shrub and the sagebrush steppe, to 7,500', in eastern California, western and central Nevada, e.g., Peavine Mountain, Toiyabe Range.

Comments: *Sphaeralcea* means "globe mallow" in reference to the round-headed fruit. *Ambigua* means "uncertain" in reference to some taxonomic difficulties with this species, which has several varieties and intergrades with several other species.

CURRANT-LEAF DESERT MALLOW
Sphaeralcea grossulariifolia
Mallow Family (Malvaceae)

Description: With flowers very similar to and as spectacular as its close relative Desert Mallow *(S. ambigua)*, Currant-Leaf Desert Mallow dazzles with its great displays of 1–1½", bowl-shaped, intense orange blossoms. Each 2–4' plant usually bears many clusters of these 5-petaled flowers. They close at night, but even in early morning before they fully open, the furled, orange torpedoes are stunning. The main difference between this species and Desert Mallow is the leaves—as the common and species names suggest, the leaves of Currant-Leaf Desert Mallow are deeply 3-lobed with each lobe again lobed or divided. The leaves, stem, and calyx are usually covered with dense, fine, grayish white hairs.

Flowering Season: April–October.

Habitat/Range: Dry washes, plains, hillsides in the sagebrush steppe, to 7,500', throughout the Great Basin, e.g., Soldier Meadow, Steens Mountain.

Comments: *Sphaeralcea (S. ambigua)*. *Grossulariifolia* means "gooseberry leaf" in reference to the deeply 3-lobed leaves resembling those of some species of gooseberry *(Ribes* genus).

85

FIREWEED
Epilobium angustifolium
Evening Primrose Family (Onagraceae)

Description: Because it is probably the most common and widespread of the *Epilobium* species and often is one of the first species to move into areas disturbed by fire or bulldozing, Fireweed's beauty and interest may not be fully appreciated. One of its gifts is that it is a late bloomer (in late summer and into fall), bringing intense color to the landscape when many of the other showy plants have gone to seed. The 2–6' stem bears many narrow, alternating, 1–8", conspicuously veined leaves. The upper part (sometimes as much as 2') of the stem is thick with horizontally branching pedicels that lead to stout, cylindrical ovaries, which support the spectacular 1–2" flowers. The 4 separate petals are clawed, rounded, and intensely rose colored. The narrow,

darker red-purple sepals alternate between the petals. Since the pollen is so stringy and sticky, you will often find strands of it (and spots of nectar) stuck to the short anthers, the 4-lobed stigma, visiting pollinators, and even the petals. In fall the leaves turn scarlet, bringing further color to the otherwise browning landscape.

Flowering Season: July–September.

Habitat/Range: Moist areas in meadows, grassy slopes, along streambanks in the montane, 6,000–12,000', throughout the Great Basin, e.g., White Mountains, Deep Creek Mountains.

Comments: *Epilobium (E. obcordatum). Angustifolium* means "narrow leafed."

SMOOTH-STEM WILLOWHERB
Epilobium glaberrimum
Evening Primrose Family (Onagraceae)

Description: Though the flowers of Smooth-Stem Willowherb are much smaller than those of many of its close relatives in the *Epilobium* genus (e.g., *E. obcordatum, E. angustifolium*), if you take the time to look closely, you will see that they are equally colorful and dramatic, just on a smaller scale. The 1–2½' plant stem bears many opposite pairs of small, ovate, clasping leaves most of its length. From the top part of this stem branch many of what appear to be long, slender pedicels (in fact, these are inferior ovaries) atop which perch the ⅛–1", rose or pink flowers. Each of the 4 petals is deeply lobed and often has noticeable darker red-purple veins. As the common name and the species name indicate, the stems (and leaves) are hairless and smooth.

Flowering Season: June–August.

Habitat/Range: Streambanks, wet meadows, seeps in the montane, 6,500–9,500' throughout the Great Basin, e.g., Toiyabe Range, Steens Mountain.

Comments: *Epilobium (E. obcordatum). Epilobium* means "upon the pod" in reference to the inferior ovary. *Glaberrimum* means "smooth stemmed."

ROCK FRINGE
Epilobium obcordatum
Evening Primrose Family (Onagraceae)

Description: In a family of plants with large, strikingly beautiful flowers, Rock Fringe certainly upholds the family tradition, for its flowers bring gorgeous color to their often rather bare, rocky habitat. As its common name indicates, it grows at the edges of rock cliffs or talus fields, adorning the rocks with thick carpets of 1–2", rose-purple blooms. The 2–6" stem creeps along the ground, so the ¼–¾", elliptic leaves tend to form a ground-hugging mat bed for the dense cluster of flowers. With its 4 heart-shaped petals and their intense red-purple or pink color, Rock Fringe is the perfect Valentine bloom. The long style and its velvety, 4-lobed stigma are even more intensely red-purple than the petals, and the small, creamy yellow anthers are at the tips of red-purple filaments. Even the velvety ovary, as it swells in fruit, is the same rich color.

Flowering Season: July–September.

Habitat/Range: Rock ledges, rocky or gravelly flats and slopes, talus in the montane, 8,000–10,000', throughout the Great Basin except western Utah, e.g., Steens Mountain, Ruby Mountains.

Comments: *Obcordatum* means "inversely heart shaped" in reference to the petals.

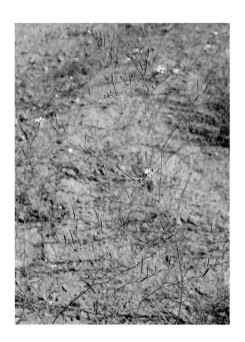

PANICLE WILLOWHERB

Epilobium paniculatum
Evening Primrose Family (Onagraceae)

Description: Willowherb flowers are usually
rather subtle—small and fragile looking on
slender stems. Panicle Willowherb takes this to
an extreme, as its ½", 4-petaled flowers are
scattered sparsely on slender, much-branched
stems that create a plant up to 3' tall and almost
as wide. Since the leaves are very narrow and
rather sparse on the stem as well, the plant
seems to be all stem—delicate, wiry, branching—
with a few pastel pink flowers floating through it!
As the flowers begin to go to fruit, the ovaries
swell and turn a dark red, now decorating the
branching stems with dabs of a deeper color.
These will soon turn into elongated, cylindrical
seedpods.

Flowering Season: July–August.

Habitat/Range: Dry slopes and roadsides, moist
meadows, openings in the sagebrush steppe and
the montane, to 8,500', in northern Nevada,
western Utah, e.g., Santa Rosa Range.

Comments: *Epilobium (E. obcordatum).*
Paniculatum means "panicled' in reference to the
much-branched stems. Also known as *E.
brachycarpum.*

LARGE-FLOWERED COLLOMIA

Collomia grandiflora
Phlox Family (Polemoniaceae)

Description: The flowers of Large-Flowered
Collomia are not only large, but grand. The 1–2",
narrow flower tubes flare out into ½–¾",
delicately pastel stars. It's sometimes a bit
difficult to figure out the color of these wonderful
flowers—it's always pastel and can be nearly
white, but usually tends more toward pink,
salmon, or peach. The blue anthers are included
in the tube or slightly project from it, while the
slender, white style with the branched stigma
sticks way out of it. Many of the flowers cluster
together in a terminal head. The ½–3' stem has
several narrow leaves alternating along most of
its length.

Flowering Season: May–August.

Habitat/Range: Dry slopes, open woods in the
sagebrush steppe and the montane, 4,500–8,500',
throughout the Great Basin, e.g., Peavine
Mountain, Deep Creek Mountains.

Comments: *Collomia* means "glue" in reference
to the sticky surface of the seeds. *Grandiflora*
means "large flowered."

SCARLET GILIA

Ipomopsis aggregata
Phlox Family (Polemoniaceae)

Description: Walking across a midelevation sagebrush slope in the Great Basin, you will occasionally see flashes of scarlet blossoms. There are several plants that could be responsible, but if the red flash is 2 or 3 feet off the ground and resembles clusters of flaring trumpets, it is probably Scarlet Gilia. The 1–3' stems rise above mostly basal leaves (with a few, needle-lobed stem leaves) and terminate in a 1-sided cluster of several showy, red, trumpet-shaped, 5-petaled flowers. The narrow, 1–1½" flowers flare out into 1" wide, slightly reflexed, red stars. Occasionally the flowers will be pale pink or even white (considered by some botanists to be a separate species); usually they will be spotted. A crushed leaf has a pungent fragrance.

Flowering Season: May–August.

Habitat/Range: Dry slopes, openings in the sagebrush steppe and the montane, to 10,000', throughout the Great Basin, e.g., Steens Mountain, Deep Creek Mountains.

Comments: *Ipomopsis* means "striking appearance." *Aggregata* means "clustered" in reference to the many-flowered inflorescence.

STANSBURY'S PHLOX
Phlox stansburyi
Phlox Family (Polemoniaceae)

Description: Very similar to Long-Leaf Phlox (and considered by some botanists to be a variety of that species), Stansbury's Phlox puts on a wonderful, varicolored, floral show on sagebrush flats in eastern California and western Nevada. Usually several of the 4–12", woody stems cluster together (having sprouted from the same underground, horizontal stem), creating a dense, shrublike growth thick with 1", pinwheel flowers. The 5 narrow, clawed petals are widely separated and vary (often on the same plant) from white to light pink to dark rose. Stansbury's Phlox differs from Long-Leaf Phlox *(P. longifolia)* in its lower,

stiffer, and more compact growth form, which typically creates a more solid mass of flowers, and its narrower, more clawed petals.

Flowering Season: April–July.

Habitat/Range: Dry, sandy or gravelly flats and slopes in the sagebrush steppe and the montane, 5,000–10,000', in eastern California, western Nevada, e.g., White Mountains.

Comments: Phlox means "flame" in reference to the showy flowers. Captain Howard Stansbury *(Purshia s.).* Sometimes known as *P. longifolia* var. *stansburyi.* Also called Pink Phlox.

LOBB'S BUCKWHEAT
Eriogonum lobbii
Buckwheat Family (Polygonaceae)

Description: Of all the many *Eriogonum* species in the Great Basin, Lobb's Buckwheat is one of the easiest to identify, for the stems bearing the large, spherical umbels of tiny flowers are usually flat on the ground. Since each plant has several of these prostrate, 1–8" stems radiating out from the dense rosette of basal leaves, the result is a unique plant with a ring of flower umbels flat on the ground encircling the clump of basal leaves. It might remind you a little of a moat of flowers protecting a castle of leaves. The stems and the oval or round, ½–2" leaves are densely white-wooly. The ⅛" flowers packed together into the 1–2", spherical umbels can be yellow, white, or rose (generally they start yellow or creamy white and age rose or raspberry).

Flowering Season: June–August.

Habitat/Range: Sandy or gravelly slopes, talus, rock ledges in the montane, 6,000–9,000', in western Nevada, e.g., Peavine Mountain. This species occurs mostly in the Sierra Nevada.

Comments: *Eriogonum (E. spergulinum).* William Lobb was a 19th-century British plant collector.

MOUNTAIN SORREL
Oxyria digyna
Buckwheat Family (Polygonaceae)

Description: It is always a bit surprising to find Mountain Sorrel growing on a rock ledge or talus slope near or above timberline. Reaching 15" tall and abundant with broad, kidney-shaped leaves, this plant seems much too robust to be living in such a harsh environment. However, the plant usually is somewhat protected from the wind by rocks, and its leaves are fleshy and juicy, which is certainly one effective way to survive arid conditions. A nibble on a leaf will give you a tangy jolt of energy, but limit yourself to one nibble for both your sake and the plant's. The tiny flowers (with no true petals) form a dense, elongated panicle of red or yellow-green. The tiny, disklike seedpods are red tinged.

Flowering Season: July–August.

Habitat/Range: Rock ledges, talus slopes in the montane and the alpine, 7,000–13,000', throughout the Great Basin, e.g., Toiyabe Range, Ruby Mountains.

Comments: *Oxyria* means "sour" in reference to the oxalic acid in the leaves. *Digyna* means "with 2 pistils."

PUSSYPAWS
Calyptridium umbellatum
Purslane Family (Portulacaceae)

Description: Pussypaws has the 2 sepals typical of the Purslane Family, however it is very difficult to discern this as the sepals and the 4 petals look almost exactly alike—papery and scalelike. Although it is difficult to tell its family, it is easy to identify Pussypaws, for its furry, almost spherical paws of papery, purple, pink, or white flowers at the tips of slender, 1–6" stems and its beautifully symmetrical, basal rosette of spoon-shaped, leathery leaves are unique. Pussypaws is, however, quite variable depending on habitat and elevation—sometimes the rosette is less pronounced and the flower clusters are less pawlike. If you observe a plant in the early morning or late afternoon and then observe it again in the heat of midday, you will notice another unique (and fascinating) feature of this plant—the stems radiate out flat to the ground when it's cold, but rise up to a steep angle when the ground heats up. The anthers are red or yellow.

Flowering Season: May–August.

Habitat/Range: Sandy or gravelly flats in the sagebrush steppe, the montane, and the alpine, to 13,000', throughout the Great Basin, e.g., Peavine Mountain, Great Basin National Park.

Comments: *Calyptridium* means "cap" in reference to the uniting of the petals in fruit into a caplike structure. *Umbellatum* means "in an umbel."

JEFFREY'S SHOOTING STAR
Dodecatheon jeffreyi
Primrose Family (Primulaceae)

Description: Wandering (carefully, of course) through a wet mountain meadow, you may come across clusters or perhaps ribbons (paralleling a creek or rivulet) of Jeffrey's Shooting Star with their beautiful and rather odd flowers. Looking at this upside-down, inside-out flower with its petals gracefully sweeping back away from the snout of reproductive parts, you will probably appreciate the common name, for the strange blossom does bear some resemblance to a shooting star or comet hurtling down out of the sky. Hanging from branching pedicels at the tip of the ½–2' tall plant stem are 3–18 of the 1–1½" flowers. The 5 (or 4) petals are pink or rose with a band of white, then yellow, then black-purple at their base. The slender style with its enlarged stigma tip sticks out from the dark snout. After the flowers are pollinated, they slowly rotate up so the shooting star is heading back to the sky. The broad, 3–20" long leaves are basal.

Flowering Season: June–August.

Habitat/Range: Streambanks, wet meadows in the montane, 6,000–11,000', throughout the Great Basin, e.g., Great Basin National Park.

Comments: *Dodecatheon* means "12 gods." John Jeffrey was a 19th-century Scottish gardener.

PARRY'S PRIMROSE
Primula parryi
Primrose Family (Primulaceae)

Description: With its cluster of gorgeous, intense rose or pink flowers held up for our admiration atop a 4–16", stout, leafless stem, Parry's Primrose is a true floral work of art. At the center of each flower is a bright yellow eye leading down into the short flower tube out of which the 5 petals flare. The flowers gracefully arch out away from the stem on slender, 1–3" pedicels as if they were being gently offered by the plant for our praise! The cluster of 2–12" leaves is basal, forming a lush cradle from which the plant stem emerges.

Flowering Season: June–July.

Habitat/Range: Grassy meadows, streambanks, rock crevices in the montane and the alpine, 8,500–13,000', in eastern Nevada, western Utah, e.g., Ruby Mountains, Deep Creek Mountains.

Comments: *Primula* means "first" in reference to early blooming. C. C. Parry was a 19th-century American botanist.

CRIMSON COLUMBINE
Aquilegia formosa
Buttercup Family (Ranunculaceae)

Description: Crimson Columbine, with its showy, bright red and yellow, long-spurred, upside-down flowers, is alluring to hummingbirds. The five 1–1½", tubular petals end in swollen, knoblike nectar sacs conspicuously amber with nectar. You may find holes in these sacs where bees pierced them to suck out the sweet liquid. The 5 red sepals flare out perpendicular to the petals like wings. Contrasting dramatically with all this red is the yellow at the mouth of the petals and of the many, long-protruding stamens. Each 1–4' plant has a few or several of these stunning flowers hanging gracefully upside down at the ends of long, arching pedicels. The flowers rise to an upright position, with their reproductive parts pointing up to the sky, after they have been pollinated. The leaves are usually deeply pinnately lobed into 2 or 3 segments.

Flowering Season: June–September.

Habitat/Range: Grassy meadows, forest openings, around trees in the montane, 5,000–10,000', throughout the Great Basin, e.g., Toiyabe Range, Ruby Mountains.

Comments: *Aquilegia* derives from the Latin for "eagle" probably in reference to the talonlike nectar spurs. *Formosa* means "beautiful."

93

OLD MAN'S WHISKERS
Geum triflorum
Rose Family (Rosaceae)

Description: If these are the Old Man's Whiskers, this must be quite some old man! The cluster of long, sinuous, feathery, red styles adorned with short white hairs is a remarkable and beautiful fruit; it would be truly amazing as facial hair! Although in fruit the plant is erect, in flower it usually nods; the 5 white or pink petals and the 5 pink sepals curve together to form a puckered kiss. The ½–2' stem sometimes bears only one flower, but often (as the species name suggests) it bears 2 or 3. The 5 narrow bractlets between the sepals splay out perpendicular to the sepals. The 2–8" leaves are pinnately compound with one terminal leaflet.

Flowering Season: June–August.

Habitat/Range: Wet meadows, forest openings in the montane, 5,000–10,000', northeastern and eastern Nevada, western Utah, southern Oregon, e.g., Ruby Mountains, Steens Mountain.

Comments: *Geum (G. macrophyllum). Triflorum* means "3-flowered" in reference to the plant's tendency to bear flowers in clusters of 3. Also called Prairie Smoke and Downy Avens.

DESERT PEACH
Prunus andersonii
Rose Family (Rosaceae)

Description: The soft pink or rose blossoms of desert peach are especially welcome to wildflower lovers, for this 2–6' shrub is one of the first conspicuous flowering plants to bloom in the spring in the sagebrush steppe. As if to make up for the long, flowerless winter, Desert Peach is a mass of blossoms, almost concealing the gray, spine-tipped branches and the ½–1", shiny green, oval leaves. At the center of the 5 narrow, clawed, widely spaced, pink petals are a darker rose eye and a dense cluster of long stamens with yellow anthers. The ovary will swell into a small, round, red-orange, peachlike fruit.

Flowering Season: April–June.

Habitat/Range: Dry, brushy flats and slopes in the sagebrush steppe, to 7,000', in eastern California, western and central Nevada, e.g., Washoe Valley.

Comments: *Prunus* is the ancient Latin name. C. L. Anderson *(Astragalus a.)*.

WILD ROSE
Rosa woodsii
Rose Family (Rosaceae)

Description: Getting snagged in a rose thicket may result in some painful scratches and even some torn clothing, but perhaps this isn't too high a price to pay for all the pleasures that will come with it! The crinkly-petaled blossoms are 1½–2½" across, delicately colored with 5 petals ranging from pale pink to dark rose surrounding a cluster of yellow stamens and pistils, and deliciously fragrant. You may be trapped by the thorns, but you'll be imprisoned by the aroma! The plant is a shrub up to 6' tall, which is thick with dark green, compound leaves (with toothed leaflets) that form a dramatic palette for the beautiful flowers and the striking, dark red, torpedo buds. Enter the Wild Rose's embrace on a hot, sunny day, and you may melt away, never to return. The juicy, round, red fruits are the familiar rose hips with nutritional and medicinal value.

Flowering Season: June–July.

Habitat/Range: Streambanks, hillsides, washes, openings in the sagebrush steppe and the montane, to 9,000', throughout the Great Basin, e.g., Soldier Meadow, Great Basin National Park.

Comments: *Rosa* is the ancient Latin name. Alphonso Wood was the 19th-century author of *Class-Book of Botany*, the first American book to use dichotomous keys. Also called Mountain Rose.

APPLEGATE'S PAINTBRUSH
Castilleja applegatei
Snapdragon Family (Scrophulariaceae)

Description: Although several of the Great Basin's paintbrush species range from red to orange to yellow, Applegate's Paintbrush is one of the only species where neighboring plants or even the same plant may show all of these color variations. It is not unusual to find places in the sagebrush steppe where seemingly every available opening between sagebrush shrubs is solid with Applegate's Paintbrush plants of almost every conceivable shade of the red end of the color spectrum. The ½–2½' plants are also identifiable by their wavy-edged leaves and glandular-sticky stems, leaves, and inflorescences. The long, yellow-green flower tube and beak protrude conspicuously beyond the colored bracts. These bracts are usually 3-lobed, and the leaves lower on the plant are usually 3-lobed or 5-lobed, though they both are sometimes unlobed.

Flowering Season: June–August.

Habitat/Range: Dry, brushy slopes and flats in the sagebrush steppe and the montane, 5,000–10,000', throughout the Great Basin, e.g., Peavine Mountain, White Mountains.

Comments: *Castilleja (C. chromosa)*. Elmer Applegate was a 20th-century American botanist.

DESERT PAINTBRUSH
Castilleja chromosa
Snapdragon Family (Scrophulariaceae)

Description: Desert Paintbrush is not limited to the desert, lighting up sagebrush slopes well up into the pinyon-juniper woodlands throughout the Great Basin. Its 1–1½' stems terminate in scarlet, 3-lobed or 5-lobed bracts, which mostly hide the atrophied, yellow-green tubular flowers. The base of the bracts is usually dark red-brown, giving the otherwise scarlet "inflorescence" (actually not the flowers at all, but flower-looking bracts) a bit of a chocolate look. The leaves, lower down on the stem than the bracts, have 3 or 5 narrow, fingerlike lobes. As with several other red-"flowered" paintbrush species, you can find Desert Paintbrush plants with bracts that are not red at all, but are yellow or orange.

Flowering Season: April–June.

Habitat/Range: Sandy or gravelly flats and slopes in the desert shrub, the sagebrush steppe, and the montane, to 9,000', throughout the Great Basin, e.g., Peavine Mountain, Soldier Meadow.

Comments: Domingo Castillejo was a Spanish botanist. *Chromosa* means "red." Some botanists consider this the same as *C. angustifolia*.

LONG-LEAF PAINTBRUSH
Castilleja linariifolia
Snapdragon Family (Scrophulariaceae)

Description: The key word in the name of this paintbrush is "long"—the stem is long (to 3') with few leaves, the leaves are long (to 3") and very narrow (almost needlelike), and the yellow-green flower tube and beak are long, sticking out very noticeably beyond the bracts. This is a rather sparse-looking plant with a few narrow leaves and a rather loose spike of bracts and flowers. The leaves are often folded or rolled inward and can have 2 or 3 lobes, though they are often unlobed. The 3-lobed bracts are usually red, though they often have a bit of a purplish tinge.

Flowering Season: June–October.

Habitat/Range: Grassy meadows, roadsides, dry flats and slopes in the desert shrub, the sagebrush steppe, and the montane, to 10,000', throughout the Great Basin, e.g., Santa Rosa Range, Great Basin National Park.

Comments: *Castilleja (C. chromosa). Linariifoilia* means "leaves like *Linaria*," which is another genus in the Snapdragon Family. Also called Wyoming Paintbrush.

GREAT RED PAINTBRUSH
Castilleja miniata
Snapdragon Family (Scrophulariaceae)

Description: Great Red Paintbrush is one of the few Great Basin paintbrush species to grow in wet areas, so it's not surprising that the plant is tall (to 3') with large, lush leaves and a robust, long (to 6") and broad spike of bracts and flowers. Unlike most of its kin, its leaves are unlobed. The stems, leaves, and bracts are usually covered with long, soft hairs. The yellow-green flower tube and beak stick out well beyond the bracts. If you look closely in among the red, upper bracts at the base of the flower tube, you can see 3 tiny, green, leaflike structures, which are the atrophied remains of the 3 petal lobes of the lower lip of the flower—atrophied because the colorful bracts have modified (over thousands of years) to do the job of the petals. Being red in this species, the bracts attract mostly hummingbirds.

Flowering Season: July–August.

Habitat/Range: Grassy meadows, streambanks in the montane, 6,000–11,000', throughout the Great Basin, e.g., Steens Mountain, Deep Creek Mountains.

Comments: *Castilleja (C. chromosa). Miniata* means "cinnabar red." Also called Streamside Paintbrush.

ALPINE PAINTBRUSH
Castilleja nana
Snapdragon Family (Scrophulariaceae)

Description: Most paintbrush species have flashy red, yellow, orange, or purple bracts that create quite showy plants that stand out conspicuously from their environment. Although Alpine Paintbrush can have showy pink-purple bracts, often the bracts are pale pink or even gray, blending in easily with the plant's rocky environment. Because of its more muted color and its very small stature (to 6"), Alpine Paintbrush can easily be overlooked. However, keep an eye out for it when you're near or above timberline, for a close look at even the grayest plant will reveal unsuspected, beautiful tinges of a variety of colors—pink, rose, purple, and perhaps salmon. As with most paintbrush species, the bracts have 3 or 5 lobes. The flower tube and beak are mostly concealed by the bracts, although you may be able to see the black tip of the stigma.

Flowering Season: June–August.

Habitat/Range: Rocky ridges, exposed slopes in the montane and the alpine, 8,000–13,000', throughout the Great Basin, e.g., Toiyabe Range, Great Basin National Park.

Comments: *Castilleja (C. chromosa). Nana* means "dwarf."

BIGELOW'S MONKEYFLOWER
Mimulus bigelovii
Snapdragon Family (Scrophulariaceae)

Description: Bigelow's Monkeyflower is one of the most gorgeous of the more than 20 *Mimulus* species in the Great Basin. The ¾–1" wide, red-purple flowers look even larger blooming on such a short (1–10") stem. With up to 10 or more of these large, showy flowers in bloom at once, Bigelow's Monkeyflower provides a spectacular bouquet to adorn desert and sagebrush flats. The red-purple flowers have 2 yellow ridges in their throat with darker red-purple lines and splotches. There are usually two red-purple eyes in the throat bordering the yellow ridges. The leaves are elliptic or widely ovate and sharp pointed.

Flowering Season: March–June.

Habitat/Range: Sandy washes, gravelly flats in the desert shrub and the sagebrush steppe, to 6,500', in eastern California, western Nevada, e.g., White Mountains. This species occurs mostly in the Mojave Desert.

Comments: *Mimulus (M. guttatus)*. John Bigelow was a 19th-century physician and plant collector.

LEWIS MONKEYFLOWER
Mimulus lewisii
Snapdragon Family (Scrophulariaceae)

Description: Lewis Monkeyflower is one of the showiest of the many *Mimulus* species in the Great Basin, for the flowers can be up to 2" wide and they grow on plants that can be up to 3' tall. The plants inhabit wet meadows and thickets along creeks, so the flowers are usually part of a multicolored floral banquet consisting of numerous robust plants with exuberant flowers. Lewis Monkeyflower definitely holds its own, for its flowers are multicolored banquets all by themselves—their pink or rose, square-tipped petals are usually streaked with darker red-purple, and the flower throat is tinged with bright yellow. The base of the lower petals has clumps of yellow or white hairs. The beige, hinged stigma pressed against the upper throat is easily noticed, so this is a great monkeyflower on which to observe the rapid closing of the stigma when touched.

Flowering Season: June–August.

Habitat/Range: Wet meadows, streambanks in the montane, 6,000–10,000', throughout the Great Basin, e.g., Steens Mountain, Great Basin National Park.

Comments: *Mimulus (M. guttatus).* Meriwether Lewis *(Lewisia pygmaea).*

DWARF PURPLE MONKEYFLOWER
Mimulus nanus
Snapdragon Family (Scrophulariaceae)

Description: Dwarf Purple Monkeyflower is one of the many *Mimulus* species in the Great Basin that has flowers some shade of red-purple, but although its 5-petaled flowers tend toward magenta, they often have hints of violet, distinguishing them from almost all of their monkeyflower kin. The flower throat is a darker rose-purple with 2 yellow ridges extending onto the petal lobes of the lower lip. Dwarf Purple Monkeyflower is not so much dwarfed in its flower (which is about ½") but in its growth form, as the plant hugs the ground, seldom reaching up more than 4". The narrow, glandular leaves form a cradle on which lie the striking flowers.

Flowering Season: May–July.

Habitat/Range: Dry, sandy or gravelly flats in the sagebrush steppe and the montane, to 10,000', throughout the Great Basin except Utah, e.g., Charles Sheldon National Wildlife Refuge, Steens Mountain.

Comments: *Mimulus (M. guttatus). Nanus* means "dwarf."

COPELAND'S OWL'S-CLOVER
Orthocarpus cuspidatus
Snapdragon Family (Scrophulariaceae)

Description: Copeland's Owl's-Clover is one of the many plants that thrive on sandy or gravelly openings between sagebrush. From a distance a mass of this Owl's-Clover looks like a pink haze, but on close inspection the 4–16" plants are fascinating in their detail. The stems end in a spike of rounded bracts with pointed, pink-purple tips. Perched delicately between the bracts are the tiny flowers. The upper lip of the tubular flower forms a pink beak which projects above and beyond the lower lip, which is reduced to a swollen, white sac. To complete this intricate display, the tiny, globular, pink-purple stigma projects just beyond the tip of the beak. With perhaps a good dose of imagination, you may be able to see a tiny pink owl sitting on the branch of a tree!

Flowering Season: June–August.

Habitat/Range: Dry, sandy or gravelly slopes and flats in the sagebrush steppe and the montane, 6,000–10,000', western and northwestern Nevada, southern Oregon, e.g., Peavine Mountain, Steens Mountain.

Comments: *Orthocarpus (O. hispidus). Cuspidatus* means "with a sharp, stiff point." Formerly known as *O. copelandii* (Edwin Copeland was a 20th-century California authority on ferns).

LITTLE ELEPHANT'S HEAD
Pedicularis attolens
Snapdragon Family (Scrophulariaceae)

Description: Little Elephant's Head is a shorter plant (4–18") with smaller flowers (¼–½") than its close relative Bull Elephant's Head *(P. groenlandica)*. Though the 5-petaled flowers still have the floppy elephant's ears (formed by the 2 outer petals of the lower lip), the trunk of Little Elephant's Head is less elephantine, curving more sideways than down and then up. Though the flowers can be the same red-purple as those of Bull Elephant's Head, they are often a lighter pink with darker red-purple veins. The inflorescence is densely covered with cobwebby, white hairs. The leaves are typical of *Pedicularis* species—fernlike and mostly basal.

Flowering Season: June–August.

Habitat/Range: Wet meadows in the montane, 8,500–10,500', in eastern California, western Nevada, southern Oregon, e.g., Steens Mountain.

Comments: *Pedicularis (P. groenlandica). Attolens* means "upraised" in reference to the petals that form the elephant's trunk.

BULL ELEPHANT'S HEAD
Pedicularis groenlandica
Snapdragon Family (Scrophulariaceae)

Description: Of the many flowering plants named after an animal, some are eaten by that animal (e.g., Antelope Brush, Burrobush, Rabbitbrush, Elk Thistle), some share habitats with that animal (e.g., Toad Lily), some share colors or markings with that animal (e.g., Tiger Lily), and some bear a remote (often very remote!) resemblance to that animal (e.g., Monkeyflower). Elephant's Head, however, is one of the very few flowers to look almost exactly like its namesake—the ½–2½' plant bears scores of ½", red-purple or pink elephant heads along its upper 6–12". Each head is a nearly perfect miniature replica—the 2 petals of the upper lip form the down-curving, then upswept trunk, while the 3 petals of the lower lip form the forehead and floppy ears. When you tell your friends that you saw a herd of pink elephants cavorting in a wet meadow, you won't be far from the truth! The 1–10" leaves are typical of *Pedicularis* species—basal and deeply divided (fernlike).

Flowering Season: June–August.

Habitat/Range: Streambanks, seeps, marshy meadows in the montane and the alpine, 7,000–12,000', throughout the Great Basin, e.g., Ruby Mountains.

Comments: *Pedicularis* means "lousewort" in reference to the belief that animals who ate some species of this genus became susceptible to infestation by lice. *Groenlandica* means "of Greenland" in reference to the circumboreal distribution of this species (although it does not occur in Greenland).

FIRECRACKER PENSTEMON
Penstemon eatonii
Snapdragon Family (Scrophulariaceae)

Description: You can understand how these narrow, 1–1½", scarlet, 5-petaled, tubular flowers would remind someone of firecrackers both in their shape and in their fiery color. Although in all *Penstemon* species the flower faces are small in comparison to the length of the flower tube, in most red-flowered species the lower lip of the flower tube is especially small. This reveals the coevolution of this red flower with its pollinator (the hummingbird), for this bird hovers as it sips nectar from the tube, so it doesn't need the lower lip landing pad that is so helpful to bees (who pollinate Blue Penstemons). In Firecracker Penstemon this lower lip is even smaller than in most red-flowered penstemons—in fact the face is just a continuation of the tube as the petal lobes hardly flare at all. The 1–3' plant bears numerous flowers and numerous opposite pairs of 1–3", narrow leaves.

Flowering Season: May–July.

Habitat/Range: Gravelly flats and slopes in the desert shrub, the sagebrush steppe, and the montane, to 11,000', in central and eastern Nevada, western Utah, e.g., Toquima Range, Deep Creek Mountains.

Comments: *Penstemon (P. deustus).* D. C. Eaton was a 19th-century Yale University botanist. Also called Eaton's Penstemon.

ROSY PENSTEMON
Penstemon floridus
Snapdragon Family (Scrophulariaceae)

Description: With almost half the length of its 1–4' stems bearing 1–1½", showy, pink, 5-petaled flowers, rosy penstemon is a stunning plant, noticeable on sagebrush flats from quite a distance as pink flags waving in the breeze. A close look at the amazing flowers will probably elicit a chuckle, for the tube is dramatically swollen into a protruding potbelly. With only a little imagination, the flowers become inflated, pink blowfish with puckered lips. The opposite pairs of leaves are fleshy, toothed, and clasping.

Flowering Season: June–July.

Habitat/Range: Gravelly flats, washes in the sagebrush steppe, 5,000–9,000', eastern California, western Nevada, e.g., White Mountains.

Comments: *Penstemon (P. deustus). Floridus* means "full of flowers." Also called Panamint Penstemon.

SCENTED PENSTEMON
Penstemon palmeri
Snapdragon Family (Scrophulariaceae)

Description: With its tall (1½–5') stems and large (1–1½" long and nearly as wide in the face) flowers, Scented Penstemon grabs your attention even from a considerable distance. The flowers are deliciously scented, interesting in structure, and beautifully marked. The upper 2 petals project to form a kind of awning for the tube, while the lower 3 petals are bent down. While the upper petals are solid pale pink or white, the lower ones are decorated with numerous red-violet lines. The protruding staminode is adorned with a dense pompom of fine, long, yellow hairs. There can be as many as 20 of these spectacular flowers in bloom at the same time on a stem and there can be several stems per plant.

Flowering Season: May–July.

Habitat/Range: Sandy or gravelly flats and slopes, washes, canyons in the desert shrub, the sagebrush steppe, and the montane, to 9,000', throughout Nevada except for the northwestern region, western Utah, e.g., Great Basin National Park, Deep Creek Mountains.

Comments: *Penstemon (P. deustus).* Edward Palmer was an ethnobotanist and plant collector for the 1861 California State Geological Survey.

BRIDGES PENSTEMON
Penstemon rostriflorus
Snapdragon Family (Scrophulariaceae)

Description: From a distance you might confuse Bridges Penstemon with one of the several other tall, red-flowered penstemons, but a close look at the flowers will leave no doubt as to this plant's identity. The 1–1½", red, 5-petaled flowers have a unique, severely reflexed lower lip, which gives the flowers the appearance of some kind of seal-like creature flippering its way through the air. The 1–3' plant is thick with these intriguing flowers floating well above the opposite pairs of small, narrow leaves, which branch off the lower parts of the plant stems. Usually you will find Bridges Penstemon in many-stemmed clumps, creating a conspicuous, scarlet patch on the landscape.

Flowering Season: June–August.

Habitat/Range: Gravelly or sandy slopes, washes in the sagebrush steppe and the montane, 5,000–11,000', in western Nevada, western Utah, e.g., White Mountains.

Comments: *Penstemon (P. deustus). Rostriflorus* means "having beaked flowers." Thomas Bridges was an Englishman who collected plants in California in the the 19th century.

MOUNTAIN FIGWORT
Scrophularia desertorum
Snapdragon Family (Scrophulariaceae)

Description: For such a tall (2–4') plant, Mountain Figwort has quite small (¼–½") flowers, but there are many of them crowding the branches of the elongated panicle. The flowers reward close inspection both for their unusual color and for their odd form. The 2 petals of the upper lip form a flat, maroon, erect canopy; while the 2 outer petals of the lower lip form lighter purple or pink, erect sides, and the third lower petal forms a creamy white or pale pink bib. The creamy anthers barely protrude above the bib, while the long pistil droops out against it. The robust stem is square and bears many opposite pairs of petioled, toothed, somewhat triangular leaves.

Flowering Season: May–July.

Habitat/Range: Rocky slopes and crevices, gravelly road edges in the sagebrush steppe, to 8,500', in eastern California, western, north-western, and central Nevada, e.g., White Mountains, Toquima Range.

Comments: *Scrophularia* is derived from "scrofula," a disease presumably cured by some species. *Desertorum* means "of the desert." Formerly known as *S. californica* var. *desertorum*.

BECKWITH VIOLET
Viola beckwithii
Violet Family (Violaceae)

Description: Violets are such cheery flowers with their happy faces and bright colors, especially since so many of them bloom in the early spring when flower lovers are craving floral companionship. Beckwith's Violet is one of the showiest and most unusual of the *Viola* species in the Great Basin, for its 1–1½" blossoms are multicolored—the upper 2 petals are a velvety purple-maroon, while the lower 3 petals are blue-purple, maroon, pink, or white. The flower throat is white and yellow with conspicuous maroon stripes or splotches. The blossoms appear even larger because they rise only 2–8" above the basal, deeply divided, rather fan-shaped leaves.

Flowering Season: March–May.

Habitat/Range: Dry slopes in the sagebrush steppe, to 7,200', western and northern Nevada, southern Oregon, e.g., Wassuk Range, Steens Mountain.

Comments: *Viola (V. macloskeyi)*. e.g., Beckwith led one of the Pacific Railroad surveys through northern Nevada.

YELLOW AND ORANGE FLOWERS

This section includes yellow and orange flowers as well as multicolored flowers where the predominant color is yellow or orange. Since yellow and orange flowers often become either paler or deeper in color with age, you should check both the White and Cream section and the Pink and Red section if you don't find the flower you are looking for here.

AROMATIC SPRING-PARSLEY
Cymopterus terebinthinus
Carrot Family (Apiaceae)

Description: Aromatic Spring-Parsley is a good name for this plant (certainly much more descriptive than its alternative common name Terebinth Pteryxia!), because its intricately divided, fernlike leaves do resemble those of domestic parsley and are very fragrant when crushed. It is a low (½–2'), spreading plant that is woody at the base and inhabits dry slopes, often around rocks. The ½–8" leaves are broadly ovate in outline and are finely pinnately dissected into tiny, rough segments. The peduncles bear 3–24 rays varying in length from ½–3". The pedicels branching off the tips of the rays are very short (usually less than ⅛") and bear the tiny, 5-petaled, yellow flowers. For a plant with such miniscule flowers, *Cymopterus terebinthinus* certainly has a ponderous name!

Flowering Season: May–July.

Habitat/Range: Sandy or rocky slopes, canyons in the sagebrush steppe and the montane, 5,000–9,000', throughout the Great Basin, e.g., Toiyabe Range, Deep Creek Mountains.

Comments: *Cymopterus* means "wavy wing" in reference to the fruit. *Terebinthinus* means "of turpentine" in reference to the plant's pungent oil. Formerly known as *Pteryxia terebinthina*. Also called Terebinth Pteryxia.

SONN'S DESERT PARSLEY
Lomatium austinae
Carrot Family (Apiaceae)

Description: In the limited area in which it occurs (western Nevada), Sonn's Desert Parsley is one of the most common of the yellow-flowered *Lomatium* species. It is easily distinguished from the other yellow-flowered *Lomatium* species frequently found in this region, Fern-Leaf Lomatium *(L. dissectum),* by its stature and by its leaves. While Fern-Leaf Lomatium is a tall (1–5'), robust plant with stout stems and long rays (the umbrella spokes) creating clearly separated umbellets of flowers, Sonn's Desert Parsley is a considerably shorter plant (only up to 1') with less separated umbellets (because the rays are shorter). If in any doubt, check the leaves, for though the leaves of both species are fernlike (i.e., deeply divided), those of Sonn's Desert Parsley are covered with downy, white hairs, creating a rather gray-green appearance.

Flowering Season: April–June.

Habitat/Range: Sandy slopes in the sagebrush steppe, to 6,500', in western Nevada, e.g., Virginia Range.

Comments: *Lomatium (L. nevadense).* Mary Austin was an amateur botanist of eastern California and the author of *Land of Little Rain.* Formerly known as *L. plummerae* var. *sonnei.* Also called Plumas Lomatium.

FERN-LEAF LOMATIUM
Lomatium dissectum
Carrot Family (Apiaceae)

Description: An early spring bloomer, Fern-Leaf Lomatium is quite conspicuous despite its tiny, pale yellow or yellow-green flowers, for it's a tall plant (1–5') with stout stems and large umbels of flowers up to 4" across. Because the rays bearing the umbellets of flowers are long and of unequal length, the umbellets are widely separated and distinct. In fruit, these umbellets are also quite conspicuous and attractive, for they are then thick with the ½–¾", elliptic, striped seeds. The deeply divided, green leaves are rough to the touch and highly aromatic when crushed.

Flowering Season: April–July.

Habitat/Range: Rocky or gravelly slopes in the sagebrush steppe and the montane, to 8,500', throughout the Great Basin, e.g., Washoe Valley, Deep Creek Mountains.

Comments: *Lomatium (L. nevadense). Dissectum* means "deeply divided" in reference to the fernlike leaves.

PESTLE LOMATIUM
Lomatium nudicaule
Carrot Family (Apiaceae)

Description: Despite its clusters of tiny flowers typical of the Carrot Family, Pestle Lomatium is a striking plant, for its "stems" (actually peduncles and rays) are quite dramatic. Rising above the widely ovate, blue-green, basal leaves are 4–16", stout, blue-green stalks with white swellings at their top out of which rise several blue-green, slender, 1–8" rays. From the end of these rays branch out the several short pedicels at the end of which, finally, are the clusters of tiny, 5-petaled flowers. All the radiating spokes and all the swellings and curves create quite an architectural wonder!

Flowering Season: April–June.

Habitat/Range: Dry meadows, openings in the sagebrush steppe and the montane, to 8,000', throughout the Great Basin, e.g., Peavine Mountain.

Comments: *Lomatium (L. nevadense). Nudicaule* means "naked stem."

WESTERN SWEET CICELY
Osmorhiza occidentalis
Carrot Family (Apiaceae)

Description: If you were to unearth the roots of plants in the *Osmorhiza* genus, you would probably notice their licorice fragrance, but of course you wouldn't want to dig up these plants, so you'll have to seek other identifying features. Though Western Sweet Cicely is a 1–4' plant resembling several other members of the Carrot Family with its umbels of tiny flowers, it does have some easily observed distinguishing features. Separating it from many of its kin are the loose umbels of greenish yellow (rather than the usual white or bright yellow) flowers. Also the large leaves are pinnately divided into several 1–5" serrated leaflets, which themselves are irregularly cut or lobed. The umbels of flowers usually have 5–12 slender 1–3" rays, from each of which branch a cluster of ⅛–¼" pedicels bearing the tiny, 5-petaled flowers. The fruits are ½–1", slender cylinders.

Flowering Season: May–July.

Habitat/Range: Grassy meadows, thickets, forest openings in the montane, 6,000–10,000', throughout the Great Basin, e.g., Charles Sheldon National Wildlife Refuge, Deep Creek Mountains.

Comments: *Osmorhiza* means "scented root." *Occidentalis* means "western."

ORANGE MOUNTAIN DANDELION
Agoseris aurantiaca
Composite Family (Asteraceae)

Description: Orange Mountain Dandelion is very much a typical dandelion with its flower head of straplike rays (no disk flowers); however, the color of these rays is quite startling—burnt orange drying to purple. The 4–24" plant bears only one ½–¾" flower head, which is subtended by long, triangular phyllaries. The 2–14" basal leaves are slender (grasslike or a bit wider) and pointed. The leaves and stem can be hairless but often have sparse, soft, white hairs. If the name "dandelion" conjures images of yellow lawn weeds for you, Orange Mountain Dandelion may be just what you need to evoke new dandelion appreciation.

Flowering Season: July–August.

Habitat/Range: Seep areas in rocks, grassy slopes, openings in the montane, 6,500–11,500', throughout the Great Basin, e.g., Steens Mountain, Ruby Mountains.

Comments: *Agoseris* means "goat chicory." *Aurantiaca* means "orange-red."

SHORT-BEAKED AGOSERIS
Agoseris glauca
Composite Family (Asteraceae)

Description: A more typical "mountain dandelion" (i.e., *Agoseris* species) than the orange-flowered *A. aurantiaca*, Short-Beaked Agoseris has a dandelion-like flower head of many, square-tipped, straplike, yellow rays. The ½–3½' tall scape bears only one of the large (to 1") flower heads. There are several varieties of this species, in most of which the narrow phyllaries and the toothed leaves are at least somewhat hairy or felty. The flowers usually dry somewhat pink. As in all *Agoseris* species, the plant has milky sap.

Flowering Season: May–July.

Habitat/Range: Dry slopes, grassy meadows in the sagebrush steppe and the montane, to 11,000', throughout the Great Basin, e.g., Peavine Mountain.

Comments: *Agoseris (A. aurantiaca). Glauca* means "glaucous" (i.e., covered with a fine, white powder).

111

SEEP-SPRING ARNICA
Arnica longifolia
Composite Family (Asteraceae)

Description: While all *Arnica* species have opposite pairs of stem leaves, most have only a few (2–5) pairs, with upper pairs that are greatly reduced in size. Seep-Spring Arnica is one of the few species to have many (5–12) pairs of leaves that are all about the same size, whether on the upper or lower part of the stem. The result is a very leafy plant. These leaves are also quite distinctively shaped and textured: They are long and narrow (almost linear), sharp tipped, and rough to the touch, being covered with short, bristly hairs. Seep-Spring Arnica, as the common name suggests, grows in seeps and along creeks and in other wet areas. You will usually find it in large, tight clumps, for the underground runner is usually abundantly and closely branched.

Flowering Season: July–September.

Habitat/Range: Wet meadows, seeps, creekbanks, damp openings in the montane, 6,000–10,500', throughout the Great Basin, e.g., Sweetwater Mountains, Deep Creek Mountains.

Comments: *Arnica (A. mollis). Longifolia* means "long leafed."

SOFT ARNICA
Arnica mollis
Composite Family (Asteraceae)

Description: Because most *Arnica* species sprout from long, underground runners, it is not uncommon to find these plants growing in great masses, their bright sunflower-like flower heads creating a large, almost solid canopy. Of the several species of *Arnica* in the Great Basin, Soft Arnica may be the champion in this regard, for you will often discover huge, solid stands of this plant dominating large portions of wet, grassy mountain meadows. Its ½–2' stem is glandular-hairy and bears 3–5 opposite pairs of leaves, which are all sessile or on very short petioles. They can vary in shape, but are usually ovate and untoothed and are, as the species name indicates, distinctively soft-hairy. The 9–18 rays are usually square and 3-lobed at the tip. The flower heads can be up to 2" wide.

Flowering Season: July–September.

Habitat/Range: Damp or wet, grassy meadows, streambanks in the montane, 6,000–11,500', throughout the Great Basin, e.g., Toiyabe Range, Deep Creek Mountains.

Comments: *Arnica* is the ancient Latin name. *Mollis* means "soft" in reference to the hairy leaves.

BUDSAGE
Artemisia spinosa
Composite Family (Asteraceae)

Description: None of the many species of sagebrush in the Great Basin has very showy flowers, but Budsage may have the least conspicuous, for the small (¼") flower heads have only 2–10 tiny disk flowers in a rather tight ball, which are somewhat obscured by the bracts and leaves. Budsage is not a very showy plant either—it's a small (½–2') shrub with small, palmately divided leaves—but nonetheless it may catch your eye, for the old flower-bearing branches become stiff, white spines, while the old bark becomes shredded. Though not very showy, Budsage is hardy—resistant to drought and heavy grazing.

Flowering Season: April–June.

Habitat/Range: Gravelly, alkali flats and slopes in the sagebrush steppe, to 6,500', throughout the Great Basin, e.g., Soldier Meadow.

Comments: *Artemisia (A. tridentata). Spinosa* means "spiny."

BIG SAGEBRUSH
Artemisia tridentata
Composite Family (Asteraceae)

Description: Big Sagebrush is the state flower of Nevada, and some would say for good reasons. It is remarkably widespread and adaptable, prospering in a variety of habitats from high, cold desert plains to dry hillsides and forest openings near timberline. Its flowers are certainly not ostentatious, but are interesting and get the job done; it takes a while to learn to appreciate it, but it does rub off on you! These familiar (and perhaps rather drab) shrubs can create vast sagebrush landscapes where very little else can grow, but can also dot hillsides where surprisingly diverse wildflower gardens flourish between them. The plant ranges from 1–10' tall depending on the moisture and soil and tends to have a crooked central trunk that branches freely above. Although this is a highly variable species with several recognized varieties, all have the distinctive silvery-hairy leaves with 3 lobes at the tip. The spikes of flowers can be 1' or so long, but even so the tiny disk flowers are easy to overlook. Not easy to "oversmell," however, is the sweet, delicious fragrance that seems embedded in our collective memories and images of the American West.

Flowering Season: July–October.

Habitat/Range: Dry flats and slopes, openings in the sagebrush steppe and the montane, to 11,000', throughout the Great Basin, practically anywhere.

Comments: *Artemisia* is probably after Artemis, mythical Greek goddess of the hunt, who so benefited from a plant of this family that she gave it her own name. *Tridentata* means "3-toothed" leaf.

HOOKER'S BALSAMROOT
Balsamorhiza hookeri
Composite Family (Asteraceae)

Description: Though having large, sunflower-like flower heads like its close relative Arrow-Leaf Balsamroot *(B. sagittata)*, Hooker's Balsamroot has a very different feel to it and is easily identified by its decidedly unarrowlike leaves. These basal leaves can be up to 16" long and are deeply pinnately divided into segments, which in turn are lobed or divided. The leafless stem, the basal leaves, and the phyllaries are densely white-wooly. The 1–3" wide flower heads have 10–21 rays, which are usually fringed at the tips. You will often find Hooker's Balsamroot in much rockier habitats than Arrow-Leaf Balsamroot,

though the two species are known to hybridize (inset photo), resulting in leaves that are broad and arrow shaped *(B. sagittata)*, but also deeply divided *(B. hookeri)*.

Flowering Season: April–July.

Habitat/Range: Dry, grassy meadows, gravelly or rocky slopes in the sagebrush steppe and the montane, to 9,000', throughout the Great Basin, e.g., Washoe Valley, Great Basin National Park.

Comments: *Balsamorhiza (B. sagittata)*. Joseph Hooker was a 19th-century English botanist and director of Kew Gardens.

ARROW-LEAF BALSAMROOT
Balsamorhiza sagittata
Composite Family (Asteraceae)

Description: Sometimes in the mountains of the Great Basin, especially on volcanic soil, you'll come across expansive slopes covered nearly solid with large, brilliant yellow "sunflowers." It is likely that many of these will be Mule Ears *(Wyethia mollis)*, but the chances are good that Arrow-Leaf Balsamroot will be mixed in. You may have some difficulty distinguishing the two at first, but a closer look will show that Arrow-Leaf Balsamroot has (surprise!) arrow-shaped (or heart-shaped) leaves. Unlike the furry, vertically oriented leaves of Mule Ears, these balsamroot leaves are mostly shiny, bright green (though they do have fine, short, silvery hairs) and tend to arch out parallel to the ground. At the tip of each ½–2' stem is a 2–4" flower head with 8–25 (often 13 or 21), somewhat overlapping, pointed rays. Arrow-Leaf Balsamroot can also occur in clearings of conifer forests—it can be a startling experience to find a clump of this plant lit up by a ray of sun in an otherwise shaded forest.

Flowering Season: April–August.

Habitat/Range: Dry hillsides and flats, openings in the sagebrush steppe and the montane, to 9,000', throughout the Great Basin, e.g., Charles Sheldon National Wildlife Refuge, Ruby Mountains.

Comments: *Balsamorhiza* means "balsam root." *Sagittata* means "arrow shaped" in reference to the leaves.

LARGE-FLOWERED BRICKELLIA
Brickellia grandiflora
Composite Family (Asteraceae)

Description: Although Large-Flowered Brickellia is a relatively tall plant (½–3½') with large, broad, distinctive leaves, it is easy to overlook because the flowers are inconspicuous both in color and in form. Each of the usually nodding, cylindrical flower heads consists of 20–40 disk flowers (no rays), which are whitish or yellowish with protruding yellow reproductive parts. The flower heads form clusters of a few to many. The large (1–4" long and up to 2" wide), showy leaves are triangular or heart shaped, toothed, and dark green. Low on the stem they are opposite, while on the upper part of the stem they alternate.

Flowering Season: July–September.

Habitat/Range: Rocky slopes, clearings in the montane, 6,000–8,000', throughout the Great Basin except western and central Nevada, e.g., Steens Mountain, Ruby Mountains.

Comments: John Brickell was an 18th-century American physician and botanist. *Grandiflora* means "large flowered."

RUBBER RABBITBRUSH
Chrysothamnus nauseosus
Composite Family (Asteraceae)

Description: Practically anywhere in the Great Basin, Rubber Rabbitbrush is likely to be your companion. This 1–6', gray-green shrub often brings a warm, golden glow to fall landscapes, otherwise mostly brown with plants dried and gone to seed, for the yellow flower heads (with their usually 5 disk flowers) are late and persistent bloomers. Though the ½–3", gray-green leaves are very narrow, they are profuse, crowding the felty stems. Since the flower heads cluster at the tips of the stems, the plants look a bit like a bundle of paintbrushes with only their tips dipped in paint.

Flowering Season: July–November.

Habitat/Range: Dry flats and slopes, washes, openings in the desert shrub, the sagebrush steppe, and the montane, to 11,000', throughout the Great Basin, practically anywhere.

Comments: *Chrysothamnus* means "golden shrub." *Nauseosus* means "sickening" in reference to the plant's strong, rather unpleasant odor. The common name Rubber Rabbitbrush refers to the high latex content of the plant, especially in its lower, woody portions.

TAPER-TIP HAWKSBEARD
Crepis acuminata
Composite Family (Asteraceae)

Description: Taper-Tip Hawksbeard is one of the many hybridizing species of *Crepis* that frequent the Great Basin. As with most species Taper-Tip Hawksbeard is a tall (to 2') plant with many-branched stems, creating a candelabra-like appearance with many flower heads and rather dandelion-like leaves. Taper-Tip Hawksbeard can be distinguished from its close kin by its much smaller and more profuse flower heads and by its leaves. As the common and species names suggest, the deeply lobed leaves have a very long and narrow, unlobed terminal spike.

Flowering Season: May–August.

Habitat/Range: Dry slopes and flats in the sagebrush steppe, to 9,000', throughout the Great Basin, e.g., Soldier Meadow, Steens Mountain.

Comments: *Crepis (C. occidentalis)*. Acuminata means "having a long tapering point" in reference to the leaves.

WESTERN HAWKSBEARD
Crepis occidentalis
Composite Family (Asteraceae)

Description: Western Hawksbeard is one of the many dandelion-like Great Basin composites with only yellow ray flowers. Though its 4–12" leaves with the ragged teeth do somewhat resemble those of dandelion, the plant has quite a different look. Its 6–24" stems are candelabra-like with many branches and many flower heads with square-tipped rays. The yellow flower heads are cupped and rise out of a vaselike calyx. The phyllaries are narrow and pointed and often are covered with short, black, gland-tipped hairs. The leaves, stems, and phyllaries are distinctly blue-green.

Flowering Season: March–July.

Habitat/Range: Dry, rocky flats and slopes in the sagebrush steppe, to 9,000', throughout the Great Basin, e.g., Carson Valley, Steens Mountain.

Comments: *Crepis,* meaning "sandal," is of uncertain reference. *Occidentalis* means "western."

WHITE-STEM GOLDENBUSH
Ericameria discoidea
Composite Family (Asteraceae)

Description: As the species name indicates, the flower heads of White-Stem Goldenbush consist of only disk flowers (as opposed to the few scattered ray flowers of its close relative Single-Head Goldenbush, *E. suffruticosus*). Whitestem Goldenbush is a low, narrow-leaved shrub with golden yellow flower heads that grows in rocky areas in the high mountains, extending up to ridges and flats above timberline. As its common name suggests, White-Stem Goldenbush has distinctive white stems. If you scratch a small area of a stem with your fingernail, you will discover that this color is created by a dense mat of appressed, white hairs that provide some defense against the intense ultraviolet and the drying winds of the high mountains.

Flowering Season: July–August.

Habitat/Range: Dry, rocky slopes in the montane and the alpine, 7,500–12,500', throughout the Great Basin, e.g., Steens Mountain, Ruby Mountains.

Comments: *Ericameria (E. suffruticosus). Discoidea* means "disklike" in reference to the flower heads with only disk flowers. Sometimes known as *Haplopappus macronema*.

SINGLE-HEAD GOLDENBUSH
Ericameria suffruticosus
Composite Family (Asteraceae)

Description: Although its flower heads have only a few ray flowers, Single-Head Goldenbush is nonetheless quite a conspicuous plant for its growth form and its foliage as well as for its interesting blooms. It is a 6–16" subshrub that often spreads out for several feet over its rocky terrain high in the mountains. It has rather odd, small, gray-green leaves that are crisped or wavy on the edges and are sticky and highly aromatic when crushed. The flower heads, though not dazzlingly showy, are distinctive and intriguing with their highly irregular and rather messy appearance. The few disk flowers seem to be heading in all directions, and the even fewer (1–6) ray flowers are haphazardly arranged. It really looks like whoever created these flower heads wasn't paying a lot of attention at the time!

Flowering Season: July–September.

Habitat/Range: Rocky flats, ledges, exposed ridges in the montane and the alpine, 8,000–12,000', throughout the Great Basin, e.g., White Mountains, Steens Mountain.

Comments: *Ericameria* refers to the resemblance of the narrow leaves (of some species) to those of some species of the *Erica* genus (in the Heath Family). *Suffruticosus* means "shrublike." Sometimes known as *Haplopappus suffruticosus*.

RAYLESS DAISY
Erigeron aphanactis
Composite Family (Asteraceae)

Description: Of the many species of *Erigeron* in the Great Basin, Rayless Daisy is certainly one of the easiest to identify, for it is very unusual for a daisy to be yellow or to be without ray flowers, and both are true in Rayless Daisy. The 3–12" plant is much-branched with one of the ½", golden, buttonlike flower heads at the tip of each branch. These flat-topped heads are crammed with scores of disk flowers (sometimes also some tiny, inconspicuous rays), which are cradled by narrow, pointed phyllaries. The 1½–3" leaves are long and narrow and mostly erect, like fingers pointing up to the flower heads. They form dense, basal clusters with smaller leaves scattered up the stems. The leaves, stems, and phyllaries are covered with spreading, silvery hairs, giving the entire plant (except the bright, golden flower heads) a soft, muted, gray-green tone.

Flowering Season: April–September.

Habitat/Range: Sandy or gravelly flats in the desert shrub and the sagebrush steppe, to 9,000', throughout the Great Basin, e.g., Peavine Mountain, Deep Creek Mountains.

Comments: *Erigeron (E. filifolius). Aphanactis* from the Greek *aphanes*, "inconspicuous" and *actis*, "a ray," thus a head with tiny, inconspicuous (or no) ray flowers.

WOOLY SUNFLOWER
Eriophyllum lanatum
Composite Family (Asteraceae)

Description: Wooly Sunflower is a widespread, complex species with much variation and numerous recognized varieties. It ranges from low-elevation sagebrush flats and forests to exposed ridges and summits above timberline. It can be a subshrub up to 3½' tall in lower elevations, while it can practically hug the ground in its higher elevations. Regardless of elevation and form, it has several to many branching stems, each topped by 1–5 of the 1–1½" flower heads. The result is usually a dense mass of golden yellow cheer. Each flower head has 8–13 rays, which are shallowly toothed at the tip. The narrow, white-wooly, ½–3" leaves, depending on the variety, can be entire or pinnately compound.

Flowering Season: May–July.

Habitat/Range: Brushy slopes, rocky ridges in the sagebrush steppe, the montane, and the alpine, 5,000–12,500', throughout the Great Basin, e.g., White Mountains, Ruby Mountains.

Comments: *Eriophyllum* means "wooly leafed." *Lanatum* means "wooly" in reference to the white, wooly hairs covering the leaves, stems, and phyllaries.

CURLY-CUP GUMWEED
Grindelia squarrosa
Composite Family (Asteraceae)

Description: This plant's common name—Curly-Cup Gumweed—doesn't seem to hold much promise, and indeed this ½–3' plant is weedy and rather unpleasant. Its flower heads are heavy with sticky, white resin, its leaves are brittle and scratchy, and it frequents roadsides and other disturbed places. It is even unpalatable to animals, so it flourishes in fields where the competing plants are heavily grazed. Despite all these unpleasantries, it does have some intriguing and even appealing features. The 1–2" flower heads are crammed with 20–40 sunny, yellow rays surrounding the central yellow disk, and the phyllaries under the flower head are an architectural delight—they are narrow and hooked and are arranged in several intricately overlapping rows. As if to announce and celebrate their fascinating structure, the phyllaries (and the 1–2", almost rectangular, toothed leaves) are varnished, glistening, and sparkling in the sun.

Flowering Season: June–October.

Habitat/Range: Dry fields, roadsides, and other disturbed places in the desert shrub and the sagebrush steppe, to 6,200', throughout the Great Basin, e.g., Washoe Valley, Ruby Mountains.

Comments: David Grindel was a Russian botanist of the late 18th and early 19th centuries. *Squarrosa* means either "scaly or rough" or "with the leaves spreading at right angles" in reference to the hooked phyllaries. Alien.

COMMON SUNFLOWER
Helianthus annuus
Composite Family (Asteraceae)

Description: Growing to over 6' tall with large (to 4"), showy flower heads, Common Sunflower is a stunning plant, especially considering that it is an annual. If you were to stand quietly by a young plant for a few hours, perhaps you could hear it grow! The central button of disk flowers alone is larger than many flowers, while the 15–35 narrow, separated rays can extend the flower head out another 2–3 inches. The stem, the phyllaries, and the 4–16", widely ovate leaves are covered with short, rough hairs. The disk is usually reddish brown, though it sometimes is

yellow. Distinguishing this sunflower from the several other species of *Helianthus* in the Great Basin are the phyllaries—they are broadly ovate (as opposed to linear) with a long, slender tip (a bit like the whiplash tail of a stingray).

Habitat/Range: Grassy fields, roadsides, and other disturbed places in the sagebrush steppe and the montane, to 8,000', throughout the Great Basin, e.g., Santa Rosa Range.

Comments: *Helianthus* means "sun flower." *Annuus* means "annual."

CUSICK'S SUNFLOWER
Helianthus cusickii
Composite Family (Asteraceae)

Description: Cusick's Sunflower is, like most sunflowers, quite a striking plant with its large (up to 3" across), bright yellow flower heads atop their ½–4' tall stems. The notched rays are pointed and tend to be somewhat disheveled, radiating out from the yellow disk in various planes. There can be up to 21 of these rays. The phyllaries under the flower head are narrow and pointed. The pairs of opposite, bright green leaves are long and narrow and slightly hairy.

Flowering Season: April–July.

Habitat/Range: Dry slopes, openings in the sagebrush steppe, to 6,500', in western Nevada, southern Oregon, e.g., Peavine Mountain, Steens Mountain.

Comments: *Helianthus (H. annuus).* William Cusick was an Oregon plant collector of the early 1900s. Also called Turnip-Root Sunflower.

SHAGGY HAWKWEED
Hieracium horridum
Composite Family (Asteraceae)

Description: Shaggy Hawkweed is a 4–12", much-branched plant with many small (½") flower heads. Though the flower heads are bright yellow, they aren't especially showy, for they have only a few (up to 20) ray flowers and no central disk. However, the plant is quite dramatically striking, for its 1–5", tongue-shaped leaves are very dense on the plant and are covered with long, shaggy, white hairs. Sometimes the leaves are so profuse and so hairy that they capture all your attention, and you may forget to even look for flowers. To see a tangled mass of these leaves seemingly sprouting out of solid granite on a rocky ridge high in the mountains is a startling and unforgettable sight, flowers or not.

Flowering Season: July–September.

Habitat/Range: Dry slopes, rocky flats and ridges, crevices, openings in the montane, 7,000–11,000', in eastern California, western Nevada, southern Oregon, e.g., Bodie Mountains, Steens Mountain.

Comments: *Hieracium* means "hawk," as the Roman naturalist Pliny believed that hawks fed on this plant and similar plants to strengthen their eyesight. *Horridum* means "spiny or bristly," in reference to the extremely hairy leaves.

ALPINE GOLD
Hulsea algida
Composite Family (Asteraceae)

Description: In the harsh, cold, windy environment near and above timberline, you expect to find miniaturized plants hugging the ground for warmth and protection, often forming dense mats or cushions to keep the wind out and the heat in. It can be quite a surprise, then, to find the relatively tall (to 16") and loose plants of Alpine Gold thriving in these challenging environments above timberline. The large size (1–2" wide) of the golden flower heads is also a bit startling. A closer look (or a touch) will explain the mystery—the entire plant (except the flowers) is densely glandular-hairy. Touch a leaf or stem or phyllary and your fingers will stick (and will pick up the plant's strong, sweet fragrance). This covering of sticky hairs helps protect the plant from dessicating wind (creating miniature

eddies around the hairs) and from damaging ultraviolet rays. Another reason why Alpine Gold can be tall for an alpine plant is that it usually grows in more protected areas behind rocks and in depressions. The long, sticky, tonguelike leaves are usually toothed and somewhat infolded.

Flowering Season: July–August.

Habitat/Range: Rocky ridges and summits, rock crevices, talus slopes in the montane and the alpine, 8,000–13,000', in eastern California, Nevada, e.g., Sweetwater Mountains, Toquima Range.

Comments: G. W. Hulse was a U.S. Army surgeon and plant collector. *Algida* means "frigid" in reference to the plant's often cold, alpine environment.

COMMON TARWEED
Madia elegans
Composite Family (Asteraceae)

Description: Although the common name
Tarweed may not inspire a desire to seek out this
plant, it really is worth finding, for it has a
beautiful and graceful flower head, which
occasionally has an added colorful surprise. The
½–3' stem, the narrow, 2–8" leaves, and the
narrow, pointed phyllaries are all glandular-sticky
and rather unpleasantly aromatic. However, the
1–2" wide flower head is showy with 5–21
deeply 3-lobed rays surrounding a small central
button of 25–50 yellow disk flowers. The black
anthers on the disk flowers provide a dash of
contrast. On some plants the base of the rays is
splotched with red-maroon, creating a gorgeous,
dark doughnut around the disk.

Flowering Season: June–September.

Habitat/Range: Dry slopes and meadows, grassy
fields, roadsides in the sagebrush steppe, to
7,000', in western Nevada, e.g., Washoe Valley.

Comments: *Madia* is from a Chilean word for the
plant. *Elegans* means "elegant."

SILVER-LEAF RAILLARDELLA
Raillardella argentea
Composite Family (Asteraceae)

Description: Silver-Leaf Raillardella is a
diminutive plant with usually only 1 small flower
head at the tip of its 1–6", leafless stem. The
flower head too is small (½" wide) and
inconspicuous with only 7–26 tubular disk flowers
(there are no showy ray flowers). Despite its
small stature and relative lack of showiness,
however, it is always a delight to find one of
these plants blooming on a rocky, exposed ridge
high in the mountains (note the elevation range),
for its clustered, ½–3", narrow, basal leaves are
densely covered with long, silvery, silky hairs that
glisten in the sun, and its yellow flower heads
bring a little sunshine to the mostly gray
landscape. The leaves and the phyllaries are
sometimes also glandular-sticky.

Flowering Season: July–September.

Habitat/Range: Exposed, rocky ridges, rocky or
sandy flats in the montane and the alpine,
8,000–14,000', in eastern California, western
Nevada, e.g., White Mountains.

Comments: *Raillardella* means "little *Raillardia*,"
another genus in the Composite Family. *Argentea*
means "silvery" in reference to the hairy leaves.

DWARF MOUNTAIN BUTTERWEED
Senecio fremontii
Composite Family (Asteraceae)

Description: Dwarf Mountain Butterweed has the usual *Senecio* look in several ways—flower heads with only a few (in this case, about 8) irregularly spaced rays and one neat row of phyllaries; and stems with alternating leaves. However, the overall look and location of the plant might fool you, for the plant is short (4–10"), it has only a few flower heads, it has thick, somewhat succulent leaves, and it lives in the rocks high in the mountains. The ½–2", ovate leaves are rather stiff and toothed. Consider yourself blessed to come across this stunning plant with its deep green leaves and bright, sunny flower heads in a pile of gray granite near timberline—it is a surprising and glorious experience.

Flowering Season: July–September.

Habitat/Range: Rocky slopes, rock ledges in the montane and the alpine, 8,000–13,000' in northwestern and northeastern Nevada, southern Oregon, e.g., Steens Mountain.

Comments: *Senecio (S. multilobatus).* J.C. Fremont *(Lepidium fremontii).*

SINGLE-STEM GROUNDSEL
Senecio integerrimus
Composite Family (Asteraceae)

Description: Single-Stem Groundsel has a single, stout, unbranched, 1–3' stem. From its upper few inches branch 6–20 of the 1" wide flower heads. The single stem is all the more noticeable because it is almost bare with only a few scattered leaves clasping it. Most of the 2–10" leaves (sometimes narrow and sometimes rounder) are basal on long petioles. The leaves and the stem are usually sparsely hairy. As with most *Senecio* species, the flower heads look rather scraggly—the few (usually 5 or 8 or 13) narrow rays are widely and irregularly spaced. The phyllaries (usually about 13 or about 21) are noticeably black tipped.

Flowering Season: May–July.

Habitat/Range: Dry or moist meadows, forest openings in the montane, to 11,000', throughout the Great Basin, e.g., Peavine Mountain, Great Basin National Park.

Comments: *Senecio (S. multilobatus). Integerrimus* means "complete," probably in reference to the single stem. Also called Single-Stem Butterweed and Single-Stem Senecio.

127

BASIN BUTTERWEED
Senecio multilobatus
Composite Family (Asteraceae)

Description: Of the many yellow-flowered composites in the Great Basin, *Senecio* species are fairly easy to distinguish by their usually flat-topped, branched inflorescence and their small flower heads with only a few scattered ray flowers. The rays often are irregularly spaced, giving the flower head a bit of a scraggly look. The narrow, pointed phyllaries are in one neat row and in many species are black tipped. Basin Butterweed is distinguished from the many other *Senecio* species by its almost fernlike, deeply pinnately lobed leaves. Most of these ¼" leaves are basal, but there are also smaller ones distributed loosely along the stem. The small flower heads often have 8 rays, sometimes 5, and occasionally about 13.

Flowering Season: April–August.

Habitat/Range: Sandy or gravelly flats and slopes in the desert shrub, the sagebrush steppe, and the montane, to 10,500', throughout the Great Basin, e.g., Great Basin National Park.

Comments: *Senecio* means "old man" in reference to the white-hairy pappus. *Multilobatus* means "with many lobes" in reference to the pinnately lobed leaves.

ARROW-LEAF SENECIO
Senecio triangularis
Composite Family (Asteraceae)

Description: Arrow-Leaf Senecio has the usual look of *Senecio* species—a branched inflorescence of many small flower heads, each of which has only a few, irregularly spaced ray flowers. It can, however, be easily distinguished from the many other Great Basin species by its broad, triangular, toothed leaves. Unlike many of its kin that have mostly basal leaves, Arrow-Leaf Senecio has many leaves alternating all the way up the stem to just below the inflorescence. With its 1–5' stem dense with the broad, 2–10", arrow-shaped leaves, this is quite an impressive, robust plant that adds a definite lushness to streambanks and wet meadows in the mountains. The 1" wide flower heads usually have 8 (sometimes 5) rays.

Flowering Season: June–September.

Habitat/Range: Streambanks, wet meadows, seeps in the montane, 7,000–11,000', throughout the Great Basin, e.g., Toiyabe Range, Ruby Mountains.

Comments: *Senecio* (*S. multilobatus*). *Triangularis* means "triangle shaped" in reference to the leaves. Also called Arrow-Leaf Groundsel and Arrow-Leaf Butterweed.

MEADOW GOLDENROD
Solidago canadensis
Composite Family (Asteraceae)

Description: It is easy to recognize Goldenrod with its long, triangular inflorescence of small, golden yellow flower heads. Whenever you see it in bloom, you may feel a tinge of sadness or sentimentality, for it blooms from late summer into fall, so its blossoms signify the tail end of summer. Meadow Goldenrod is a 1–5', leafy plant with distinctive broad, 2–6", pointed, toothed leaves that alternate all the way up the stems to just under the 4–12" inflorescence, which is thick with scores of the ¼–½" yellow flower heads. Each flower head consists of only a few (8–15, commonly 12 or 13) rays and fewer (5–12) disk flowers.

Flowering Season: July–October.

Habitat/Range: Streambanks, seeps, wet meadows, drainage areas in the sagebrush steppe and the montane, to 10,000', throughout the Great Basin, e.g., Sweetwater Mountains, Deep Creek Mountains.

Comments: *Solidago* means "make whole" in reference to the reputed medicinal qualities of these plants. *Canadensis* means "of Canada."

MISSOURI GOLDENROD
Solidago missouriensis
Composite Family (Asteraceae)

Description: The more-or-less triangular inflorescence of small, golden yellow flower heads blooming in late summer or early fall identifies Missouri Goldenrod as a species of *Solidago*. What distinguish it from the more common Meadow Goldenrod *(S. canadensis)* are its smaller stature (1–2'), its shorter and usually broader inflorescence, and its less leafy stems. The leaves are longer (to 10") and broader and are mostly basal, though there are some smaller stem leaves. The ¼–½" flower heads have the same spindly look as those of Meadow Goldenrod, but usually have fewer rays (usually 7 or 8, though up to 10).

Flowering Season: July–September.

Habitat/Range: Moist places in the sagebrush steppe and the montane, to 8,000', in eastern Nevada, western Utah, southern Oregon, e.g., Steens Mountain, Ruby Mountains.

Comments: *Solidago (S. canadensis)*. *Missouriensis* means "of Missouri."

SHORT-STEM STENOTUS
Stenotus acaulis
Composite Family (Asteraceae)

Description: Finding a mat of Short-Stem Stenotus adorning some otherwise barren rock ledge high in the mountains is a wonderful surprise, for the bright yellow flower heads and dark green leaves bring joyful vitality to this difficult and rather harsh environment. The crowded leaves create a beautiful bed for the brilliant, yellow, ½–1½" wide flower heads that seem almost oversized for their diminutive (2–6") stems. The 6–15 ray flowers are often a bit asymmetrically placed—these alpine suns frequently appear to be missing a few of their rays.

Flowering Season: June–August.

Habitat/Range: Rocky flats and slopes, ridges, ledges in the montane and the alpine, 6,000–11,500', throughout the Great Basin, e.g., Steens Mountain, Great Basin National Park.

Comments: *Stenotus* means "narrow ear." *Acaulis* means "stemless." Formerly known as *Haplopappus acaulis.*

COMMON DANDELION
Taraxacum officinale
Composite Family (Asteraceae)

Description: Although you may be inclined to dismiss Common Dandelion as a persistent and unwanted weed in your lawn or in other disturbed areas, in the wild it might be possible to perceive it somewhat differently. As if to make up for its reputation as an undesirable, it is one of the very first wildflowers to bloom, bringing dazzling yellow splotches to grassy fields and meadows that are rapidly greening as winter fades. Though it is an invasive weed, it usually doesn't take over a wild area as it does a lawn, so it can be more appreciated for its restraint. Atop each of the 4–16" smooth or hairy scapes (i.e., leafless flower stem) is one of the ¾–1½", yellow-rayed flower heads. The pointed phyllaries underneath the rays are reflexed. The 2–16" leaves are broad and highly variable but are always toothed or lobed in some fashion. The fruits form the familiar, cottony sphere of parachutes just waiting for the first breath of wind (or breath of breath) to spread the seeds far and wide.

Flowering Season: April–November.

Habitat/Range: Meadows, lawns, grassy disturbed places in the sagebrush steppe and the montane, to 10,000', throughout the Great Basin, e.g., Washoe Valley, Great Basin National Park.

Comments: *Taraxacum* is of uncertain origin, perhaps from a word meaning "to stir up" in reference to its medicinal qualities. *Officinale* means "medicinal."

131

LITTLE-LEAF HORSEBRUSH
Tetradymia glabrata
Composite Family (Asteraceae)

Description: Like its close relative Thorny
Horsebrush *(T. spinosa)*, Little-Leaf Horsebrush is
a rather scratchy-looking, 1–4' shrub with small
flower heads of only a few yellow disk flowers
projecting out of a cylindrical, white-felty vase of
narrow phyllaries. There are some obvious
differences between the two horsebrush species,
though, primarily in the leaves and in the flower
heads. Whereas in Thorny Horsebrush many of
the leaves have modified into sharp spines, Little-
Leaf Horsebrush is spineless, though the narrow
leaves can be stiff and scratchy. The flower heads
of Little-Leaf Horsebrush are even fewer-flowered
than those of its spiny kin, having only 4 disk
flowers (the meaning of the genus name
Tetradymia), though the plant often appears to be

more flowery as many of the flower heads can
cluster together. This plant is highly toxic to
livestock, especially to light-colored animals,
causing extreme sensitivity to sun—sunburn,
swelled heads, and even death.

Flowering Season: May–July.

Habitat/Range: Gravelly or sandy slopes in the
sagebrush steppe, to 6,200', throughout the Great
Basin, e.g., Charles Sheldon National Wildlife
Refuge.

Comments: *Tetradymia (T. spinosa). Glabrata*
means "glabrous" (i.e., hairless) in reference to
the leaves that are less hairy than those of most
Tetradymia species.

THORNY HORSEBRUSH
Tetradymia spinosa
Composite Family (Asteraceae)

Description: Thorny Horsebrush, as you might suppose from its common and scientific names, is a decidedly unpleasant-looking plant. It is an intricately branched, 1½–4' shrub armed with numerous straight, sharply pointed, ½–2", straw-colored spines. There isn't much green on the plant as the stems are covered with a mat of white, felty hair and the green leaves are small (½" long) and needlelike, forming inconspicuous whorls around the stem. The flower heads are small too, consisting of only a few (4–9) tiny, yellow disk flowers. Perhaps more noticeable than the flowers is the cylindrical vase of 4–6, narrow, white-felty phyllaries. You will often find swellings on the stems (caused by a gallfly particular to *Tetradymia* species).

Flowering Season: April–June.

Habitat/Range: Dry slopes in the desert shrub and the sagebrush steppe, to 7,200', throughout the Great Basin, e.g., Fly Canyon, Steens Mountain.

Comments: *Tetradymia* means "four together" in reference to some species having heads of only 4 disk flowers. Spinosa means "with spines." Also called Catsclaw-Horsebrush and Cotton-Thorn. Sometimes known as *T. axilaris*.

YELLOW SALSIFY
Tragopogon dubius
Composite Family (Asteraceae)

Description: Yellow Salsify is an invasive weed that frequents disturbed places. The 1–3' stem bears many 8–20" clasping, grasslike leaves and is topped by a single 1–2" flower head. The 15–25 or so narrow, pointed, lemon-yellow rays appear at first to be more than that because the green phyllaries are of similar shape and radiate out under and beyond the rays. There is no disk, though the reproductive parts arching up from the base of the rays bear some resemblance to disk flowers. In fruit Yellow Salsify is at least as striking as it is in flower, for the huge, dandelion-like sphere of plumed seeds is fascinatingly intricate and beautiful. When you look at this 1–2", fluffy ball of parachuted seeds, you'll easily understand how this plant has spread so widely across the United States and Canada.

Flowering Season: May–September.

Habitat/Range: Roadsides and other disturbed places in the sagebrush steppe and the montane, to 10,000', throughout the Great Basin, e.g., Steens Mountain, Great Basin National Park.

Comments: *Tragopogon* means "goat beard" in reference to the bristly pappus. *Dubius* means just that in reference to some taxonomic difficulties. Alien.

133

NORTHERN MULE EARS
Wyethia amplexicaulis
Composite Family (Asteraceae)

Description: As beautiful as is a western Nevada hillside nearly solid with Wooly Mule Ears *(W. mollis)*, an eastern Nevada or western Utah meadow thick with Northern Mule Ears might be even more stunning. The bright yellow flower heads of Northern Mule Ears are quite similar to those of its close relative but can be a little larger (to 4" wide), and the 13–21 rays are a bit more pointed at the tip. The most dramatic difference between the two species, however, is the leaves: While those of Wooly Mule Ears are muted by their soft, silvery hairs, those of Northern Mule Ears are a glossy, varnished, deep green. Since these leaves are up to 2' long and ½' wide and they crowd along almost the full height of the plant stem, the flower heads can almost seem to be floating on a lush, shiny green, leaf "sea." This green "sea" and its bright yellow "islands" are especially stunning when they flow among a grove of white-barked aspen!

Flowering Season: May–July.

Habitat/Range: Grassy meadows, around trees (especially aspen) in the sagebrush steppe and the montane, to 9,000', northeastern and eastern Nevada, western Utah, southern Oregon, e.g., Steens Mountain, Great Basin National Park.

Comments: *Wyethia (W. mollis). Amplexicaulis* means "clasping the stem" in reference to the leaves.

WOOLY MULE EARS
Wyethia mollis
Composite Family (Asteraceae)

Description: Especially along the western edge of northern Nevada, you can find great expanses of volcanic hillsides covered with the large, sunny flower heads of Wooly Mule Ears (often with a few scattered Arrow-Leaf Balsamroot, *Balsamorhiza sagittata*). With their extremely deep roots (sometimes to over 30'), Wooly Mule Ears is able to thrive in porous volcanic soil, where the moisture seeps down to bedrock. Since the ½–1½', broad leaves tend to be erect on long petioles, and the flowering stem only reaches 1–3' tall, the bright yellow, 2–3" flower heads are often displayed against a background of gray-green, wooly leaf. The large flower heads make it easy to see clearly not only the 8–17 showy rays, but also the many tubular disk flowers with their protruding reproductive parts. The delicately 2-branched stigma is particularly lovely.

Flowering Season: May–August.

Habitat/Range: Dry, volcanic slopes and flats in the sagebrush steppe and the montane, to 8,500', in western, northwestern, and central Nevada, southern Oregon, e.g., Peavine Mountain, Toiyabe Range.

Comments: Nathaniel Wyeth was a 19th-century explorer of the American West. *Mollis* means "soft" in reference to the leaves. The common name Mule Ears is also in reference to these broad, softly hairy leaves.

CREEPING OREGON GRAPE
Berberis aquifolium
Barberry Family (Berberidaceae)

Description: Creeping Oregon Grape is a striking plant, its clusters of bright yellow flowers providing flashes of contrast to the various shades of green of the forest floor. The many flower clusters are attached along the usually prostrate stems between where the leaves attach. Each flower itself appears to be a whole bouquet of blossoms, for it has 9 flaring yellow sepals (in 3 whorls of 3) and 6 cupped, yellow petals (in 2 whorls of 3). The hollylike leaves are almost as showy as the flowers, each with 5–9 deep green, waxy, serrated, 1–3", pinnate leaflets. The creeping stems and profuse leaves can be very effective in reducing soil erosion.

Flowering Season: March–June.

Habitat/Range: Conifer and aspen forests in the montane, 5,000–10,000', in eastern Nevada, western Utah, southern Oregon, e.g., Steens Mountain, Ruby Mountains.

Comments: *Berberis* is the ancient Arabic name for barberry. *Aquifolium* is the ancient Latin name for holly in reference to the hollylike leaves. Formerly known as *Mahonia repens*. Also called Creeping Mahonia and Creeping Barberry.

135

GOLDEN CRYPTANTHA
Cryptantha confertiflora
Borage Family (Boraginaceae)

Description: There are many species of *Cryptantha* in the Great Basin, most of which are very difficult to distinguish from each other. Most are bristly-hairy plants with tight clusters of caterpillar-like coils of ¼–½", white flowers. The 5 petal lobes flare out of a short tube and usually have a raised appendage at their base, creating a kind of lip around the flower throat. Golden Cryptantha has all these characteristics except for one, but that one (as indicated by the name) makes it easy for even the nonbotanist to distinguish this plant from all the other cryptanthas— its flowers are golden yellow rather than white. Golden Cryptantha has several ½–1½' stems that rise well above the clusters of narrow, 1–4", basal leaves. The stem, leaves, and calyx are all covered with bristly, silver hairs. Many of the ½"

pale yellow or golden yellow flowers are clustered at the tip of each stem and in the axils of the few upper stem leaves. The lip around the flower throat is pronounced through it is usually the same color as the rest of the petals.

Flowering Season: April–June.

Habitat/Range: Sandy or rocky slopes or flats, washes in the desert shrub and the sagebrush steppe, to 9,000', in eastern California, western and central Nevada, western Utah, e.g., White Mountains, Deep Creek Mountains.

Comments: *Cryptantha (C. humilis). Confertiflora* means "crowded with flowers" in reference to the dense-flowered inflorescences. Also called Golden Forget-Me-Not.

AMERICAN WINTERCRESS
Barbarea orthoceras
Mustard Family (Brassicaceae)

Description: There are numerous mustards with terminal racemes of small, yellow flowers. Many of them are plants of dry environments, so American Wintercress's preference for wet environments helps distinguish it. In addition, the leaves are very distinctive—rounded, shiny green, and pinnately lobed with 2–3 pairs of small, lateral lobes and 1 much larger, usually slightly toothed terminal lobe. The basal leaves are on long petioles, while the smaller stem leaves are usually less lobed and often clasp the plant's stout, 1–2', succulent stem. The ¼–½" yellow, 4–petaled flowers grow in dense, 1–2" clusters that become looser spikes of narrowly cylindrical, straight seedpods that are erect or horizontal.

Flowering Season: May–July.

Habitat/Range: Wet meadows, streambanks in the montane, 5,000–10,000', throughout the Great Basin, e.g., Wahoe Valley, Great Basin National Park.

Comments: *Barbarea* is after Saint Barbara. *Orthoceras* means "straight horned" in reference to the long, straight seedpods.

WALLFLOWER
Erysimum capitatum
Mustard Family (Brassicaceae)

Description: Although many mustards are more notable for their showy seedpods than for their flowers (which are often inconspicuous), Wallflower is one mustard with very showy flowers. The plant has one or several ½–3' stems that are topped by a cylindrical or round inflorescence of many 1–1½" flowers. There may be a few other flowers branching off the stem lower down. Each flower has 4 round, separated, lemon-yellow (sometimes orange) petals. The 1–6", narrow, ascending fruits are mostly straight and are 4-sided or slightly flattened. This is a widespread and complex species with several recognized varieties and subspecies, some of which are considered separate species by some botanists. Whatever its subspecies and location, this plant is a very early bloomer—a joy to see, for it forecasts the wildflower season to come.

Flowering Season: March–August.

Habitat/Range: Sandy or gravelly flats, washes, shrubby slopes in the desert shrub, the sagebrush steppe, and the montane, to 10,000', throughout the Great Basin, e.g., Charles Sheldon National Wildlife Refuge, Great Basin National Park.

Comments: *Erysimum* means "to help" in reference to medicinal properties. *Capitatum* means "rounded head" in reference to the inflorescence.

SHIELD PEPPERGRASS
Lepidium perfoliatum
Mustard Family (Brassicaceae)

Description: One of the many mustards with small, inconspicuous flowers, Shield Peppergrass is nonetheless easily distinguishable and notable for its leaves as well as for its seedpods. As the species name and common name suggest, the leaves along most of the ½–2' stem are heart shaped (shieldlike) and completely surround the stem. The leaves on the lower part of the stem are completely different—pinnately lobed or divided into narrow, needlelike segments. The many, tiny, 4-petaled, yellow flowers in the long inflorescence become flat, ovate, or diamond-shaped seedpods with a minute notch at the tip. Shield Peppergrass is a widespread and common weed usually found mixed in with various grasses in disturbed places.

Flowering Season: April–June.

Habitat/Range: Moist, grassy fields, roadsides, and other disturbed places in the sagebrush steppe and the montane, to 8,500', throughout the Great Basin, e.g., Soldier Meadow, Deep Creek Mountains.

Comments: *Lepidium (L. fremontii). Perfoliatum* means "perfoliate" in reference to the upper stem leaves that completely surround the plant stem. Alien.

TOWER MUSTARD
Sisymbrium altissimum
Mustard Family (Brassicaceae)

Description: Tower Mustard is one of the highly invasive weeds of the Mustard Family that has spread throughout most of the United States. The 1–5' tall (hence the names "tower" and *"altissimum"*), grayish stem has many slender branches and branchlets that form a rather tangled mass that supports a scattering of small (½"), pale yellow flowers. The 2–10", basal leaves are pinnately lobed and toothed. The smaller stem leaves have threadlike divisions. The 2–4" seedpods are narrowly cylindrical and are attached to 2–4" pedicels of equal thickness. The seedpods usually extend horizontally. As the alternative common name Tumbling Mustard suggests, this plant can break free and tumble in the wind, spreading its seeds far and wide.

Flowering Season: April–September.

Habitat/Range: Dry roadsides, disturbed places in the desert shrub and the sagebrush steppe, to 6,500', throughout the Great Basin, e.g., Soldier Meadow.

Comments: *Sisymbrium* is the ancient Greek name. *Altissimum* means "very tall" in reference to the plant's height. Also called Tumbling Mustard. Alien.

PRINCE'S PLUME
Stanleya pinnata
Mustard Family (Brassicaceae)

Description: Many of the mustards are weedy plants with inconspicuous flowers and more conspicuous fruits, but Prince's Plume is nothing of the sort. Its woody, unbranched, 1–3' stems bear 4–12", densely flowered spikes of ¾–1½", delicate, lemon-yellow, 4-petaled blossoms. These flower spikes give the plant a graceful, feathery appearance, for they have a gentle up curve and are crammed with 100 or more flowers, each with slender, long-protruding stamens and white, wooly hairs at the base of the petals. These spikes are especially interesting part way through the blooming season when they are adorned with buds, blooms, and fruits on their upper, middle, and lower portions, respectively.

The 2–6" leaves are pinnately divided into very narrow leaflets (except those on the upper stem, which are narrow and undivided). The basal leaves often dry up and fall off the plant early in the blooming season.

Flowering Season: March–July.

Habitat/Range: Gravelly flats and slopes in the desert shrub and the sagebrush steppe, to 7,000', throughout the Great Basin, e.g., Pyramid Lake, Steens Mountain.

Comments: Edward Stanley, earl of Derby, was a 19th-century English ornithologist. *Pinnata* means "feathery" in reference to the plumelike flower stalks. Also called Golden Prince's Plume.

PLAINS PRICKLY PEAR
Opuntia polyacantha
Cactus Family (Cactaceae)

Description: Plains Prickly Pear is a low (½–1'), clump-forming cactus with the flat, oblong stem segments (i.e., pads) typical of prickly pears. The ¼–3", straw-colored spines are in clusters of 5–11 that are loosely distributed on the pads. The flowers are so large (2–3" wide) and colorful (bright yellow or intense red) that the plant is likely to catch your eye even from a speeding car. The many petals are silky and almost translucent, forming a gorgeous bowl around the numerous yellow stamens and the globular, green stigma. Although it does grow in the Mojave Desert and on sagebrush plains, it might surprise you to find this beautiful cactus also at fairly high elevations in some of the Great Basin's northern mountains.

Flowering Season: May–June.

Habitat/Range: Sandy or gravelly flats, scrubby slopes, rock crevices in the desert shrub and the sagebrush steppe, to 8,000', throughout the Great Basin except northwest Nevada and southern Oregon, e.g., Bodie Mountains, Great Basin National Park.

Comments: *Opuntia* (*O. polyacantha*, red section). *Polyacantha* means "many spines."

YELLOW BEE PLANT
Cleome lutea
Caper Family (Capparaceae)

Description: Although Yellow Bee Plant often grows along roads and in other disturbed places, it is a beautiful plant with a very appealing, graceful symmetry. Up the 1–4' stem alternate long, slender petioles terminating in palmately compound leaves, each with 3–7 (usually 5) narrow, pointed, ½–2½" leaflets. The stem terminates in a dense, round-topped raceme of many ½" yellow flowers with long-protruding reproductive parts. The flowers resemble mustards with 4 petals, 4 sepals, 6 stamens, and a superior ovary. When the flowers go to seed, the narrow, 1–3" pods hang down gently off slender pedicels. In the middle of the blooming season, you can find many of the hanging pods circling the stem under the cluster of flowers, which itself is topped by tight, oval buds. It almost looks like golden fireworks with falling green streamers.

Flowering Season: May–October.

Habitat/Range: Sandy flats, roadsides, disturbed places in the desert shrub and the sagebrush steppe, to 7,500', throughout the Great Basin, e.g., Pyramid Lake, Steens Mountain.

Comments: *Cleome* was an early European name for a mustardlike plant.

141

BROAD-PODDED BEE PLANT
Cleome platycarpa
Caper Family (Capparaceae)

Description: As you would expect, Broad-Podded Bee Plant is quite similar to its close relative Yellow Bee Plant *(C. lutea)*. Both plants are tall (though Broad-Podded is a bit shorter, reaching only 2') and bear a long, round-topped raceme of bright yellow, 4-petaled flowers with long-protruding reproductive parts. Both have palmately compound leaves with wide-spreading, elliptic or ovate leaflets, though Broad-Podded typically has 3 leaflets, while Yellow Bee Plant typically has 5. The major difference between the two species (as indicated by the common name Broad-Podded) is with the fruits. Whereas Yellow Bee Plant has narrow, smooth, banana-like pods, those of its close kin are oval or almost rectangular and slightly hairy. Whatever the pod and whatever the species, bee plant is an intriguing and attractive plant, as much to wildflower lovers as to bees.

Flowering Season: May–July.

Habitat/Range: Dry plains and slopes in the sagebrush steppe, to 7,500', western and northwestern Nevada, southern Oregon, e.g., Peavine Mountain, Steens Mountain.

Comments: *Cleome (C. lutea)*. *Platycarpa* means "broad fruited."

HILLMAN'S CLEOMELLA
Cleomella hillmanii
Caper Family (Capparaceae)

Description: Plants in the genus *Cleomella,* as the name suggests, are quite similar to those in the closely related genus *Cleome.* Plants in both genera have racemes of showy, 4-petaled flowers (usually yellow, see *Cleome serrulata* for an exception) with long-protruding stamens and palmately compound leaves. From a distance, and perhaps even from up close as well, you could easily confuse Hillman's Cleomella for a species of *Cleome;* however, Hillman's Cleomella tends to be a shorter plant (2–12" as compared to several feet) and has very different seedpods. Whereas the fruits of *Cleome* species are definitely longer than wide (e.g., the banana-like fruits of *C. lutea* and the ovals or rectangles of *C. platycarpa*), the fruits of Hillman's Cleomella are tiny (⅛–¼") circles or diamonds. The leaves generally have 3 elliptic or oval leaflets. This plant can grow in huge masses, creating a spectacular, golden landscape in spring or early summer.

Flowering Season: April–June.

Habitat/Range: Sandy flats and hillsides in the sagebrush steppe, to 7,000', in western Nevada, e.g., Virginia Range.

Comments: *Cleomella* is diminutive of *Cleome,* a closely related genus in the Caper Family *(Cleome lutea).* Fred Hillman was a 19th-century Nevada agriculturist, plant collector, and botanical illustrator.

143

BLACK TWINBERRY
Lonicera involucrata
Honeysuckle Family (Caprifoliaceae)

Description: You are most likely to encounter Black Twinberry in dense thickets along the border of a damp mountain meadow and adjoining woods. Black Twinberry is a leafy, 2–8' shrub with fascinating and unusual flowers, especially when they go to fruit. The 1–5" leaves are broadly ovate, deep green, and strongly veined. They occur thickly all the way to the top of the plant stems. The 5–petaled, yellow flowers are narrow, ½–¾" tubes that occur in pairs cradled within a green, leafy bract. When they go to fruit, this bract turns a deep crimson. From a distance you could easily think this gorgeous bract was a spectacular flower in full bloom, but when you look closely, you'll see that the bract now cradles a connected pair of black or purple, ¼" berries. In fruit this plant is truly a twinberry; in flower it's a twinbloom.

Flowering Season: April–August.

Habitat/Range: Damp meadows, thickets, streambanks in the montane, 5,500–10,000', throughout the Great Basin, e.g., Steens Mountain, Ruby Mountains.

Comments: Adam Lonitzer was a 16th-century German herbalist. *Involucrata* means "with an involucre," a ring of bracts surrounding several (in this case, two) flowers. Also called Bear-Berry Honeysuckle and Bracted Honeysuckle.

WEAK-STEM STONECROP
Sedum debile
Stonecrop Family (Crassulaceae)

Description: Creeping along rock ledges and talus slopes in the high mountains, Weak-Stem Stonecrop can carpet the rocks with its small, pale green, round leaves. As with all *Sedum* species, the leaves are succulent, able to hold water and to sustain the plant through long periods of drought. Rising only 2–6" above the mat of leaves (and sometimes not rising at all but decumbent) are the weak (easily broken) stems bearing a few opposite stem leaves and the bright yellow, ½", starlike, 5-petaled blossoms. Enhancing the stellar effect of the flowers are the 5 stamens that radiate out between the 5 pointed petals.

Flowering Season: June–August.

Habitat/Range: Rock ledges, talus slopes in the montane, 6,000–10,500', in central and eastern Nevada, southern Oregon, western Utah, e.g., Steens Mountain, Ruby Mountains.

Comments: *Sedum* probably means "to sit" in reference to the rock-hugging growth form. *Debile* means "weak" in reference to the stems, which are usually decumbent and are easily broken.

NARROW-LEAF STONECROP
Sedum lanceolatum
Stonecrop Family (Crassulaceae)

Description: As with all members of the Stonecrop Family, Narrow-Leaf Stonecrop has distinctive, succulent leaves; however, this won't always be so apparent in this species, for its alternating stem leaves, as the common and species names indicate, are narrow and often shrivel up by the time the flowers bloom. If you look at the base of the plant, however, you will find a cluster of basal leaves that are definitely succulent. The 1–8" stems bear terminal clusters of 3–24 bright yellow, ½–¾", starlike, 5-petaled flowers. Since the plants rarely occur singly, the rocky ground where they grow will usually be lit up by a large patch of brilliant yellow.

Flowering Season: June–August.

Habitat/Range: Gravelly or rocky flats and slopes in the sagebrush steppe and the montane, 6,000–11,000', throughout the Great Basin, e.g., Steens Mountain, Deep Creek Mountains.

Comments: *Sedum (S. debile). Lanceolatum* means "lancelike leaves."

YELLOW SWEET CLOVER
Melilotus officinalis
Pea Family (Fabaceae)

Description: Extremely similar in appearance and habitat to its close relative White Sweet Clover *(M. alba)*, Yellow Sweet Clover is also a tall (to 5'), weedy plant with spikes of small, reflexed, 5-petaled pea flowers. The pale yellow flowers offer a soft contrast to the rich green leaves. As with White Sweet Clover, the leaves of Yellow Sweet Clover have 3 toothed leaflets, though they are a bit broader than those of its white-flowered relative. The only other noticeable difference between the two *Melilotus* species (in addition, of course, to the color of the flowers) is the relative size of the banner and wings. In Yellow Sweet Clover, they are about the same length, while in White Sweet Clover the banner is distinctly longer than the wings.

Flowering Season: May–September.

Habitat/Range: Grassy meadows, roadsides, disturbed places in the sagebrush steppe and the montane, to 8,000', throughout the Great Basin, e.g., Carson Valley.

Comments: *Melilotus (M. alba). Officinalis* means "medicinal." Alien.

GOLDEN PEA
Thermopsis rhombifolia
Pea Family (Fabaceae)

Description: As the genus name *Thermopsis* indicates, Golden Pea does indeed closely resemble a yellow-flowered lupine. The ½–2½' stems are topped by a 4–12" loose raceme of 7–30 lupinelike flowers complete with banner, wings, and keel. The ¾–1" flowers are bright yellow, sometimes drying purplish. The leaves are also lupinelike in that they are palmately compound, but they are more cloverlike in that there are only 3 leaflets. These leaflets are 1–4" long, narrow, and somewhat infolded. This colorful and fragrant flower often attracts butterflies such as the Tiger Swallowtail to savor its nectar and pollen.

Flowering Season: May–August.

Habitat/Range: Grassy meadows, aspen woods in the sagebrush steppe and the montane, to 8,000', throughout the Great Basin, e.g., Steens Mountain, Great Basin National Park.

Comments: *Thermopsis* means "resembling *Lupinus*," another genus in the Pea Family. *Rhombifolia* means "diamond-shaped leaves."

GOLDEN PHACELIA
Phacelia adenophora
Waterleaf Family (Hydrophyllaceae)

Description: The beautiful, ¼–½", golden yellow flowers of Golden Phacelia can carpet openings in sagebrush flats, bringing bright color to the dry, sandy, or clay soil. The 4–16", much-branched and many-flowered stems usually spread out near the ground, creating a tangle of stems, leaves, and flowers. The small, narrowly bell-shaped, golden flowers often have delicate, rather faint purplish veins on their 5 petals. The ½–1", somewhat fleshy leaves are deeply pinnately lobed into rounded segments. The whitish stems, the leaves, the fingerlike sepals, and the back of the petals are covered with short hairs that are often glandular.

Flowering Season: May–July.

Habitat/Range: Sandy flats in the sagebrush steppe, to 7,000', in western and northwestern Nevada, e.g., Charles Sheldon National Wildlife Refuge, Peavine Mountain.

Comments: *Phacelia (P. heterophylla).* *Adenophora* means "gland bearing." Sometimes considered the same as *P. lutea* though distinguished from this species by some botanists on the basis of the short hairs on the corolla.

SCOULER'S ST. JOHN'S WORT
Hypericum scouleri
St. John's Wort Family (Hypericaceae)

Description: It's always a delight to find Scouler's St. John's Wort, for its ½–2½' branching stems bear clusters (3–25) of ½–1", bright yellow flowers. To add to their exuberance, exploding out of the center of these floral stars are scores of yellow, threadlike filaments. Because of the 5 regular petals and numerous stamens, your first thought might be a species of *Potentilla* in the Rose Family, but the clasping leaves, the (subtle) clumping of the stamens, and the lack of bractlets alternating with the sepals distinguish this plant from the numerous *Potentilla* species in the Great Basin. Often the leaves, sepals, and/or anthers of this plant will have black dots.

Flowering Season: June–August.

Habitat/Range: Streambanks, moist openings in aspen groves in the sagebrush steppe and the montane, 5,500–10,000', throughout the Great Basin, e.g., Steens Mountain, Ruby Mountains.

Comments: *Hypericum* is the ancient Greek name. John Scouler accompanied David Douglas *(Silene douglasii)* on his botanical expeditions in the Pacific Northwest in the early 19th century.

WHITE-STEM STICKLEAF
Mentzelia albicaulis
Loasa Family (Loasaceae)

Description: The common name White-Stem Stickleaf certainly points out some of the key identifying features of this 4–20" plant—its white (or straw) stems and its glandular-sticky leaves— but it may not do justice to the exquisite, satiny, yellow flowers. The 5 shiny, separate petals flare out of a long, cylindrical, inferior ovary that you could easily mistake for a flower stem. At the center of the flower is a cluster of many delicate stamens. The ½–4" leaves are quite distinctive— glossy green, fleshy, and irregularly lobed with comblike teeth.

Flowering Season: March–July.

Habitat/Range: Gravelly or sandy flats in the desert shrub and the sagebrush steppe, to 8,000', throughout the Great Basin, e.g., Steens Mountain, Great Basin National Park.

Comments: Christian Mentzel was a 17th-century German botanist. *Albicaulis* means "white stemmed." Also called White-Stem Blazing Star.

FLOWER BASKETS
Mentzelia congesta
Loasa Family (Loasaceae)

Description: Flower Baskets is an appropriate name for this lovely *Mentzelia*, as several of the yellow, 5-petaled, ½" flowers are held within a basket of papery white and green bracts in the leaf axils and atop the ½–1½' stems. Typical of the *Mentzelia* genus, the petals are shiny yellow with a darker (orangish) throat out of which protrude the clump of yellow stamens. The characteristic thick, inferior ovaries are difficult to see, for they are mostly concealed by the cluster of flowers and bracts. The narrow, 1–3" leaves are deeply lobed and toothed.

Flowering Season: May–June.

Habitat/Range: sandy flats and slopes, dunes, roadsides in the sagebrush steppe and the montane, 5,000–9,000', in eastern California, western and central Nevada, e.g., Peavine Mountain, White Mountains.

Comments: *Mentzelia (M. albicaulis). Congesta* means "congested" in reference to the cluster of flowers within each cradle of bracts.

SMOOTH-STEM BLAZING STAR
Mentzelia laevicaulis
Loasa Family (Loasaceae)

Description: Of the numerous species of *Mentzelia* in the Great Basin, Smooth-Stem Blazing Star has the largest, showiest flowers—blazing stars indeed! It is an imposing plant with its many-branched, 2–3½' stem, its 8–10", sawtooth leaves, and its very large (to 6"), lemon-yellow flowers. The 5 narrow, pointed, widely separated, flaring petals form a golden star bursting with color and energy. In the center of the flower is a dense cluster of stamens of the same golden yellow color as the petals. The stem is a sleek, smooth white that contrasts sharply with the dark green, clasping leaves. In bud the flowers are long, pale yellow torpedoes cradled by long, narrow, pointed, green sepals.

Flowering Season: June–August.

Habitat/Range: Sandy flats, canyons, roadsides in the sagebrush steppe, to 7,000', throughout the Great Basin, e.g., Toiyabe Range, Ruby Mountains.

Comments: *Mentzelia (M. involucrata). Laevicaulis* means "smooth stemmed."

YELLOW POND LILY
Nuphar luteum
Pond Lily Family (Nymphacaceae)

Description: To see an "armada" of Yellow Pond Lilies covering a pond or a patch of a mountain lake is a stunning experience, for the leaves and flowers are exceptionally large and showy. Even before the blooming, the 1½' long and almost as broad heart-shaped leaves can form an almost solid, deep green cover over the water. Then, when the flowers bloom … wow! Rising a foot or so above the leaves on thick, hollow stems are the 2–3" wide, bright yellow, globe-shaped flowers with their 7–9 leathery, petal-like sepals cupping the many showy, bright yellow reproductive parts—a broad, disklike stigma surrounded by scores of stamens. These amazing flowers look like 1-eyed sea creatures with long necks!

Flowering Season: June–August.

Habitat/Range: On lakes and ponds in the montane, 6,500–10,500', northwestern and northeastern Nevada, southern Oregon, e.g., Steens Mountain.

Comments: *Nuphar* is an old Arabic name. *Lutea* means "yellow." Formerly known as *N. polysepalum.*

TINY EVENING PRIMROSE
Camissonia pusilla
Evening Primrose Family (Onagraceae)

Description: Tiny Evening Primrose is well named, for the plant is short (1–8") and the flowers are only ¼" across. The plant stem can be unbranched, bearing only 1 flower, or (with sufficient rain) can be much-branched, with many flowers. Though the flowers are tiny, they are surprisingly showy, for each of the 4 bright yellow petals contrasts dramatically with the reddish stems and sepals. With age the yellow petals often become orange, lavender, or purple, and the sepals reflex. The globular stigma protrudes only slightly beyond the anthers.

Flowering Season: April–June.

Habitat/Range: Dry slopes in the sagebrush steppe, to 8,000' throughout the Great Basin, e.g., Carson Valley.

Comments: *Camissonia (C. claviformis). Pusilla* means "very small."

NORTHERN SUN CUP

Camissonia subacaulis
Evening Primrose Family (Onagraceae)

Description: There are many stemless, yellow-flowered evening primroses in the Great Basin (both *Oenothera* and *Camissonia* genera) with showy flowers that rest almost directly on a rosette of green leaves. In most of these plants, the flowers are very large (to 3" or even 4" wide), almost dwarfing the leaf rosette. In Northern Sun Cup, however, the leaves dominate your attention, for they are up to 12" long and 2" wide, fleshy, and mostly undivided, while the 4-petaled flowers are relatively small (1–1½" wide). As with most *Camissonia* species, the flowers open in the morning and wilt later that same day. The globular (often shallowly 4-lobed), yellow stigma sticks out just a little beyond the yellow anthers.

Flowering Season: May–July.

Habitat/Range: Damp meadows, forest openings in the montane, 5,000–8,500', in central and northwestern Nevada, southern Oregon, e.g., Charles Sheldon National Wildlife Refuge, Steens Mountain.

Comments: *Camissonia (C. claviformis).* *Subacaulis* means "without much of a stem."

TANSY-LEAF EVENING PRIMROSE

Camissonia tanacetifolia
Evening Primrose Family (Onagraceae)

Description: Tansy-Leaf Evening Primrose is easy to distinguish from the several other Great Basin species of *Camissonia* by its deeply pinnately lobed leaves. The 1–1½", bright yellow (sometimes orange) flowers rest on a rosette of these ground-hugging leaves. Sometimes in the early spring in meadows or fields just drying out from winter, you will find huge masses of these 4-petaled flowers painting vast canvasses of ground bright yellow or orange—a floral work of art visible from a long way off. The flowers open in the morning and wilt later that same day. The globular, yellow stigma is elevated above the yellow anthers by its slender, yellow style.

Flowering Season: May–July.

Habitat/Range: Damp meadows and fields, edges of drying ponds in the sagebrush steppe and the montane, to 7,500', in western and northwestern Nevada, southern Oregon, e.g., Washoe Valley, Fly Canyon.

Comments: *Camissonia (C. claviformis).* *Tanacetifolia* means "tansy leaved" in reference to the deeply divided leaves.

HOOKER'S EVENING PRIMROSE
Oenothera elata
Evening Primrose Family (Onagraceae)

Description: One of the several Great Basin evening primroses with large (to 3"), yellow flowers, Hooker's Evening Primrose is one of the few of these species with tall stems, often exceeding 3' and sometimes reaching 6'. Of these tall species Hooker's Evening Primrose is by far the most common, occurring throughout the area. The single stem (sometimes with a few branches) bears many 1–16", tonguelike, hairy leaves throughout its length. Several of the large, 4-petaled, bright yellow flowers branch off the upper part of the stem (the branches are actually long, slender, inferior ovaries and floral tubes). The yellow, slightly heart-shaped petals fade reddish orange or purplish after their one afternoon and night of blooming.

Flowering Season: May–September.

Habitat/Range: Damp meadows, near springs in the sagebrush steppe and the montane, to 10,000', throughout the Great Basin, e.g., Washoe Valley, Ruby Mountains.

Comments: *Oenothera (O. deltoides). Elata* means "noble."

EARLY EVENING PRIMROSE
Oenothera primiveris
Evening-Primrose Family (Onagraceae)

Description: There are many large-flowered species of *Oenothera* in the Great Basin, several of which are ground-hugging desert and sagebrush steppe dwellers (e.g., *O. deltoides, O. caespitosa*). To come across such large flowers practically prone on the ground is a startling and exhilarating sight, even the more appreciated for its brevity—most *Oenothera* species (including Early Evening Primrose) open at dusk and last only one night and part of the following day. Early Evening Primrose has bright yellow flowers that can be up to 3" across; the 4 petals are heart shaped and slightly separated. The flowers rest almost directly on the rosette of long (up to 10"), basal leaves, which are wavy margined or deeply pinnately lobed. As with all *Oenothera* species,

the stigma is deeply lobed into 4 fingerlike segments. The bud is white-hairy. After their brief blooming, the flowers fade to reddish orange or purple and wither. As the common and species names suggest, Early Evening Primrose is indeed early, being one of the first showy flowers to greet the spring in the desert shrub.

Flowering Season: March–May.

Habitat/Range: Sandy flats, washes, roadsides in the desert shrub, to 4,800', in central Nevada, e.g., Toiyabe Range. This species occurs mostly in the Mojave Desert.

Comments: *Oenothera (O. deltoides). Primiveris* means "first spring" in reference to its early blooming. Also called Sundrop.

LADIES TRESSES
Spiranthes romanzoffiana
Orchid Family (Orchidaceae)

Description: You may have to get wet knees and elbows to find Ladies Tresses, as it grows low to the ground, often hidden among grass, in very wet meadows. But it's definitely worth the effort to see the exquisite ¼–½" flowers twisting around their 2–6" spike. A close look shows an orchid flower—5 perianth parts (3 sepals and 2 petals) alike and the 6th part (the lower petal) different. In the case of Ladies Tresses, all 6 parts are the same pale yellow (sometimes almost white), but the lower petal is broader. The plant has narrow, basal leaves.

Flowering Season: July–September.

Habitat/Range: Marshy meadows, streambanks in the montane, to 8,000', in northern Nevada, southern Oregon, e.g., Steens Mountain.

Comments: *Spiranthes* means "coiled flowers." N. von Romanzoff was a Russian count who promoted the Russian expedition to California in 1816.

CLUSTERED BROOMRAPE
Orobanche fasciculata
Broomrape Family (Orobanchaceae)

Description: At first glance you might think Clustered Broomrape was a Snapdragon Family member, perhaps a penstemon with its long, tubular, 2-lipped flowers, but then you would notice that the flowers are at the end of leafless, fleshy, glandular-sticky stems. In fact, the plant has no leaves at all—it is a root parasite. Clustered Broomrape can have solitary stems, but usually it has a cluster of many 3–10", branched stems, each branch of which is topped by a solitary, ¾–1¼", tubular, 5-petaled flower. In some plants the flowers are straw-yellow; in others they are purplish or pink.

Flowering Season: April–June.

Habitat/Range: Sandy or rocky slopes, washes in the sagebrush steppe and the montane, to 10,500', throughout the Great Basin, e.g., Charles Sheldon National Wildlife Refuge.

Comments: *Orobanche* means "strangle vetch," an appropriately horrible reference to the parasitic nature of plants in this genus. *Fasciculata* means "clustered" in reference to the densely flowered inflorescences.

CALIFORNIA POPPY
Eschscholzia californica
Poppy Family (Papaveraceae)

Description: California Poppy puts on a truly spectacular golden yellow display in sagebrush slopes of western Nevada and in the Mojave Desert (the desert flower is considered by some botanists to be a subspecies of *E. californica*, while other botanists consider it a separate species—*E. mexicana*). Perched atop the ½–2' stem is one of the glorious, 4-petaled, 2–3" blossoms, sometimes golden yellow and sometimes orange. The leaves are typical of *Eschscholzia* species—blue-green and deeply dissected. The plant's many leaves and stems give it a bushy appearance—a bush amply adorned with gorgeous, sunny jewels. The buds are erect (not nodding as in many poppies) and under the flower is a conspicuous, enlarged rim.

Flowering Season: March–June.

Habitat/Range: Dry flats, brushy slopes in the desert shrub and up into the sagebrush steppe, to 6,500', in western Nevada, e.g., Peavine Mountain, Washoe Valley.

Comments: J. F. Eschscholtz was a 19th-century Russian naturalist. *Californica* means "of California" where it is abundant in great masses in the Central Valley and the western foothills of the Sierra.

BREWER'S NAVARETTIA
Navarettia breweri
Phlox Family (Polemoniaceae)

Description: One of the many delightful but demanding "belly flowers" (i.e., those you have to get down on your belly to see) of the Great Basin, Brewer's Navarettia looks a bit like yellow stars perched on a spiny, evergreen tree. The clumps of needlelike leaves extend beyond the tiny ($\frac{1}{4}$" long and $\frac{1}{8}$" wide), 5-petaled, yellow, tubular flowers partially concealing them, but their bright yellow color grabs your attention and invites your careful examination. If you look very closely, you will see a further dash of color—tiny, white anthers slightly protruding from the flower tube. As you get back to your feet, you may be able to brush the sand and gravel from your body, but the image of these delicate flowers nestled in their prickly bed will probably still cling to you!

Flowering Season: May–July.

Habitat/Range: Sandy or rocky flats and slopes, dried vernal pools in the sagebrush steppe and the montane, 6,000–11,000', throughout the Great Basin, e.g., Peavine Mountain, Steens Mountain.

Comments: F. Navarete was an 18th-century Spanish physician. William Brewer *(Cardamine b.)*.

CUSHION DESERT BUCKWHEAT
Eriogonum caespitosum
Buckwheat Family (Polygonaceae)

Description: One of the many yellow-flowered, mat-forming buckwheats in the Great Basin, Cushion Desert Buckwheat is an exceptionally beautiful plant that can be distinguished from its many close kin by close inspection. As with some other species, it forms large (1–4' in diameter), tight mats of tiny, elliptical or spatulate leaves covered with densely matted, white hairs. Rising above the leaves are very short (1–4"), un-branched, leafless stems, each topped with a single, tightly packed, spherical or flat-topped umbel of tiny flowers with 6 petal-like sepals. The flowers start deep red in bud and usually turn to bright yellow in flower, often returning to red late in the bloom. All these characteristics taken together narrow down identification to a few species, but the characteristic that distinguishes Cushion Desert Buckwheat is the involucre (i.e., the group of connected bracts that is directly under the flower) that is noticeably white-hairy.

Flowering Season: April–July.

Habitat/Range: Dry, rocky or sandy slopes in the sagebrush steppe, the montane, and the alpine, to 11,000', throughout the Great Basin, e.g., Virginia Range.

Comments: *Eriogonum (E. spergulinum)*. *Caespitosum* means "cespitose," i.e., in a tufted growth form.

DOUGLAS BUCKWHEAT
Eriogonum douglasii
Buckwheat Family (Polygonaceae)

Description: Douglas Buckwheat offers a beautiful, pastel mix of colors: Its 1–5", nearly naked stems bearing round clusters of yellow, papery flowers with 6 petal-like sepals rise above a dense mat of blue-gray, spoon-shaped leaves. The slightly bluish tinge to the leaves is due to the white, matted hairs covering the green beneath. As the season progresses, the flowers begin to turn red, so you'll often find the yellow cluster tinged with red or rust, eventually becoming entirely red or orange. The "nearly" of "nearly naked stems" is a great help in identifying this species of buckwheat, for near the middle of the stem is a very distinctive whorl of narrow, leaflike bracts.

Flowering Season: May–June.

Habitat/Range: Dry, rocky or sandy flats and slopes in the sagebrush steppe, 5,000–7,000', in western Nevada, only on Peavine Mountain.

Comments: *Eriogonum (E. spergulinum)*. David Douglas *(Silene d.)*.

KING'S BUCKWHEAT

Eriogonum kingii
Buckwheat Family (Polygonaceae)

Description: One of the several yellow-flowered, mat-forming buckwheats of high elevation in the Great Basin, King's Buckwheat is a Nevada endemic that can be found only in a few mountain ranges in the northeastern part of the state. Its small, oval leaves are often in erect clusters. The flower clusters on the tips of the 1–4" stems are dense but not spherical, and they vary greatly in size and shape, creating a rather messy, asymmetrical appearance. The flowers are pale yellow or sometimes even yellow-green.

Flowering Season: June–August.

Habitat/Range: Rocky flats and slopes in the montane, 8,000–10,500', in eastern Nevada, e.g., Ruby Mountains.

Comments: *Eriogonum (E. spergulinum)*. Clarence King *(Arenaria kingii)*.

OCHER-FLOWERED BUCKWHEAT

Eriogonum ochrocephalum
Buckwheat Family (Polygonaceae)

Description: Of the many mat-forming, yellow-flowered buckwheats of the Great Basin, Ocher-Flowered Buckwheat is one of the showiest, for its umbels of flowers are large and spherical, tightly packed, and bright yellow. Though the stems can be relatively tall (4–16"), the overall appearance of the plant is anything but sparse (as in Blue Mountain Buckwheat, *E. strictum*), for the spheres of flowers with their 6 petal-like sepals are large and usually are staggered on different length stems, so there's yellow pretty much everywhere you look! The blue-green, basal leaves (covered with a mat of gray hair) are often erect and usually have somewhat wavy edges.

Flowering Season: May–July.

Habitat/Range: Rocky slopes and flats in the sagebrush steppe and the montane, 4,000–8,000', Peavine Mountain, Steens Mountain.

Comments: *Eriogonum (E. spergulinum)*. *Ochrocephalum* means "yellow head" in reference to the bright yellow, spherical flower clusters.

OVAL-LEAF BUCKWHEAT
Eriogonum ovalifolium
Buckwheat Family (Polygonaceae)

Description: As with Sulphur Flower *(E. umbellatum)*, Oval-Leaf Buckwheat has a remarkable elevational range—from sagebrush flats to exposed ridges considerably above timberline. At lower elevations the stems may rise to 15" above the mat of basal leaves; above timberline the stems are miniaturized, rising only a couple inches. In either case the basal, oval leaves are tiny and are covered with white, wooly hairs. The ⅛–¼" flowers with the 6 petal-like sepals are at the tips of leafless, bractless stems and form ball-like clusters, which can be bright yellow, cream colored, or dark red. On high alpine ridges, you'll often find the bluish gray matted leaves of this plant flowing over rocks, while the various colors of flowers match the various species (and colors) of rock lichen. Especially in the harsh, alpine environment, mats of Oval-Leaf Buckwheat are a stirring and comforting sight.

Flowering Season: April–August.

Habitat/Range: Brushy slopes, openings, rocky ridges in the sagebrush steppe, the montane, and the alpine, to 12,000', throughout the Great Basin, e.g., Charles Sheldon National Wildlife Refuge, Deep Creek Mountains.

Comments: *Eriogonum (E. spergulinum). Ovalifolium* means "oval leaf." Also called Butterballs in reference to their yellow color.

BLUE MOUNTAIN BUCKWHEAT
Eriogonum strictum
Buckwheat Family (Polygonaceae)

Description: Although there are many quite similar yellow-flowered buckwheats in the Great Basin, you'll start to get a feel for different species probably before you can pinpoint the characteristics that distinguish them. You'll probably notice right away that Blue Mountain Buckwheat has a sparser look to it than most of the yellow-flowered buckwheat species. This is partly because of somewhat fewer-flowered clusters than in many species, but the main factors contributing to this less robust appearance are leafless stems and relatively tall (4–16') stems that are all more-or-less the same height. These characteristics taken together create a lot of space between the leaves and the flowers, imparting a sparser look to the plant. The rather loose mat of basal leaves only reinforces this impression. These grayish, wooly, elliptic leaves are often held upright (vertical) by their 1–2" petioles.

Flowering Season: May–August.

Habitat/Range: Rocky or sandy flats and slopes in the sagebrush steppe and the montane, 5,500–8,500', in western and northwestern Nevada, southern Oregon, e.g., Peavine Mountain, Steens Mountain.

Comments: *Eriogonum (E. spergulinum). Strictum* means "erect" in reference to the tall, straight plant stem (it could also refer to the often vertical, basal leaves).

SULPHUR FLOWER
Eriogonum umbellatum
Buckwheat Family (Polygonaceae)

Description: Along with Oval-Leaf Buckwheat *(E. ovalifolium)*, Sulphur Flower is one of the most common and widespread of the *Eriogonum* species in the Great Basin. It is also highly variable with over 30 recognized varieties. The woody, much-branched stems can form low mats (more common at upper elevations) or shrubs (more common at lower elevations) up to several feet tall and about as wide. This plant has a remarkable elevational range from near sea level to above timberline. The bright, sulphur-yellow flowers form large, umbel-like or headlike clusters at the tips of leafless stems, although directly under the rays of the flower cluster are several leaflike bracts. The actual leaves (small, ovate, and olive green with whitish hairs on the undersurface) occur low on the stems. The bright yellow flowers become reddish (sometimes cream or purple) with age.

Flowering Season: May–October.

Habitat/Range: Brushy slopes, rocky ridges in the sagebrush steppe, the montane, and the alpine, to 11,000', throughout the Great Basin, e.g., White Mountains, Great Basin National Park.

Comments: *Eriogonum (E. spergulinum). Umbellatum* means "in an umbel" in reference to the inflorescence. The common name Sulphur Flower refers to the color of the flowers.

WATER PLANTAIN BUTTERCUP
Ranunculus alismifolius
Buttercup Family (Ranunculaceae)

Description: Water Plantain Buttercup is one of the floral treasures of early spring, often carpeting wet meadows and streambanks just thawing out from winter with great masses of bright yellow blooms. The 2–20" stems are often decumbent, so the ½–1½" flowers are frequently on or near the ground. They sometimes have 5 petals, but can have as many as 15. Regardless of the number of petals, the flowers are glorious yellow beacons glistening in the sun. Water Plantain Buttercup is one of the few buttercups with narrow, undivided, mostly basal leaves. When you see a large patch of these buttercups in a mountain meadow still fringed by snow, the day and your heart seem to warm with joy and anticipation.

Flowering Season: April–June.

Habitat/Range: Creekbanks, soggy meadows in the sagebrush steppe and the montane, to 12,000', throughout the Great Basin, e.g., Steens Mountain, Great Basin National Park.

Names: *Ranunculus* means "little frog" in reference to the wet habitats of many species. *Alismifolius* means "leaf like *Alisma*," a genus in the Water Plantain Family.

ALPINE BUTTERCUP
Ranunculus eschscholtzii
Buttercup Family (Ranunculaceae)

Description: It is always a surprise and a delight to come across Alpine Buttercup, for its 1–1½", shiny, yellow flowers seem as warm as they are bright—both welcome attributes in their usually rather harsh (though wet) habitat in the rocks near and above timberline. You wouldn't expect much wet habitat around timberline, but Alpine Buttercup finds the seeps and moisture collection spots in and around rocks. The 5 broad, glistening petals curl up slightly, forming a bowl, which holds the mass of radiating, yellow stamens and green pistils. The 2–10" stems are leafy with shiny, broad, fanlike leaves.

Flowering Season: July–August.

Habitat/Range: Seeps around rocks in the montane and the alpine, 9,000–14,000', throughout the Great Basin except Utah, e.g., Steens Mountain, Ruby Mountains.

Comments: *Ranunculus (R. alismaefolius).* J. F. Eschscholtz *(E. californica).*

LARGE-LEAF AVENS
Geum macrophyllum
Rose Family (Rosaceae)

Description: Although the flowers of Large-Leaf Avens are fairly typical of the Rose Family and might be confused with those of cinquefoil (e.g., *P. gracilis*), the leaves and fruits clearly distinguish this species. The ½–3½' stem seems to be mostly leaves, for the leaves are large and extend far up the stem to directly under the clusters of flowers. Although many of these leaves are pinnately divided, you might not notice this as the lateral lobes are small, while the terminal lobe is 3–4" long and almost as broad. The leaves also attract attention for their color and shape—they are dark green, deeply veined, and deeply toothed. The clusters of ¼–½", yellow, 5-petaled flowers are especially striking in contrast to the bed of dark leaves lying directly beneath them. However, the plant is even more striking in fruit when the plant is festooned with fuzzy, spherical pincushions of threadlike, hooked styles.

Flowering Season: June–July.

Habitat/Range: Grassy streambanks, damp meadows in the montane, 6,000–9,200', throughout the Great Basin, e.g., Steens Mountain, Great Basin National Park.

Comments: *Geum* is the ancient Latin name. *Macrophyllum* means "large leaf."

ALPINE AVENS
Geum rossii
Rose Family (Rosaceae)

Description: Alpine Avens is a lovely component of high mountain meadow (and talus slope) plant communities—lovely both for its bright, yellow flowers and for its delicately pinnately compound leaves. The plants tend to form large, dense clumps of several square yards in areas where very little else intrudes, creating a wonderful tapestry of shiny yellow (petals) and soft green (leaves). The 4–12" stems bear one or a few of the ½–1" flowers with their 5 rounded petals and numerous stamens. You might confuse Alpine Avens with a cinquefoil, for the flowers are quite similar, but the unusual, almost fernlike leaves and the few flowers per stem will help you distinguish it.

Flowering Season: July–August.

Habitat/Range: Meadows, rocky ledges, talus slopes in the montane and the alpine, 6,500–12,500', in eastern Nevada, western Utah, e.g., Great Basin National Park.

Comments: *Geum (G. macrophyllum)*. James Ross was a 19th-century explorer of the polar regions. Also called Ross' Avens.

GORDON'S IVESIA
Ivesia gordonii
Rose Family (Rosaceae)

Description: Gordon's Ivesia is a beautiful and intriguing member of the montane and alpine flora in the Great Basin with its cluster of starlike, yellow flowers and its basal, pinnately divided leaves. Each 2–10" stem of Gordon's Ivesia ends in a ball of 10–20 of the ½" flowers, each with 5 narrow, rounded petals alternating with 5 pointed, yellow-green sepals. The leaves are divided into many tiny leaflets (10–25 opposite pairs) that give a delicate grace to this plant in sharp contrast to its rough, rocky environment.

Flowering Season: June–August.

Habitat/Range: Talus slopes, rocky flats, ledges in the montane and the alpine, 7,000–12,000', throughout the Great Basin, e.g., Steens Mountain.

Comments: Joseph Ives was a 19th-century American explorer. George Gordon was a 19th-century London horticulturist.

BASALT CINQUEFOIL
Potentilla basaltica
Rose Family (Rosaceae)

Description: Of the numerous species of *Potentilla* in the Great Basin, more than half are rarely or uncommonly found. Basalt Cinquefoil is one of those species with very limited distribution—it occurs in Nevada only in Soldier Meadow (and only in one other place in the world—Lassen County, California). It is easily recognized as a cinquefoil with its 5 yellow petals between which can be glimpsed the pointed, green sepals, the tiny, green bractlets between the sepals, and the many reproductive parts. As with many *Potentilla* species, the leaves are pinnately compound. The unusual features are the prostrate growth form (the long stems bearing the ½–¾" flowers radiate out close to the ground) and the number of leaflets (each 3–5" leaf consists of 14–36 tiny, opposite leaflets plus one terminal one). With its network of blue-green leaves and its sprinkles of bright yellow flowers, Basalt Cinquefoil brings quite a showy display to its rather bare, sandy environment.

Flowering Season: May–August.

Habitat/Range: Dry, basalt flats, streambanks in the sagebrush steppe, 4,500–5,000', in northwestern Nevada, only in Soldier Meadow.

Comments: *Potentilla (P. glandulosa). Basaltica* means "basalt" in reference to this plant's habitat.

MOUNTAIN MEADOW CINQUEFOIL
Potentilla diversifolia
Rose Family (Rosaceae)

Description: The bright yellow flowers of Mountain Meadow Cinquefoil are a delight to encounter, especially on some rocky slope near timberline. The 5 petals are broadly heart shaped and separated enough to see a glimpse of the green sepals between them. As with all *Potentilla* species, the leaves are compound, but as with only a few other Great Basin species, they are divided into 5–7 *palmate* leaflets. The leaflets are toothed but only on the distal half (i.e., the tip). The leaves are usually distinctively blue-green, being covered with a bluish or whitish film. The 2–16" stems usually curve upward, but can be decumbent.

Flowering Season: June–August.

Habitat/Range: Grassy meadows, rocky slopes, forest openings in the montane, 8,000–11,000', throughout the Great Basin, e.g., White Mountains, Ruby Mountains.

Comments: *Potentilla (P. glandulosa). Diversifolia* means "variable leaves." Also called Diverse-Leaf Cinquefoil.

SHRUBBY CINQUEFOIL
Potentilla fruticosa
Rose Family (Rosaceae)

Description: There are many species of *Potentilla* in the Great Basin, almost all of which have bright yellow flowers. However, Shrubby Cinquefoil is very easy to distinguish from the others, for it is the only woody (shrubby) species. The plants are generally 1–4' tall and usually at least as wide. The ½" flowers occur singly or in small clusters at the tips of the stems and in the leaf axils. The 5 petals are round and slightly overlapping. In the center of the flower is a cluster of 20–25 stamens and several pistils. The small leaves are divided into 3–7 (usually 5) narrow leaflets. Shrubby Cinquefoil is a circumboreal species, widespread in northern latitude mountains of the world.

Flowering Season: July–September.

Habitat/Range: Moist or wet areas on rocky slopes and cliffs in the montane and the alpine, 6,000–12,000', throughout the Great Basin, e.g., Steens Mountain, Great Basin National Park.

Comments: *Potentilla (P. glandulosa)*. *Fruticosa* means "shrubby." Also known as *Pentaphylloides fruticosa*.

FIVE-FINGER CINQUEFOIL
Potentilla gracilis
Rose Family (Rosaceae)

Description: Along with buttercups and some of the yellow composites, cinquefoils have some of the most dazzling, sunniest, yellow flowers in the Great Basin. Five-Finger Cinquefoil is a complex and varied species with several varieties, but it is distinguishable from most other Great Basin *Potentilla* species by its combination of tall growth form (½–3') and palmately compound, toothed leaves. The 2–10" leaves are divided into 5–9 narrow, deeply toothed leaflets. The 5 petals of the ½–¾" flowers are heart shaped and are slightly overlapping. The yellow flowers are amazingly bright, especially in contrast with the dark green foliage and the often reddish stems. In the center of the flower is a cluster of about 20 stamens and many pistils.

Flowering Season: June–August.

Habitat/Range: Grassy meadows, roadsides, openings in the sagebrush steppe and the montane, to 9,000', throughout the Great Basin, e.g., Washoe Valley, Deep Creek Mountains.

Comments: *Potentilla (P. glandulosa). Gracilis* means "graceful."

BITTERBRUSH
Purshia tridentata
Rose Family (Rosaceae)

Description: One of the first shrubs to bloom extensively in the sagebrush steppe, Bitterbrush can cover entire hillsides with a delightful, pale yellow or creamy froth and a delicious, spicy, cinnamon-like fragrance. Although it can become prostrate in higher, more exposed environments, it usually is a 3–9', much-branched, gray-barked shrub. The ½–1", pale yellow (cream) flowers have the 5 separate petals and the central cluster of many reproductive parts characteristic of the Rose Family. The petals are spoon shaped with narrow "handles" and are widely separated. Despite its bitter taste Bitterbrush is one of the most important browse plants in the Great Basin, especially for deer, antelope, and livestock.

Flowering Season: April–August.

Habitat/Range: Sandy or gravelly slopes, canyons in the sagebrush steppe and the montane, to 9,000', throughout the Great Basin, e.g., Charles Sheldon National Wildlife Refuge, Great Basin National Park.

Comments: *Purshia (P. stansburiana). Tridentata* means "3-toothed" in reference to the 3-lobed leaves. Also called Antelope Brush.

COMMON YELLOW MONKEYFLOWER
Mimulus guttatus
Snapdragon Family (Scrophulariaceae)

Description: Of the many species of monkeyflowers in the Great Basin, Common Yellow Monkeyflower is the most common and widespread, often growing in great masses in wet areas throughout the area from the desert shrub to the high mountains. Although it is a complex species with many variations (e.g., it can range from 2" to 5' tall!), it has several reliable characteristics. Its 5-petaled, ½–1½" flowers are yellow with small red spots, mostly on the lower petals. The strongly ribbed calyx tube is also red spotted and swells noticeably in fruit, the shorter lower lip curving up and nearly closing the throat. The pedicels are longer than the calyx, sometimes reaching 3". The broad, oval, serrated, often glossy leaves form opposite pairs, which (especially on the upper stem) often fuse at their base around the stem. Common Yellow Monkeyflower may be common, but it is still a joy to see every time.

Flowering Season: March–August.

Habitat/Range: Creekbanks, seeps, marshy meadows in the desert shrub, the sagebrush steppe, and the montane, to 9,500', throughout the Great Basin, e.g., Soldier Meadow, Deep Creek Mountains.

Comments: *Mimulus* means "mime" in reference to the resemblance of the corolla to a face. *Guttatus* means "spotted" in reference to the red spots frequently found on the petals and calyx.

YELLOW-OR-PURPLE MONKEYFLOWER
Mimulus mephiticus
Snapdragon Family (Scrophulariaceae)

Description: Many of the Great Basin's monkeyflower species have yellow flowers (often with red splotches, lines, or spots), while many others have flowers some shade of red or purple (usually with yellow lines or ridges). *Mimulus mephiticus* is unusual in that it has flowers of both types—yellow with 1 or a few reddish splotches on the lower middle petal and numerous red spots in the throat, and magenta with yellow and purple splotches and spots. Often you will find both types in the same population. Also a bit unusual is the growth form of this plant—either up to 9" or so with many flowers or almost directly on the ground with usually only 1 or a few flowers. The ½–1" leaves are slightly rounded or narrowly tonguelike and emit a pungent odor if crushed.

Flowering Season: March–July.

Habitat/Range: Sandy or gravelly flats and slopes in the sagebrush steppe and the montane, 4,500–10,000', in western Nevada, e.g., Carson Valley.

Comments: *Mimulus (M. guttatus). Mephiticus* means "foul smelling." Sometimes considered the same as *M. densus.*

PRIMROSE MONKEYFLOWER
Mimulus primuloides
Snapdragon Family (Scrophulariaceae)

Description: One of the loveliest early morning floral sights in the high mountains of the Great Basin is an expanse of yellow Primrose Monkeyflowers carpeting a wet meadow or fringing a mountain pond. Although each short (1–5"), slender stem bears only 1 flower at its tip, you will usually find great masses of these flowers, for long underground or on-the-ground runners connect many stems. The 5 bright yellow, delicately red-spotted petals are shallowly lobed, creating a bit of a heart shape. The round, beige, hinged stigma is prominently displayed. Adding to the delight of these plants are the basal rosettes of round leaves with their long, silvery hairs. Especially in the early morning, you may find each leaf bejeweled with dewdrops.

Flowering Season: June–August.

Habitat/Range: Wet meadows, seeps, creekbanks in the montane and the alpine, 7,000'–12,500', throughout the Great Basin, e.g., Steens Mountain, Ruby Mountains.

Comments: *Mimulus (M. guttatus). Primuloides* means "primroselike."

MOUNTAIN MONKEYFLOWER
Mimulus tilingii
Snapdragon Family (Scrophulariaceae)

Description: Mountain Monkeyflower is quite similar to its close kin, Common Yellow Monkeyflower *(M. guttatus)* and can easily be confused with it. Both plants grow in wet areas, have large (to 1½"), bright yellow, 5-petaled flowers with small red spots on the lower petals, and have opposite pairs of broad, serrated leaves. In addition, in both species the calyx strongly inflates in fruit. However, if you look closely, you can notice some distinguishing features. Mountain Monkeyflower is often a low plant, topping out at about 1½' (while Common Yellow Monkeyflower can be low, but can reach 5'). The pairs of opposite leaves of Mountain

Monkeyflower are usually noticeably slimy to the touch, and though (on the upper stem) they can be petioleless, unlike the leaves of Common Yellow Monkeyflower, they never fuse together.

Flowering Season: July–August.

Habitat/Range: Marshy meadows, seeps, creekbanks in the montane and the alpine, 7,000–11,000', throughout the Great Basin, e.g., White Mountains, Steens Mountain.

Comments: *Mimulus (M. guttatus).* Heinrich Tiling was a 19th-century Baltic physician and botanist who collected plants in the American West. Also called Subalpine Monkeyflower.

HAIRY OWL'S-CLOVER
Orthocarpus tenuis
Snapdragon Family (Scrophulariaceae)

Description: With its narrow leaves and bracts, its small flowers, and its short (4–16") stature, Hairy Owl's-Clover can be difficult to find among its usually taller grass neighbors. But it's well worth finding, for its flowers are interesting with a subtle beauty. Unlike its close kin, paintbrush, with its leaves that have modified to be colorful and flowers that have mostly atrophied, Hairy Owl's-Clover has mostly green leaves with only a few darker bracts and has noticeable, though small, flowers. The tubular flowers nestled in the bracts have 3 yellow, saclike lower petals, above which project the 2 upper petals, which are fused into a narrow, pale yellow or white spike. As the common name indicates, the stems, leaves, and bracts are covered with short hairs (and are usually sticky).

Flowering Season: June–August.

Habitat/Range: Grassy meadows in the sagebrush steppe and the montane, 5,000–8,000', in western and northwestern Nevada, e.g., Charles Sheldon National Wildlife Refuge.

Comments: *Orthocarpus* means "straight fruit." *Tenuis* means "slender." Formerly known as *O. hispidus.*

MOTH MULLEIN
Verbascum blattaria
Snapdragon Family (Scrophulariaceae)

Description: Moth Mullein resembles its close relative Wooly Mullein *(V. thapsus)* in several ways—it is a weedy biennial that produces a rosette of leaves the first year and a tall, stout flowering stem the second (and last) year, and its stem is topped by a raceme of ½–1", 5-petaled, yellow flowers. However, it is a shorter plant (1–4'); its leaves are not wooly and do not extend as far up the stem; and the flowers are not crammed into a dense spike, but are scattered loosely along the upper part of the stem. You don't have to look very closely at the flowers to see a dramatic difference here too—all the filaments are covered with long, dense, purple hairs, creating a purple eye at the center of the flower. For a weedy plant Moth Mullein certainly has gorgeous and intricate flowers!

Flowering Season: June–September.

Habitat/Range: Roadsides and other disturbed places in the sagebrush steppe, to 6,500', thoughout the Great Basin, e.g., Washoe Valley.

Comments: *Verbascum (V. thapsus). Blattaria* is derived from a word meaning "moth," perhaps in reference to the presumed resemblance of the stamens and styles to the antennae and tongue of a moth.

WOOLY MULLEIN
Verbascum thapsus
Snapdragon Family (Scrophulariaceae)

Description: Along roadsides, in disturbed fields, and sometimes on dry edges of reservoirs, you may find stands of the stout, wooly, 1–7' stalks of Wooly Mullein. At the base of the stalk is a rosette of very large (3–20"), broad, densely wooly leaves. Smaller leaves clothe much of the height of the stalk. Often mixed in with these towering stalks will be stemless rosettes of these same wooly leaves. This is because Wooly Mullein is a biennial, producing a rosette of leaves the first year and the stout flower stem the second year. Whether in its first or second (and last) year, you will recognize the plant by these soft, wooly leaves—the very good reason why some hikers call this plant mountain toilet paper! The top 6–12" of the stalk is a spike crammed with scores of bright yellow, ½–1", 5-petaled flowers. The long filaments are of two types—the upper 3 are yellow-hairy, while the lower 2 are mostly hairless. The anthers are orange.

Flowering Season: June–September.

Habitat/Range: Dry fields, roadsides and other disturbed places in the sagebrush steppe and the montane, to 8,500', throughout the Great Basin, e.g., Peavine Mountain, Great Basin National Park.

Comments: *Verbascum* is a variation on an ancient Latin word for "bearded" in reference to the hairy filaments. *Thapsus* was the name of an ancient Mediterranean town.

MOUNTAIN VIOLET
Viola purpurea
Violet Family (Violaceae)

Description: There's something so heartwarming about the violets, especially since they are one of the first flowers to bloom in the spring. Their bright faces light up the landscape with the promise of all the flowers and sun soon to come. Mountain Violet is a highly variable species with several subspecies, but it can be recognized by its ½–1", lemon-yellow, 5-petaled flowers with 2 upper petals that are brown-purple on the back and a lower middle petal that is purple veined. The leaves vary by subspecies, but are dark green, deep veined, and ovate or round. They can be smooth edged or slightly toothed. Each flower is at the tip of a 1–8" slender peduncle.

Flowering Season: April–June.

Habitat/Range: Dry slopes, openings in the sagebrush steppe and the montane, to 10,000', throughout the Great Basin, e.g., Steens Mountain, Deep Creek Mountains.

Comments: *Viola (V. macloskeyi). Purpurea* means "purple" in reference to the brown-purple backs of the upper two petals.

This section includes flowers that range from creamy to bright white. Some plants produce flowers that tend toward pale yellow or pale green. Check the sections for yellow and green flowers if you don't find your flower here.

SODA STRAW
Angelica lineariloba
Carrot Family (Apiaceae)

Description: Soda Straw is an especially delicate and lovely member of the Carrot Family—its umbels of flowers and its leaves are graceful and airy. The rays bearing the small, ball-shaped umbellets of tiny, white, 5-petaled flowers are long enough (to 3") to spread the umbellets out so they are clearly distinct. The stout, 1–5' stems are also clearly seen, for the leaves are deeply and delicately divided into very narrow, needlelike segments, so they don't hide the stem. The entire plant, then, despite its large size has an almost wispy look to it. When it goes to fruit, the bouquet of white flowers becomes a greenish "skeleton" with even more clearly visible "bones" (i.e., rays).

Flowering Season: June–August.

Habitat/Range: Streambanks, moist meadows, talus slopes in the montane, 7,500–9,500', in eastern California, western Nevada, e.g., Sweetwater Mountains.

Comments: *Angelica* means "angelic" in reference to this plant's medicinal uses, which are said to have been revealed to a monk by an angel who told him it was a cure for the plague. *Lineariloba* means "linear lobed" in reference to the leaves.

DOUGLAS WATER HEMLOCK
Cicuta douglasii
Carrot Family (Apiaceae)

Description: Douglas Water Hemlock is one of the several tall members of the Carrot (Umbel) Family with umbels of tiny, white, 5-petaled flowers. Like Poison Hemlock *(Conium maculatum),* it is a *highly poisonous* plant that has been responsible for numerous human and livestock deaths. Although its hollow stem can reach 8' or so tall, it is a less substantial plant than Poison Hemlock, for its stem is not as stout, and it is much less leafy. Its leaves can be up to 1' long but are divided into only a few, narrow, widely spaced, serrated leaflets that are usually not further dissected, so they do not have the fernlike appearance that the leaves of Poison Hemlock have.

Flowering Season: June–October.

Habitat/Range: Streambanks, wet meadows, roadside ditches in the sagebrush steppe, to 6,500', in eastern California, western and northwestern Nevada, southern Oregon, e.g., Charles Sheldon National Wildlife Refuge, Wassuk Range.

Comments: *Cicuta* is the ancient Latin name. David Douglas *(Silene douglasii).*

POISON HEMLOCK
Conium maculatum
Carrot Family (Apiaceae)

Description: Although Poison Hemlock is a robust plant with a thick, hollow, branching, 1–8' stem, its leaves and flowers create a delicate, airy appearance. Its leaves can be up to a foot long and almost as wide, but they are deeply twice-pinnately dissected into tiny, serrated, fernlike leaflets. The inflorescence is an open double umbel—the tiny, white, 5-petaled flowers are at the tips of short rays, which radiate out from the tips of longer (1–4") rays, which in turn radiate out from the tips of the branching stem. As if to announce its extreme toxicity—this is the plant that killed Socrates and that has *poisoned* many livestock—the stem is often speckled with purple spots or splotches.

Flowering Season: May–July.

Habitat/Range: Streambanks, roadside ditches and other disturbed places in the sagebrush steppe and the montane, to 7,000', throughout the Great Basin, e.g., Washoe Valley, Steens Mountain.

Comments: *Conium* is the ancient Greek name. *Maculatum* means "spotted" in reference to the purple splotches on the plant stem. Alien.

COW PARSNIP
Heracleum lanatum
Carrot Family (Apiaceae)

Description: Of all the tall, white-flowered plants of the Carrot Family that grow in the Great Basin, Cow Parsnip is probably the most robust. Its hollow, ribbed stem is stout and can reach 8' tall, and its leaves are huge (to almost 2' wide). These leaves make Cow Parsnip easy to distinguish from all its Great Basin relatives—they are round in outline and palmately (not pinnately) lobed into serrated segments. Their maplelike shape differs dramatically from the fernlike or arrow-shaped leaves of other white-flowered Carrot Family members you are likely to find in the area. Much of the plant is covered with long, white hairs. Although most of its kin prefer damp soil, Cow Parsnip usually grows in wet, even boggy, areas.

Flowering Season: June–August.

Habitat/Range: Streambanks, wet meadows in the montane, to 9,500', throughout the Great Basin, e.g., Santa Rosa Range, Ruby Mountains.

Comments: *Heracleum* is derived from Hercules, probably in reference to the large size of several species. *Lanatum* means "wooly" in reference to the white hairs on the stems and peduncles.

GRAY'S LOVAGE
Ligusticum grayi
Carrot Family (Apiaceae)

Description: Although Gray's Lovage has the umbels of tiny white, 5-petaled flowers characteristic of so many of the Carrot Family genera, it is a much smaller and more delicate plant than many of its relatives, reaching up to only about 2½' tall. The stem is mostly leafless, the majority of the lacy leaves occurring on their own basal, 1–12" petioles. The 4–10" leaves are delicately twice-pinnate. There is only 1 terminal umbel of flowers with 1 or 2 axillary umbels, each consisting of 5–18 widely spaced, 1–1½" rays.

Flowering Season: June–August.

Habitat/Range: Meadows, forest openings in the montane, 6,500–10,000', throughout the Great Basin, e.g., Santa Rosa Range, Ruby Mountains.

Comments: *Ligusticum* is after Liguria, the Italian town where a closely related genus, *Levisticum*, was first found. Asa Gray was a renowned 19th-century American botanist.

NEVADA LOMATIUM
Lomatium nevadense
Carrot Family (Apiaceae)

Description: Although its flowers are not especially showy or colorful, Nevada Lomatium has a special place in my affections, for in northern Nevada it is among the very first plants to bloom. In February (sometimes even early in the month) when the snow still lies heavy at our house at about 7,700' on the east side of Mt. Rose, and I'm starting to get desperate for spring, I can drive a few miles east and about 3,000' down to the Carson Valley area and cheer my soul with the first blooms of this white-flowered lomatium. It is a prostrate plant with finely divided leaves crowded with short, somewhat fleshy, pointed segments. The umbels of tiny, white, 5-petaled flowers are also densely crowded and lie nearly flat on the ground. There is sometimes a touch of red at the center of the flowers. From a distance you might think these prostrate flower umbels were just more patches of snow, but what a delight to discover that they are, instead, spring's floral messengers!

Flowering Season: February–March.

Habitat/Range: Dry, sandy or rocky places in the sagebrush steppe and the montane, 4,500–9,500', throughout the Great Basin, e.g., Carson Valley, Steens Mountain.

Comments: *Lomatium* means "bordered" in reference to the prominent margins on the fruits. *Nevadense* means "of Nevada."

BOLANDER'S YAMPAH
Perideridia bolanderi
Carrot Family (Apiaceae)

Description: *Perideridia* is one of the very few genera in the Carrot Family with plants that have leaves divided into smooth, linear segments (as opposed to broad, maplelike leaves or deeply divided, rough-edged, fernlike leaves). Bolander's Yampah can grow to 3' tall, its slender, often branching stem terminating in a dense, round-topped cluster of tiny, white, 5-petaled flowers with protruding, white reproductive parts that give the cluster a fuzzy appearance. The few leaves are divided into very narrow, unlobed segments. The roots are short and radishlike (whereas most *Perideridia* species have longer, more carrotlike roots). As with many of the yampahs, Bolander's Yampah sometimes grows alone, but often cloaks hillsides with an airy garment of white fuzz.

Flowering Season: May–August.

Habitat/Range: Dry or moist meadows, washes, rocky ridges in the montane, to 10,000', throughout the Great Basin, e.g., Soldier Meadow, Deep Creek Mountains.

Comments: *Perideridia* means "around the neck," probably in reference to the bracts under the umbels. H.N. Bolander was a 19th-century California botanist.

RANGER'S BUTTONS
Sphenosciadum capitellatum
Carrot Family (Apiaceae)

Description: Another of the seemingly endless number of tall, white-flowered plants of the Carrot Family, Ranger's Buttons is, however, very easily distinguished from all its relatives with even the most cursory glance. Although it has the umbels of tiny white, 5-petaled flowers characteristic of so many of its kin, these umbels are unique—the 4–18 rays end in nearly spherical, buttonlike "umbellets" of flowers that are widely separated from each other. The flowers often have a pink or purplish tinge. The 4–16" leaves are typical of the Carrot Family, being large and pinnately divided into serrated leaflets, but the leaflets are longer (to 4½"), narrower, and more widely separated than are those of most of its relatives.

Flowering Season: July–August.

Habitat/Range: Streambanks, marshy meadows, lake shores in the montane, 6,500–9,500', eastern California, western and northern Nevada, southern Oregon, e.g., White Mountains, Steens Mountain.

Comments: *Sphenosciadum* means "wedge umbrella" in reference to the large flower umbel. *Capitellatum* means "with heads" in reference to the spherical flower clusters. The common name Ranger's Buttons also refers to these buttonlike heads of flowers.

YARROW
Achillea millefolium
Composite Family (Asteraceae)

Description: Yarrow is a daisylike composite in that it has ray flowers and disk flowers, but it certainly doesn't look much like a daisy. At first glance you might not even recognize it as a composite. The flower heads are very small (¼–½" wide) and group together to form large, flat-topped clusters. Each flower head has only a few (3–8) small, round rays surrounding the several tubular disk flowers. The rays are usually white (sometimes pink), and the disks are usually beige or brownish but can be pink or purplish. The leaves are fernlike with hundreds of tiny, pinnate, threadlike lobes (as alluded to by the species name). The plant stem and leaves are white-wooly. Crush a leaf and you will notice the strong, medicinal smell. You might want to consult a book on herbal and medicinal uses of plants to learn the many healing uses of yarrow—some books will even have preparations and doses. However, be aware that using any wild plant as medicine can be risky and should be tried only after careful study, with absolute certainty about identification of the plant, and using extreme caution.

Flowering Season: May–September.

Habitat/Range: Grassy fields and meadows, disturbed places, rocky slopes in the sagebrush steppe and the montane, to 9,500', throughout the Great Basin, e.g., White Mountains, Ruby Mountains.

Comments: *Achillea* is after the mythological hero Achilles. *Millefolium* means "1,000 leaves" in reference to the deeply dissected, fernlike leaves with the hundreds of leaflets.

ALPINE EVERLASTING
Antennaria media
Composite Family (Asteraceae)

Description: Alpine Everlasting is a miniaturized (2–6"), white-wooly plant of high elevations. As you would expect of a plant that occurs high in the mountains, the ½", spoon-shaped leaves are mostly basal, in this case forming a wooly mat. There are occasional stem leaves that are typically pressed up against the stem. At the tip of the stem is a small, tight, ball-shaped cluster of 2–7 flower heads, each of which consists of many white, furry disk flowers. The upper part of the phyllaries is black or dark brown (which helps distinguish this species from other everlastings). The alternative common name Pussytoes refers to the soft, round flower heads, especially charming when you lie on the ground and look at them at eye level. Alpine Everlasting is certainly not a flamboyant or even showy plant, but its soft

texture and intricate structure definitely reward a close look.

Flowering Season: June–September.

Habitat/Range: Rocky slopes and ridges, dry meadows in the montane and the alpine, 8,000–13,000', throughout the Great Basin, e.g., Toiyabe Range, Santa Rosa Range.

Comments: *Antennaria* means "antenna" in reference to the swollen tip of the pappus, which bears some resemblance to a butterfly's antenna. *Medea* means "intermediate.' The common name Everlasting refers to the fact that the flower heads look pretty much the same fresh or dried. Formerly known as *A. alpina*. Also called Alpine Pussytoes.

ROSY PUSSYTOES
Antennaria rosea
Composite Family (Asteraceae)

Description: Rosy Pussytoes is a plant that is easy to overlook, for it is short (2–16") and has only a small cluster of rather inconspicuous flower heads of ¼", white, disk flowers. It has mostly basal leaves that are also small (¼–1" long and narrow) and a few even smaller stem leaves. However, Rosy Pussytoes does have some intriguing and attractive features, well worth inspecting up close. Its white, round-topped flower heads are delicate and soft, made even more so by the tiny, fingerlike, pink bracts holding them. And the rest of the plant matches this softness—the leaves and stem are matted with soft, white hairs.

Flowering Season: June–July.

Habitat/Range: Grassy meadows, rocky slopes in the montane, 5,000–10,000', throughout the Great Basin, e.g., Steens Mountain, Deep Creek Mountains.

Comments: *Antennaria (A. media). Rosea* means "rosy" in reference to the rose (or pink) bracts beneath the flower heads. Also known as *A. microphylla.*

BLEPHARIPAPPUS
Blepharipappus scaber
Composite Family (Asteraceae)

Description: Most dry sagebrush flats have occasional openings in the sagebrush, sometimes several square yards in area, where other plants can dominate. One of the species that can put on a dazzling show in such openings is Blepharipappus—hundreds of these beautiful, white-flowered composites can fill an opening almost to the exclusion of any other species. Each ½–1' plant bears one or several of the striking ½–¾" flower heads, each of which has 2–8 (often 5) white, 3-lobed rays surrounding the central button of 6–25 white, tubular disk flowers. Be sure to examine these disk flowers closely, for their structure and colors are fascinating. Projecting from the star-shaped lobes of the flower tube are beautiful, black-purple anthers and feathery, bristly, pink-purple styles. The leaves are very small and narrow and occur along almost the entire length of the stem.

Flowering Season: May–August.

Habitat/Range: Dry, sandy or gravelly flats and slopes in the sagebrush steppe, to 7,000', in western and northern Nevada, southern Oregon, e.g., Peavine Mountain, Pyramid Lake.

Comments: *Blepharipappus* means "eyelash pappus" in reference to the feathery bristles on the seeds. *Scaber* means "rough" in reference to the short, sticky hairs on the stems and leaves.

DUSTY MAIDEN
Chaenactis douglasii
Composite Family (Asteraceae)

Description: Dusty Maiden has several recognized varieties with wide elevational range from the sagebrush steppe all the way up to the alpine. As you might expect, the growth form varies, then, from tall (to 15") with loosely spaced branches and leaves to short (2–3") and unbranched with a tight mat of leaves. Regardless of form, Dusty Maiden is a glandular-sticky, somewhat cobwebby plant with deeply pinnately divided leaves that tend to curl up a bit. The ½" wide flower heads are crammed with tubular disk flowers with long-protruding reproductive parts. It is these reproductive parts projecting from the flower tubes that give the flower heads the pincushion look acknowledged in its alternative name Pincushion Flower. The flowers are usually creamy white but can be yellow or pink. The phyllaries under the flower head are narrow and pointed and sticky to the touch.

Flowering Season: June–August.

Habitat/Range: Dry, gravelly ridges, sandy slopes and flats, washes in the sagebrush steppe, the montane, and the alpine, to 11,000', throughout the Great Basin, e.g., Peavine Mountain, Great Basin National Park.

Comments: *Chaenactis* means "gaping ray" in reference to the enlarged, almost raylike, outer disk flowers of some species. David Douglas *(Silene douglasii).*

187

STEMLESS THISTLE
Cirsium scariosum
Composite Family (Asteraceae)

Description: Although Stemless Thistle can have a stem up to 3' tall, as the common name suggests, you will usually find these 1–2" wide flower heads sitting almost directly on the ground. One or several of the flower heads nestle on a rosette of broad, 4–16", spiny leaves. The leaves and the phyllaries are usually covered with white, wooly hair. The long, tubular disk flowers are usually creamy white (sometimes lavender or pinkish). As with all thistles, there are no ray flowers. This is a highly variable species both in height and in color, which some botanists separate into several species with frequent hybridization.

Flowering Season: June–August.

Habitat/Range: Meadows, dry flats, openings in the sagebrush steppe and the montane, 5,000–10,000', western Nevada, southern Oregon, western Utah, e.g., Peavine Mountain, Steens Mountain.

Comments: *Cirsium* means "swollen" in reference to the reputed medicinal use of thistles to treat swollen joints. *Scariosum* means "membranous and translucent" in reference to the phyllaries. Also called Elk Thistle.

CUT-LEAF DAISY
Erigeron compositus
Composite Family (Asteraceae)

Description: There is no mistaking Cut-Leaf Daisy for any of the many other daisylike composites. Although its 1–1½" wide flower heads with the 30–60 narrow, crowded, white rays surrounding the yellow disk are not unusual, it is a plant that reaches high above timberline and so is dwarfed (only 1–2" in plants at the highest elevations) and densely hairy. The stem, phyllaries, and leaves are covered with short, bristly, white hairs. The leaves are mostly basal, small, and mittenlike (i.e., divided into three round leaflets). The rays are usually bright white (often with tinges of purple) but sometimes are pinkish or lavender. There is a variety that has only the yellow disk with no rays or with poorly developed rays (inset photo).

Flowering Season: June–September.

Habitat/Range: Rocky ridges, gravelly flats, talus slopes in the montane and the alpine, 7,000–13,000', throughout the Great Basin, e.g., Toiyabe Range, Steens Mountain.

Comments: *Erigeron (E. filifolius). Compositus* means "compound."

THREAD-LEAF DAISY
Erigeron filifolius
Composite Family (Asteraceae)

Description: A lovely daisy with subtle and variable coloration, Thread-Leaf Daisy is all the more showy for its habit of growing in large clusters from a branched, woody caudex (i.e., a vertical stem at or beneath ground level). The 1–1½" wide flower heads dazzle with their raised, yellow disk and the 15–50 rounded rays that range from white (with tinges of pink or lavender) to lavender or bluish. As the common and species names indicate, the ½–3" leaves are very narrow. Most of the leaves occur in a dense basal cluster, though there are some smaller stem leaves. The ½–1½' stems are covered with fine, short, stiff, white hairs.

Flowering Season: April–July.

Habitat/Range: Dry, rocky or sandy slopes and flats in the sagebrush steppe and the montane, to 7,000', in western and northwestern Nevada, southern Oregon, e.g., Charles Sheldon National Wildlife Refuge, Washoe Valley.

Comments: *Erigeron* means "early old age," probably in reference to the white seed "parachutes," which can look like graying whiskers. *Filifolius* means "threadlike leaves."

WHITE LAYIA
Layia glandulosa
Composite Family (Asteraceae)

Description: White Layia is a delightful, cheery inhabitant of desert shrub and sagebrush steppe, bringing bright color and interesting form to the dry landscape. Each plant stem bears only 1 flower head, which consists of many bright yellow disk flowers surrounded by broad, bright white, 3-lobed rays. There is considerable variation in the number of these rays from plant to plant—some flower heads are crowded with up to 14 overlapping rays, while other flower heads may have only 5 or fewer widely separated ones. The stems (ranging from 2" to 2') and the narrow leaves are covered with glandular hairs and sometimes emit a spicy scent. Although you may find a single plant (with a single flower head) growing alone, it is not at all unusual to encounter a large patch of plants, creating a dazzling bouquet of flower heads.

Flowering Season: March–July.

Habitat/Range: Dry, open places in the desert shrub and the sagebrush steppe, to 8,000', throughout the Great Basin, e.g., Carson Valley.

Comments: George T. Lay was a 19th-century English plant collector. *Glandulosa* means "glandular." Alternative common names are White Tidy Tips or Desert Tidy Tips.

LOW CRYPTANTHA
Cryptantha humilis
Borage Family (Boraginaceae)

Description: With its dense, cylindrical cluster of rather large, white, almost flat pinwheel-like, 5-petaled flowers with the raised teeth around the throat, Low Cryptantha is easily identified as a species of *Cryptantha;* however, with over 40 species of this genus in the Great Basin, identifying the species is usually quite difficult. In this case, though, identification is relatively easy for (as the alternative common name Round-Spike Cryptantha suggests) this plant has a distinctive round or cylindrical inflorescence that rises above the mostly basal leaves and is crammed thick with unusually large (for a *Cryptantha*) flowers that can be ½" or more across. The raised teeth around the flower throat are bright yellow. The densely gray-hairy, tonguelike leaves can be up to 2½" long and ½" wide.

Flowering Season: April–June.

Habitat/Range: Dry, gravelly, or rocky flats and slopes in the sagebrush steppe and the montane, to 9,500', throughout the Great Basin, e.g., Peavine Mountain, Deep Creek Mountains.

Comments: *Cryptantha* means "hidden flower." *Humilis* means "low" in reference to the mound of basal leaves. Also called Round-Spike Cryptantha.

PALE STICKSEED
Hackelia patens
Borage Family (Boraginaceae)

Description: Like their close relatives of the Borage Family in the genus *Cryptantha,* species in the *Hackelia* genus have flowers with 5 petals united in a pinwheel or shallow bowl, often with a raised ring around the flower tube. However, while most *Cryptantha* species are densely hairy or prickly over most of the plant (leaves, stems, and sepals), *Hackelia* species often have soft-hairy leaves but are usually hairless over the rest of the plant. Most *Hackelia* flowers are intensely blue (e.g., *H. micrantha*), though a few (including Pale Stickseed) are pale blue or even white with darker blue markings. Pale Stickseed has a yellow eye in the center of the flower surrounded by a white or yellowish raised ring. The ½–2½' plant has mostly basal, 2–12", tonguelike, soft-hairy leaves.

Flowering Season: June–August.

Habitat/Range: Dry slopes in the sagebrush steppe and the montane, 6,000–10,200', throughout the Great Basin, e.g., Steens Mountain (rare), Great Basin National Park.

Comments: Joseph Hackel was a 19th-century Czech botanist. *Patens* means "spreading." Also called Spotted Forget-Me-Not.

191

SALT HELIOTROPE
Heliotropium curassavicum
Borage Family (Boraginaceae)

Description: Salt Heliotrope is a fascinating plant of harsh saline areas. The 4–30" stems sprout at intervals from stout, creeping roots, so you will often see several stems clustered together. Often each stem will bear only one opposite pair of 2–5" flower spikes, but in very wet years you may find plants with many more flowering spikes, each crowded with many flowers. The flower spikes resemble scorpion tails, which uncoil as the flowers open. The 5-petaled, ¼" flowers are white with a yellow or purplish star (nectar guides) in the center. The ½–2", tonguelike leaves are smooth and fleshy, as is the thick stem.

Flowering Season: May–October.

Habitat/Range: Sandy, saline flats, along streambanks in the desert shrub and the sagebrush steppe, to 6,200', scattered throughout the Great Basin, e.g., Charles Sheldon National Wildlife Refuge, Steens Mountain.

Comments: *Heliotropium* means "sun turning" in reference to the summer solstice, the blooming time of the first species described. *Curassavicum* means "of Curacao," the site of the first named plant.

BREWER'S BITTERCRESS
Cardamine breweri
Mustard Family (Brassicaceae)

Description: Brewer's Bittercress is quite similar to Heart-Leaf Bittercress *(C. cordifolia)*: The ½–2' plants grow in wet meadows and along creeks in montane forests and bear bright white, 4-petaled flowers. Although the flowers of Brewer's Bittercress are a bit smaller (½") than those of their close relative, the main difference between these two species is the leaves. Those of Brewer's are not heart shaped and are undivided or divided into 3 or 5 leaflets, consisting of 2 (or 4) small, pointed, opposite ones and one larger, squarish terminal one. Both species of bittercress create a crisp, fresh look along creeks that complements the rich reds, yellows, and blues of their frequent creekside neighbors—various paintbrush, monkeyflowers, senecios, and lupines, among many others.

Flowering Season: June–July.

Habitat/Range: Streambanks, shallow creeks, marshy meadows in the montane, to 8,500', in central and eastern Nevada, western Utah, e.g., Toiyabe Range.

Comments: *Cardamine (C. cordifolia).* William Brewer was a professor of agriculture at Yale who botanized in the American West in the late 1800s.

HEART-LEAF BITTERCRESS
Cardamine cordifolia
Mustard Family (Brassicacea)

Description: Heart-Leaf Bittercress is somewhat similar to Watercress *(Rorippa nasturtium-aquaticum),* another 4-petaled, white-flowered mustard that grows near or in water. However, it is easily distinguished by its larger flowers (½–1") and its broad, lush, unlobed, heart-shaped or kidney-shaped leaves. You will usually find this ½–2' plant standing erect (not sprawled like Watercress) beside a creek or in a wet meadow. Although you may occasionally find it with its "feet" in standing water, it rarely occurs in a moving creek and never chokes or covers the water as Watercress does. The narrow, ¾–1¼" seedpods angle up off the stem.

Flowering Season: May–August.

Habitat/Range: Streambanks, seeps, marshy meadows in the montane and the alpine, 5,000–12,000', in eastern Nevada, western Utah, e.g., Ruby Mountains, Deep Creek Mountains.

Comments: *Cardamine* is the ancient Greek name for a cress with medicinal purposes. *Cordifolia* means "heart-shaped leaves." Formerly known as *C. lyallii.*

WHITE-TOP
Cardaria pubescens
Mustard Family (Brassicaceae)

Description: Although White-Top is one of the many mustards that can become a troublesome or even noxious weed, it really can put on quite an eye-catching floral show. The plants tend to grow in great masses (they spread by rhizomes), and the densely flowered, relatively flat-topped inflorescences can create an almost solid, soft-looking canopy of hundreds of square feet. The ½–1½' plant is also thick with large, broad leaves clasping the stem and alternating up it. The stem, leaves, and sepals are softly hairy. The 4-petaled, ¼" flowers are bright white, while the tiny, round, or ovate seedpods are green.

Flowering Season: May–July.

Habitat/Range: Grassy fields, ditches, roadsides, disturbed places in the sagebrush steppe, to 6,500', throughout the Great Basin, e.g., Washoe Valley, Toiyabe Range.

Comments: *Cardaria* means "heart shaped" in reference to the seeds of one species *(C. draba)*. *Pubescens* means "with soft, downy hair." Alien.

SPRING WHITLOWGRASS
Draba verna
Mustard Family (Brassicaceae)

Description: Knowing that the species name *verna* means "spring," you probably won't be surprised to discover that *Draba verna* is one of the first flowers to bloom in the sagebrush steppe. Its diminutive stature (1–5") and tiny (⅛–¼"), 4-petaled flowers don't make much of a splash, but they do let us know that spring with all its colorful blooms is on its way. The slender, branching stem rises above small, oval, glandular, basal leaves and bears several of the white flowers cradled by their tiny, often reddish brown sepals. Each petal is deeply 2-lobed. The seedpods are oval.

Flowering Season: February–March.

Habitat/Range: Dry flats, disturbed areas in the sagebrush steppe, to 6,500', in western Nevada, southern Oregon, e.g., Carson Valley, Steens Mountain.

Comments: *Draba* means "acrid" in reference to the taste of the leaves. *Verna* means "spring" in reference to the early appearance of the plant and its blooms. Alien.

FREMONT'S PEPPERGRASS
Lepidium fremontii
Mustard Family (Brassicaceae)

Description: Although it's easy to understand the reason for the common name Peppergrass (just take a nibble on a leaf), this delightful shrub might more aptly be called pearlbush. Especially in the spring when the round, BB-sized, pearly white buds are thick on the plant, but also a bit later when the plant is dense with the tiny (¼"), pearly white, 4-petaled flowers, this 1–3' shrub sparkles like a mass of pearls glinting in the sun. The slender, gray-green stems bear many needlelike, pinnately lobed leaves below the densely flowered inflorescences. The fruits are round, notched, ¼" disks. This early-blooming shrub fills the air with its gentle, sweet scent.

Flowering Season: March–August.

Habitat/Range: Sandy or gravelly flats, washes in the desert shrub and the sagebrush steppe, to 6,000', throughout the Great Basin, e.g., White Mountains, Toiyabe Range.

Comments: *Lepidium* means "small scale" in reference to the plant's supposed ability to cure diseases forming scales on the skin. Captain John C. Fremont was an early explorer of the American West. Also called Desert Alyssum.

WATERCRESS
Rorippa nasturtium-aquaticum
Mustard Family (Brassicaceae)

Description: Watercress is one of the numerous mustards that can dazzle you with great masses of plants and flowers despite the small size (¼") of its flowers. You will often find slow-moving streams and ditches clogged and covered with this plant as the ½–2' spreading stems can be submersed or floating or can lie prostrate in the mud. The small, bright white, 4-petaled flowers crowd together in tight, roundish inflorescences that can form extensive overlapping, tangled thickets of flowers. The small leaves are pinnately compound with 3–9 leaflets. The plants are widely cultivated for their edible, pungent leaves, but you might want to think twice about

giardia and other biotic hazards before eating any in the wild.

Flowering Season: May–August.

Habitat/Range: Slow-moving streams, ditches, marshy meadows in the sagebrush steppe and the montane, to 8,000', throughout the Great Basin, e.g., Washoe Valley, Charles Sheldon National Wildlife Refuge.

Comments: *Rorippa* is the ancient Saxon name for this plant. *Nasturtium-aquaticum* means "water cress." Sometimes known as *Nasturtium officinale*. Alien.

CUT-LEAF THELYPODIUM
Thelypodium laciniatum
Mustard Family (Brassicaceae)

Description: With its tall (to 3½'), stout stems, its large, thick, pinnately lobed leaves, and its hundreds of rather odd, conspicuous, 4-petaled, white flowers, Cut-Leaf Thelypodium will probably catch your eye from afar. The densely flowered inflorescence, which can extend down more than half the length of the stem, resembles a massive bottlebrush, for the flowers are kept close to the stem by their short pedicels. Especially in fruit with its long, threadlike seedpods, but even in bloom with its crinkly, twisted petals, this plant has a distinctive, scraggly, ragged look.

Flowering Season: April–July.

Habitat/Range: Rocky ledges, crevices, banks in the sagebrush steppe, to 8,000', western and northwestern Nevada, southern Oregon, e.g., Virginia Range, Charles Sheldon National Wildlife Refuge.

Comments: *Thelypodium* means "woman foot" in reference to the appendage at the base of the ovary. *Laciniatum* means "torn," probably in reference to the ragged appearance of the inflorescence in seed when it's covered with hundreds of wiry seedpods, or perhaps in reference to the somewhat twisted petals.

BLUE ELDERBERRY
Sambucus mexicana
Honeysuckle Family (Caprifoliaceae)

Description: An imposing shrub (or small tree) that can reach 20' tall and about as wide, Blue Elderberry is thick with 2–13", flat-topped clusters of ¼", 5-petaled, white flowers. The flower clusters are at the ends of branchlets that also bear large leaves, each with 3–9 narrow, 2–6", toothed, slightly infolded leaflets (2–8 of the leaflets are in opposite pairs with 1 terminal). The base of each leaflet is usually asymmetrical, one side touching the petiole further down than the other side. The round, ¼", juicy berries are bluish black but are covered with a whitish, waxy film that gives them a pale, powdery blue appearance.

Flowering Season: May–July.

Habitat/Range: Openings, shrubby slopes, streambanks in the sagebrush steppe and the montane, to 10,000', throughout the Great Basin, e.g., Santa Rosa Range, Steens Mountain.

Comments: *Sambucus* is the Greek name for a musical instrument made from wood of this genus. *Mexicana* means "of Mexico." Formerly known as *S. cerulea*.

RED ELDERBERRY
Sambucus racemosa
Honeysuckle Family (Caprifoliaceae)

Description: Red Elderberry is quite similar to its close relative Blue Elderberry *(S. mexicana)* with its large, thick clusters of small, white, 5-petaled flowers and its pinnately compound leaves. There are some very conspicuous differences, however, that make it easy to distinguish the two species. As the common name indicates, the fruits (berries) of Red Elderberry are usually red (though they sometimes are dark purple or black), and they are not covered with a bluish film. In bloom, the most noticeable differences are the size of the plant and the shape of the inflorescence— Red Elderberry is a much smaller shrub (rarely exceeding 6' tall) with dome-shaped (instead of flat-topped) flower clusters. The 5–7, serrated leaflets are usually crinkly and strongly infolded. They are usually more or less symmetric at the base.

Flowering Season: June–July.

Habitat/Range: Streambanks, moist openings in the montane, 6,000–11,000', throughout the Great Basin, e.g., Steens Mountain, Great Basin National Park.

Comments: *Sambucus (S. mexicana). Racemosa* means "in a cluster" in reference to the flowers.

MOUNTAIN SNOWBERRY
Symphoricarpos rotundifolius
Honeysuckle Family (Caprifoliaceae)

Description: Snowberry is a very descriptive and rather romantic name for this 2–4' shrub with its round, ½", pasty, white berries. In bloom, the ½", white or pink, tubular flowers hang in pairs or in few-flowered clusters from the leaf axils. The young stems are reddish. With age, they gray, and the bark tends to shred. The ½–¾" leaves, as the species name indicates, are round (or elliptic) and are usually smooth edged. The veins, especially on the underside of the leaf, are prominent. The leaves are often finely, white-hairy (though you may need a magnifying glass to see the actual hairs).

Flowering Season: June–July.

Habitat/Range: Open slopes, dry meadows, forest openings in the montane, 5,000–11,000', throughout the Great Basin, e.g., Great Basin National Park, Deep Creek Mountains.

Comments: *Symphoricarpos* means "to bear fruit together" in reference to the clusters of berries. *Rotundifolius* means "round leafed." Sometimes called *S. oreophilus.*

SPINY SANDWORT
Arenaria aculeata
Pink Family (Caryophyllaceae)

Description: Most of the many species of *Arenaria* in the Great Basin are difficult to distinguish. They are all relatively short plants with slender stems, narrow (often needlelike) leaves, and small, white (to pink) flowers with 5 separated petals. Spiny Sandwort has several features that when taken together, make identification fairly easy: (1) it is mat-forming with mostly basal leaves (with only 1 or 2 pairs of stem leaves, which tend to spread out almost perpendicular to the stem); (2) the leaves are stiff and sharp-spiny; and (3) the leaves are distinctly blue-green. Since the mats tend to die in the middle as they grow outward, you will often find "fairy rings"—"moats" of leaves surrounding a central circle of dead plants. The ½", white flowers have narrow, widely separated petals; the reddish brown anthers often appear to "spot" the petals.

Flowering Season: June–August.

Habitat/Range: Rocky places, openings in the sagebrush steppe and the montane, 6,000–10,000', in western, northern, and eastern Nevada, southern Oregon, e.g., Peavine Mountain, Ruby Mountains.

Comments: *Arenaria (A. kingii). Aculeata* means "prickly."

199

KING'S SANDWORT
Arenaria kingii
Pink Family (Caryophyllaceae)

Description: There are numerous species (and numerous varieties of those species) of sandwort in the Great Basin, all of which have small, star-shaped, white (occasionally pinkish) flowers and most of which are low-growing, tufted or matted plants with needlelike leaves. King's Sandwort is a 4–12" plant (2–6" at its higher elevations) with stems and ¼–1", needlelike leaves that are glandular-hairy. The leaves can get quite dense toward the base of the plant, but the ¼–½", white flowers are loosely scattered at the tips of nearly leafless, branching pedicels. Since the upper stems and pedicels are very slender, it almost looks like the flowers are floating above the plant. Unusual for a species of the Pink Family, but common for the *Arenaria* genus, the 5 narrow

petals are not lobed (though they sometimes have a tiny notch at the tip). The 10 slender, radiating filaments are tipped with tiny, reddish anthers that early in the blooming seem to be red spots on the petals.

Flowering Season: June–August.

Habitat/Range: Sandy, gravelly, or rocky slopes and ridges in the montane and the alpine, 8,000–12,000', throughout the Great Basin except western Utah, e.g., White Mountains, Great Basin National Park.

Comments: *Arenaria* means "sand" in reference to the sandy habitats of some species. Clarence King was a 19th-century California geologist and renowned mountain climber.

STICKY STARWORT
Pseudostellaria jamesiana
Pink Family (Caryophyllaceae)

Description: Sticky Starwort closely resembles Mountain Chickweed, *Stellaria longipes* (and used to be considered in the same genus), but it is a taller (4–18"), more robust plant. The flowers are also quite similar with their 5 separate, bright white petals, but they have a bit of a different look because the petal lobes of Sticky Starwort are shallower. Rather than appearing to be 10 petals (as with Mountain Chickweed) they are obviously 5, each one somewhat heart shaped. As in Mountain Chickweed, the anthers are red when ripe and lie against the petals, so the petals appear to be red spotted. A bit later in the blooming cycle, the stamens rise up above the petals and the anthers dry black, so the red

"spots" disappear. The narrow, pointed, 1–4" leaves (as well as the stems and sepals) are covered with short, rough hairs and are sticky to the touch.

Flowering Season: May–July.

Habitat/Range: Forest openings, grassy meadows, bushy slopes in the montane, 5,500–11,000', throughout the Great Basin, e.g., Toiyabe Range, Steens Mountain.

Comments: *Pseudostellaria* means "false *Stellaria*" in reference to its close resemblance to the *Stellaria* genus *(S. longipes)*. Edwin James was a 19th-century Colorado botanist.

BOUNCING BET
Saponaria officinalis
Pink Family (Caryophyllaceae)

Description: Bouncing Bet is an imposing plant—it is tall (1–3') and is thick with 1–3", tonguelike leaves and many-flowered (20–40) clusters of 1–3" flowers. Although it's not surprising to come across large, somewhat coarse plants in disturbed places, Bouncing Bet can be a bit startling to encounter, for it's "choked" with large leaves and large, beautiful flowers. The 5 white or pink petals flaring out of the thick, tubular, red-purple calyx are widely separated and often somewhat heart shaped with small, fringed appendages at the base.

Flowering Season: July–September.

Habitat/Range: Grassy fields, roadsides and other disturbed places in the sagebrush steppe, to 6,000', throughout the Great Basin, e.g., Carson Valley.

Comments: *Saponaria* means "soap" in reference to the juice of the plant, which lathers with water. *Officinalis* means "medicinal." Alien.

MAGUIRE'S CATCHFLY
Silene bernardina
Pink Family (Caryophyllaceae)

Description: The ½–2' plant of Maguire's Catchfly is thick with linear leaves in its lower portion, but you may not pay much attention to these since the upper portion of the plant is a tangle of intricate, intriguing flowers. The most colorful part of the 5-petaled flowers is the swollen, yellow-green, ½" long calyx tube with its 10 red-purple stripes. Flaring out of this tube is a ½" wide, pinwheel-like, white flower with deeply pinked (the origin of the family name) petals. Distinguishing Maguire's Catchfly from many of its close kin is the nature of the petal lobes—there are 4 lobes of almost equal length (as opposed to the more typical 2 lobes or 4 lobes of greatly unequal length). The upper stem and especially the sepals are very noticeably glandular-sticky (the origin of the common name Catchfly).

Flowering Season: May–July.

Habitat/Range: Dry slopes in the sagebrush steppe, the montane, and the alpine, 5,000–12,000', in eastern California, western Nevada, e.g., White Mountains.

Comments: *Silene (S. douglasii). Bernardina* is of uncertain origin (it appears not to refer to the San Bernardino Mountains).

DOUGLAS CATCHFLY
Silene douglasii
Pink Family (Caryophyllaceae)

Description: Although the petals of Douglas Catchfly are interesting and worth a close look, the calyx is probably the most noticeable feature of this plant. The ½" yellowish or greenish calyx is a swollen tube decorated with 10 showy, dark reddish brown ribs running its length. Flaring out of this tube is the ½", starlike, white flower. As with most members of the Pink (as in "pinked") Family and almost all catchfly species, the 5 separate petals are lobed. However, whereas the petals of most *Silene* species are deeply cut into 2 or 4 distinct lobes, the petals of Douglas Catchfly are cut very shallowly, creating barely biloped petals. The inner teeth of the petals are very narrow and deeply bilobed. The petals are white or cream, becoming pink tinged or purple tinged with age. The slender, 4–16" stems with their opposite pairs of leaves tend to grow in clusters, so you'll usually see the flowers in bunches.

Flowering Season: May–July.

Habitat/Range: Dry slopes, rocky ridges in the montane, 6,000–10,000', throughout the Great Basin, e.g., Steens Mountain, Deep Creek Mountains.

Comments: Silenus was the foster father of Bacchus (god of wine) in Roman mythology. David Douglas was a British horticulturist and explorer who made several botanizing trips to America in the early 1800s. The common name Catchfly refers to the glandular-sticky calyx, which presumably could ensnare flies.

MOUNTAIN CHICKWEED
Stellaria longipes
Pink Family (Caryophyllaceae)

Description: Since many species in the Pink Family have pink or reddish blossoms, you might think that this was the origin of the family name, but you'd be wrong. It wasn't because of pink petals, but rather because of pinked (i.e., lobed or fringed) petals. Although there are many species in the Pink Family that don't have pink or red flowers (including Mountain Chickweed), there are only a few that don't have lobed, notched, or fringed petals. Mountain Chickweed is a delicate 4–12" plant with 1–7 small (¼–½"), white flowers at the tips of its branching stem. The 5 separate petals are so deeply lobed that they may appear to be 10 petals until you notice that the lobes don't go all the way to the base. The linear leaves are widely spaced on the stem.

Flowering Season: May–August.

Habitat/Range: Grassy meadows, streambanks in the sagebrush steppe and the montane, 5,500–11,000', throughout the Great Basin, e.g., Washoe Valley, Ruby Mountains.

Comments: *Stellaria* means "star" in reference to the flaring petals. *Longipes* means "long stalked." Also called Long-Stalk Starwort.

FIELD BINDWEED
Convolvulus arvensis
Morning Glory Family (Convolvulaceae)

Description: The common name Field Bindweed conveys a hint of tangled weediness; and indeed this plant is an alien, ground-hugging vine that can take over a field and create quite a tangled mess. However, its other common name, White Morning Glory, suggests the beauty of the funnel-shaped, white or pink flowers with the 5 fused petals. Many of these 1–1½" wide flowers branch off the trailing stem (that can be up to 3' long) on short pedicels from the leaf axils. The many leaves are dark green and broadly arrow shaped. The large number of leaves and flowers and the startling contrast between the soft white or delicate pink flowers and the dark green leaves create quite a showy and dramatic mat despite the plant's weedy nature.

Flowering Season: May–September.

Habitat/Range: Dry roadsides and fields, disturbed places in the sagebrush steppe, to 6,500', throughout the Great Basin, e.g., Santa Rosa Range.

Comments: *Convolvulus* means "to twine." *Arvensis* means "of the field." Also called White Morning Glory. Alien.

CREEK DOGWOOD

Cornus sericea
Dogwood Family (Cornaceae)

Description: Broad, lush, deep green leaves, smooth red stems, and large clusters of showy, creamy white flowers—Creek Dogwood puts on quite a fresh, colorful show along creeks in montane forests. This 5–20' shrub is heavy with tonguelike, deeply veined, 2–4" leaves in opposite pairs or in whorls on the stems. Above the leaves are 1–2", nearly flat-topped clusters of scores of the ¼", 4-petaled, white flowers. The four white stamens alternate with the petals and stick up quite noticeably. The ¼", roundish fruit is also white or cream colored. Although in some dogwood species the showy parts of the flowers are actually bracts, in Creek Dogwood they are true petals.

Flowering Season: May–August.

Habitat/Range: Streambanks, moist woods in the montane, to 9,000', throughout the Great Basin, e.g., Steens Mountain, Great Basin National Park.

Comments: *Cornus* means "horn" in reference to the hard wood. *Sericea* means "silky." Sometimes known as *C. stolonifera*. Also called Red Osier Dogwood.

PINE-MAT MANZANITA
Arctostaphylos nevadensis
Heath Family (Ericaceae)

Description: As its name suggests Pine-Mat Manzanita is a mat-forming plant that grows in openings in montane forests. Other than its ground-hugging growth form (it rarely exceeds 2' tall), it closely resembles its close kin Green-Leaf Manzanita *(A. patula)* and often grows with it. Its flowers are the same white (or pinkish), 5-petaled urns that hang in clusters off the slender stems. The branches are the same red-brown color, and the stiff leaves are the same smooth texture, bright green color, and tipped-on-edge orientation. However, the leaves of Pine-Mat Manzanita are a bit smaller (½–2"), a little narrower, and more pointed at the tip. In both manzanitas, the branches often root from where they touch the ground (they are frequently pushed to the ground in places by the snowpack).

Flowering Season: May–July.

Habitat/Range: Dry slopes, forest openings in the montane, 7,500–10,000', in western Nevada, e.g., Virginia Range. This species occurs mostly in the Sierra Nevada.

Comments: *Arctostaphylos (A. patula). Nevadensis* means "of the Sierra Nevada."

GREEN-LEAF MANZANITA
Arctostaphylos patula
Heath Family (Ericaceae)

Description: Green-Leaf Manzanita joins various *Ceanothus* species as the main components of the chapparal community (see *Ceanothus velutinus*) on dry, mid-elevation slopes in many parts of the Great Basin. Though this 3–6' shrub can form nearly impenetrable thickets, making off-trail walking extremely difficult, it has many gifts to offer as compensation. Its 5-petaled blossoms are charming, ½", hanging urns, as delightful for their "puckered kiss" form as for their bright, clean, white (sometimes pink-tinged) color and their delicious nectar. These flowers are even more appreciated for their early appearance—they are always one of the first plants to bloom every spring, ushering in warm weather and warm thoughts. Later in the summer when the blossoms have gone, the ovaries become small (½"), tasty, tart apples. As one final gift many of the stems are sensually smooth and dazzlingly red. The bright green, 1–2", ovate leaves are usually tipped up on edge.

Flowering Season: May–July.

Habitat/Range: Dry slopes, openings in the sagebrush steppe and the montane, 5,500–9,000', in western and eastern Nevada, western Utah, e.g., Peavine Mountain, Deep Creek Mountains.

Comments: *Arctostaphylos* means "bear berries." *Patula* means "spreading." Manzanita means "little apple" in reference to the tasty fruit.

207

PINEDROPS
Pterospora andromedea
Heath Family (Ericaceae)

Description: It can be rather startling to come across a stalk or a cluster of stalks of Pinedrops in the deep woods. The 1–4' stalks are reddish and clammy-sticky and appear leafless (they actually have small, scattered, reddish, scalelike leaves). Off all sides of the upper part of the stem hang many ¼–½", white (or yellowish), bell-shaped, 5-petaled flowers. The arching, red pedicels and the fingerlike red sepals (along with the reddish stalk) create quite a striking (and perhaps rather ominous) look. Having no green leaves, Pinedrops is a saprophyte, receiving its nourishment, with the help of root fungus, from decaying matter in the soil. The dead, reddish brown stalks with dried, reddish brown seedpods hanging from them can stand for a year or two in the forest, silent sentinels and poignant reminders of past blooming. You can sometimes find clusters of new stalks growing up around one of these standing "skeletons"—quite a dramatic image of the cycles of life, death, and rebirth.

Flowering Season: June–August.

Habitat/Range: Deep forest in the montane, 6,500–10,000', in western and eastern Nevada, western Utah, e.g., Peavine Mountain, Ruby Mountains.

Comments: *Pterospora* means "winged seed" in reference to the plant's many wind-dispersed seeds. Andromeda was the daughter of Cassiopeia in Greek mythology.

SPURRED LUPINE
Lupinus arbustus
Pea Family (Fabaceae)

Description: At first glance, spurred lupine looks much like so many of the other *Lupinus* species in the Great Basin. It grows to almost 3' tall, its (1–10") racemes are packed with ½", banner-wings-keel, 5-petaled flowers, and it is quite leafy with many palmately compound leaves on long petioles. However, its flowers do have a characteristic or two that aid immensely in identification. First, though the flowers can be the usual blue, they are often white or yellow, frequently creating masses of bright color in grassy meadows or on dry hillsides. However, even if a lupine has white flowers, it could be several other species, so you need to look carefully at the base of an individual flower for certain identification. As the common name suggests, Spurred Lupine has a very distinct spur at the base of the calyx resembling a rather sharp elbow.

Flowering Season: May–July.

Habitat/Range: Meadows, dry slopes in the sagebrush steppe and the montane, 5,000–10,000', throughout the Great Basin, e.g., Steens Mountain, Great Basin National Park.

Comments: *Lupinus (L. malacophyllus). Arbustus* means "like a small tree."

SOFT LUPINE
Lupinus malacophyllus
Pea Family (Fabaceae)

Description: Soft Lupine is a wonderful name for this plant for at least two reasons: 1) the long, silky hairs covering the leaves, stems, and sepals are soft on the eye and soft to the touch; and 2) the flowers are a creamy white with a hint of blue or are a soft blue. Whether white or blue, the banner often has a pale yellow splotch at its center, frequently with a few blue or black dots. The 3–8" raceme is packed with up to 30 of the 5-petaled flowers. The leaves are mostly basal, each comprised of 5–7 broad leaflets up to 1" long. With its pastel colors and soft hairs, this lupine is one of the most delightful and softly attractive members of the Pea Family.

Flowering Season: April–June.

Habitat/Range: Sandy or gravelly places in the sagebrush steppe, to 6,000', in western Nevada, e.g., Peavine Mountain.

Comments: *Lupinus* is derived from the word for wolf in reference to the mistaken belief that plants of this genus "wolfed up" soil nutrients. (The truth is quite the contrary—being nitrogen fixing, these plants can grow in infertile soil because they fertilize it.) *Malacophyllus* means "soft leaved." Nevada endemic.

209

WHITE SWEET CLOVER
Melilotus alba
Pea Family (Fabaceae)

Description: Plants that grow along roadsides, in vacant lots, or in tangled fields are likely to be invasive weeds and are often viewed with distaste. No doubt weeds can be troublesome and can be threatening to native vegetation (and sometimes to livestock). However, from another point of view, they can be appreciated as individuals with their own beauty and sometimes even with their own contributions. White Sweet Clover can be invasive, but it does have a delicate beauty and (being a pea) can help fertilize the soil. The thick, 1–6' branching stem bears slender, 2–7" racemes of 20–80 tiny, 5-petaled, white flowers that nod (especially in bud) off their peduncle. From the axils where the peduncles branch off the stem are short pedicels bearing a compound leaf with 3 slender, serrated leaflets.

Flowering Season: May–October.

Habitat/Range: Grassy fields, roadsides and other disturbed places in the sagebrush steppe, to 6,500', throughout the Great Basin, e.g., Washoe Valley.

Comments: *Melilotus* means "honey lotus" in reference to another genus *(Lotus)* also in the Pea Family. *Alba* means "white."

SHASTA CLOVER
Trifolium kingii
Pea Family (Fabaceae)

Description: In many ways Shasta Clover is a typical clover with its heads of narrow, tubular flowers, its long, sweeping banner and small wings, and its 3-parted, toothed leaves. You can get lucky with this clover, for sometimes you'll find 4 leaflets (or even 5). Each ½–1½', slender stem bears one ½–1", dense, roundish flower head. The sepals are rose or pink, while the 5 petals tend to be white with a pink tinge. Despite all the many similar species of clover with heads of flowers, Shasta Clover is relatively easy to distinguish, for its flowers are usually hanging downward in a rather moplike head.

Flowering Season: May–August.

Habitat/Range: Grassy meadows, along streambanks in the sagebrush steppe and the montane, to 10,000', throughout the Great Basin, e.g., Charles Sheldon National Wildlife Refuge.

Comments: *Trifolium* means "3-leafed." Clarence King was a 19th-century California geologist and renowned mountaineer. Also known as *T. productum.*

ALPINE GENTIAN
Gentiana newberryi
Gentian Family (Gentianaceae)

Description: One of the very few white-flowered gentian species, Alpine Gentian is an especially spectacular plant despite its small stature (1–4" tall). Most of the plant is flower, as the funnel-shaped bloom can be up to 1½" long. The 5 slightly flaring petal lobes are white (or pale blue) with green spots and with dark, purple-brown bands on the underside. Between the petal lobes are delicate, often blue-tinged fringes (triangular, ragged "sinuses"). The long stamens and the branched pistil are conspicuous inside the open funnel. The ½–2", spoon-shaped leaves are thick and mostly basal. Despite the size and beauty of the flowers, Alpine Gentian can be difficult to spot, for growing so close to the ground, it is often partly hidden by grass and leaves. It sometimes hybridizes with Explorer's Gentian *(G. calycosa)*, producing a blue flower.

Flowering Season: July–September.

Habitat/Range: Grassy meadows, rocky flats in the montane and the alpine, 6,000–12,000', in eastern California, western Nevada, e.g., White Mountains.

Comments: Gentius was a king of ancient Illyria who purportedly used gentians medicinally. John Newberry was a 19th-century American physician and botanist.

MONUMENT PLANT
Swertia radiata
Gentian Family (Gentianaceae)

Description: It is always a surprise to come across Monument Plant, especially on a rocky slope near timberline, for this plant seems much too monumental and ornate for such a harsh environment. Its stout stem can reach 6–7' tall (though 3–4' is more common) and bears scores and scores of 1–2", intricate, flamboyant flowers. Each flower has 4 greenish white petals adorned with red-purple spots along their edges. At the base of the flower is the large, gourdlike, green ovary bordered by pink nectar glands, which are partly concealed by yellow or white hairs. Adding to the amazing show are whorls of long, tonguelike leaves at intervals up the stem interspersed with the blooms. In the first year, usually only the basal leaves appear.

Flowering Season: June–August.

Habitat/Range: Dry flats and slopes, forest openings in the montane, 5,500–11,000', in central and eastern Nevada, southern Oregon, western Utah, e.g., Toiyabe Range, Steens Mountain.

Comments: Emmanuel Sweert was a 16th-century Dutch herbalist. *Radiata* means "radial" in reference to the wheel-like flowers or to the whorled leaves. Also called Deer's Tongue.

RICHARDSON'S GERANIUM
Geranium richardsonii
Geranium Family (Geraniaceae)

Description: The 1–3' plant stem of Richardson's Geranium bears many 2–10", broad, palmately compound leaves, the 5–7 wedge-shaped segments again lobed. In the fall these leaves will turn brilliant scarlet. Toward the tips of the stems are clusters of 1–1½", flat flowers with 5 broad, overlapping, slightly clawed petals. The petals range from white to pale pink with darker red or purple veins. The style column and the pink or red anthers project up ½" or so above the petals. The stems are covered with tiny, bristly hairs tipped with yellow glands. The fruits are narrow, beaked pods.

Flowering Season: June–August.

Habitat/Range: Moist meadows, openings in the sagebrush steppe and the montane, 6,500–10,000', in eastern Nevada, western Utah, e.g., Ruby Mountains.

Comments: *Geranium* means "crane" in reference to the beaklike fruit. John Richardson was a 19th-century Scottish botanist.

WAX CURRANT
Ribes cereum
Gooseberry Family (Grossulariaceae)

Description: Wax Currant is a 1–6' tall, spineless shrub with large, thin, round, shallowly lobed leaves that are delightfully spicy smelling when crushed. As the common and species names suggest, the leaves (on the upper surface) have a waxy sheen. Although this shrub is usually several feet tall and robust at lower elevations, it is often nearly prostrate on exposed, rocky ridges above timberline. The ½–¾", tubular, white or pink flowers hang in clusters of 3–7. The 5 petal lobes are very small and frequently bend back. If you look closely inside the flower tube, you will see the inserted stamens with anthers that have tiny, cuplike depressions. The fruits are ½", red, smooth or sparsely glandular berries that are somewhat toxic, sometimes causing illness if eaten.

Flowering Season: April–August.

Habitat/Range: Dry, rocky slopes, openings in the montane and the alpine, to 12,500', throughout the Great Basin, e.g., Peavine Mountain, Deep Creek Mountains.

Comments: *Ribes* is the ancient Arabic name for plants of this genus. *Cereum* means "waxy" in reference to the upper surface of the leaves.

CALIFORNIA HESPEROCHIRON
Hesperochiron californicus
Waterleaf Family (Hydrophyllaceae)

Description: California Hesperochiron is one of those plants for which no one has thought of a good common name, so the common name was taken directly from the scientific one. It is a charming, ground-hugging plant with 1", funnel-shaped flowers sitting directly on rosettes of shiny, tonguelike, 2–3", basal leaves. The flowers are usually white, often with faint, purplish veins, but the 5 petals are sometimes pink or pale purple. California Hesperochiron is a very unusual member of the Waterleaf Family, for it is not densely hairy, the flowers are not packed into caterpillar-like coils (but are born singly on slender, basal peduncles), and the reproductive parts do not project beyond the petals. Since this plant grows in grassy meadows and its flowers are almost directly on the ground, it can be difficult to spot, but it is well worth finding, for the flowers have a beautiful, delicate color and a satisfying symmetrical form.

Flowering Season: April–June.

Habitat/Range: Damp, grassy meadows in the sagebrush steppe and the montane, 4,500–9,000', in eastern California, Nevada except for the eastern region, southern Oregon, e.g., Washoe Valley, Steens Mountain.

Comments: *Hesperochiron* derives from a word meaning "evening" and from the word Chiron, a mythical centaur skilled in medicine. The significance of these allusions is not clear. *Californicus* means "of California."

DWARF HESPEROCHIRON
Hesperochiron pumilis
Waterleaf Family (Hydrophyllaceae)

Description: Like its close relative California Hesperochiron *(H. californicus)*, Dwarf Hesperochiron is a ground-hugging plant with somewhat bowl-shaped flowers of 5 overlapping petals, which is missing most of the characteristics typical of the Waterleaf Family (the caterpillar-like coils of flowers, the long-protruding reproductive parts, and the hairy stems and sepals). Distinguishing Dwarf Hesperochiron from California Hesperochiron are the smaller, flatter (less funnel-shaped) flowers, the narrower leaves, and the color of the petals—bright white with dark purple veins and a yellow throat instead of faintly veined pale white, pink, or purple. The flowers are usually 5-petaled, but it is not uncommon to find one with 6 petals.

Flowering Season: April–June.

Habitat/Range: Grassy meadows, moist openings in the sagebrush steppe and the montane, to 9,000', in central and northeastern Nevada, southern Oregon, western Utah, e.g., Toiyabe Range, Steens Mountain.

Comments: *Hesperochiron (H. californicus)*. Pumilis means "dwarf."

SILVER-LEAF PHACELIA
Phacelia hastata
Waterleaf Family (Hydrophyllaceae)

Description: There are over 50 species of *Phacelia* in the Great Basin, almost all of which have caterpillar-like cymes of 5-petaled, bowl-shaped flowers with long-protruding reproductive parts. The densely packed clusters of flowers, the long, delicate reproductive parts, and the often hairy leaves create quite an identifiable fuzzy appearance. Silver-Leaf Phacelia has several recognized varieties, some of which inhabit sagebrush flats of relatively low elevations and others of which grow on exposed, rocky ridges above timberline. As you would expect, the higher elevation variety is a smaller (2–8"), more compact plant, while the lower elevation varieties can reach 2' tall. Regardless of variety, Silver-Leaf Phacelia is distinguished from its close kin Vari-Leaf Phacelia *(P. heterophylla)* by its spread-out growth form (branching stems as opposed to

Vari-Leaf Phacelia's stout, unbranched stem) and terminal clusters of 5-petaled flowers (instead of flowers occurring along most of the length of the stem). Often several plants grow together, creating a bed of leaves out of which emerge the stems. The flowers are white, dirty white, or lavender. The elliptic leaves are usually unlobed and are silvery hairy.

Flowering Season: May–August.

Habitat/Range: Sandy, gravelly, or rocky slopes, washes, rocky ridges in the sagebrush steppe, the montane, and the alpine, 5,000–12,000', throughout the Great Basin, e.g., White Mountains, Great Basin National Park.

Comments: *Phacelia (P. heterophylla). Hastata* means "spear shaped" in reference to the pointed leaves. Formerly known as *P. frigida.*

VARI-LEAF PHACELIA
Phacelia heterophylla
Waterleaf Family (Hydrophyllaceae)

Description: The many Great Basin species of *Phacelia* range in habitat from the lowest elevations to the highest windswept peaks above timberline. Many of these species have showy blue or purple flowers, but a few have relatively inconspicuous creamy white or dirty white ones. Vari-Leaf Phacelia is one of these latter species, with coils of ½", creamy white, 5-petaled flowers along most of the length of its ½–3', stout stem. The plant has the usual fuzzy *Phacelia* look to it due to both the bristly hairs on the stem, leaves, and sepals and to the long-protruding reproductive parts. The 2–6", ovate leaves are prominently veined. Some of the lower leaves have small, lateral segments, while others of the lower leaves and most of the upper ones are simple (i.e., without segments).

Flowering Season: May–August.

Habitat/Range: Dry flats and slopes in the sagebrush steppe and the montane, to 8,500', in eastern California, western and northern Nevada, e.g., Sweetwater Mountains, Santa Rosa Range.

Comments: *Phacelia* means "cluster" in reference to the densely flowered inflorescences. *Heterophylla* means "variable leaved."

SEGO LILY
Calochortus bruneaunis
Lily Family (Liliaceae)

Description: In a genus of spectacular, colorful flowers, Sego Lily certainly doesn't disappoint. Its three 1–1½", overlapping petals are bright white and provide a dramatic backdrop for the array of colors inside the flower. The base of the bowl (on all 3 petals) is intense yellow; the round nectar glands are tinged red; and above the glands are maroon arches or spots. To complete the colorful display, the long, oblong anthers are pink or reddish brown (sometimes yellowish or bluish) and the 3-parted stigma is pink or rose. Often there will be a pale green, vertical stripe down the center of the underside of the petals. The 4–16" plant bears 1–4 flowers and a few, long, grasslike leaves that wither early.

Flowering Season: May–July.

Habitat/Range: Sandy or rocky flats and slopes in the sagebrush steppe, to 7,000', throughout the Great Basin, e.g., Sweetwater Mountains, Great Basin National Park.

Comments: *Calochortus* means "beautiful grass." *Bruneaunis* refers to the Bruneau River in Idaho, where the plant was first named. Sometimes considered a variety of *C. nuttallii*.

BIGPOD MARIPOSA LILY
Calochortus eurycarpus
Lily Family (Liliaceae)

Description: Great Basin mariposa lilies can be pink, lavender, orange, or white. Regardless of their primary color, they are usually multicolored, for the nectar gland at the base of each of the 3 petals and/or the band or splotch over each gland is usually a different color than the petals. In no Great Basin mariposa lily species is this color contrast more strikingly beautiful than in Bigpod Mariposa Lily. In the middle of each bright white petal is a somewhat triangular splotch of intense red-purple. At the base of each of the petals is a circular, yellow gland over which are a few very slender, squiggly hairs. Look carefully at one of these hairs and you will notice that even it is multicolored—purple at the base and yellow at the tip.

Flowering Season: June–August.

Habitat/Range: Grasslands, dry hillsides, openings in the sagebrush steppe and the montane, to 7,000', in eastern Nevada, southern Oregon, e.g., Steens Mountain, Ruby Mountains.

Comments: *Calochortus (C. bruneaunis)*. *Eurycarpus* means "broad-fruited."

LEICHTLIN'S MARIPOSA LILY
Calochortus leichtlinii
Lily Family (Liliaceae)

Description: Leichtlin's Mariposa Lily is the highest elevation species of *Calochortus* in the Great Basin. What a delight to find this showy, multicolored beauty brightening up a sandy slope high in the mountains (e.g., the Sweetwaters) along the western edge of the basin. The 3 rounded petals are bright white with yellow splotches at their base. The nectar glands are largely hidden by short, yellow hairs above which are dark maroon or almost black triangular splotches. The long, arrow-shaped anthers and the 3-branched stigma are creamy white or yellowish. The 8–24" plant bears 1–5 flowers and a few scattered, 4–6", grasslike leaves.

Flowering Season: June–August.

Habitat/Range: Sandy or gravelly slopes and ridges in the montane, 6,000–10,000', in eastern California and western Nevada, e.g., Sweetwater Mountains, Peavine Mountain.

Comments: *Calochortus (C. bruneaunis)*. Max Leichtlin was a 19th-century German horticulturist.

STAR-FLOWERED FALSE SOLOMON'S SEAL
Smilacina stellata
Lily Family (Liliaceae)

Description: With its broad, smooth, parallel-veined, dark green leaves and its loose racemes of pure white, star-shaped flowers, Star-Flowered False Solomon's Seal looks almost preppy—clean and crisp and freshly scrubbed. Several of the 2–8" long, pointed leaves, which can be up to 2" wide, clasp and alternate up the stout, 1–2½' stem. The leaves are often infolded. Just above the top leaves rises the loose, 1–4" raceme of 5–20 flowers, each one of which is at the end of an up-angled, ¼–½" pedicel. The 6 tepals and the pistil of each ½" flower are pure white, while the anthers are yellow. A particularly graceful touch is the slight zigzagging of the plant stem between the leaves and the echoing zigzagging of the raceme stem between the flowers. Since these plants sprout from rhizomes, you will often find great thickets of them in moist openings in the woods. The berries are black at maturity.

Flowering Season: April–July.

Habitat/Range: Shaded moist places in the montane, to 10,500', throughout the Great Basin, e.g., White Mountains, Great Basin National Park.

Comments: *Smilacina* means "little *Smilax*," which is another genus in the Lily Family. *Stellata* means "star" in reference to the 6-pointed flowers.

HYACINTH BRODIAEA
Triteleia hyacintha
Lily Family (Liliaceae)

Description: Although its leaves, like many plants in the Lily Family, are decidedly grasslike and so easily blend in with the grass in the fields and meadows where it grows, Hyacinth Brodiaea still stands out and can be spotted at quite a distance because of its showy cluster of white flowers with black-purple midveins (more conspicuous on the undersides of the 6 tepals, so more noticeable on flowers in bud). The ½" flowers (up to 30) are arranged in a beautiful, tight umbel with each flower at the end of its own ½–1½" "umbrella spoke." For much of the blooming season, the umbel will include some flowers wide open in bloom (around the periphery) and some still tight in bud (toward the center). The combination of bright white, open flowers and the dramatically black-purple striped buds creates a stunning bouquet. The 1 or 2 grasslike leaves can be up to 1½' long, while the plant stem can reach 2'.

Flowering Season: May–July.

Habitat/Range: Wet meadows, grassy fields, rocky flats in the sagebrush steppe, to 7,000', in western and northwestern Nevada, southern Oregon, e.g., Charles Sheldon National Wildlife Refuge, Steens Mountain.

Comments: *Triteleia* means "3 complete," probably in reference to the 3 stigma lobes. *Hyacintha* means "hyacinth-like." Formerly known as *Brodiaea hyacintha*. Also called Wild Hyacinth.

CORN LILY
Veratrum californicum
Lily Family (Liliaceae)

Description: In early spring (which can be as late as July in very high elevations) in meadows still soggy from snowmelt, you will often come across clumps or even huge masses of the unfurling leaves of Corn Lily. Some people have confused these large (up to 16" long and 8" wide) leaves with those of Skunk Cabbage (which are edible). Do not make this mistake—Corn Lily is *toxic* and can poison or even kill! Even drinking water in which the plants grow can cause serious stomach cramps. As the leaves unfold, their resemblance to skunk cabbage disappears, for Corn Lily leaves are smooth, pointed, and (as all lily leaves) parallel veined. Since Corn Lily grows from a rhizome, you will usually find masses or even entire fields of this plant; however, this might not result in a field of flowers, for the plants don't flower every year and some of the plants are just leaf stalks and so will never flower. But when the plants do flower, you are in for a spectacular treat—the 1–2' raceme can bear hundreds of the 1", star-shaped flowers. At the base of each of the 6 white tepals is a Y-shaped, green gland giving the flowers a greenish tint.

Flowering Season: June–August.

Habitat/Range: Streambanks, wet meadows, lake edges in the montane, to 11,500', throughout the Great Basin, e.g., White Mountains, Steens Mountain.

Comments: *Veratrum* means "true black" in reference to the black rhizomes of some species. *Californicum* means "of California."

ELEGANT CAMAS
Zigadenus elegans
Lily Family (Liliaceae)

Description: Elegant Camas has the same general look as the other two Great Basin species of *Zigadenus (Z. paniculatus, Z. venenosus)* with its long, infolded, grasslike leaves, its ½–2½' fleshy stem, and its cluster of ½" white flowers. However, it tends to have a sparser look than the other 2 species with its shorter leaves and (usually) fewer flowers in the cluster. As with the other two species, the glands at the base of the 6 tepals are yellow-green, but the anthers of Elegant Camas are the same white as the tepals, giving the flowers a subtler, more delicate appearance than the yellow-anthered *Z. paniculatus*. As with all *Zigadenus* species, Elegant Camas is *poisonous,* so don't get any ideas about eating its bulbs (or any part of the plant).

Flowering Season: June–August.

Habitat/Range: Marshy meadows, grassy openings in the montane and the alpine, 5,000–13,000', in central and eastern Nevada, southern Oregon, western Utah, e.g., Toiyabe Range, Great Basin National Park.

Comments: *Zigadenus (Z. paniculatus). Elegans* means "elegant."

SAND CORM
Zigadenus paniculatus
Lily Family (Liliaceae)

Description: Of the 3 species of death camas you will find in the Great Basin, *Z. paniculatus* is distinguishable by its bright yellow-orange anthers and its dry, sagebrush habitat. Otherwise, it is quite similar to the other two *Zigadenus* species *(Z. elegans, Z. venenosus)* with its long, infolded, grasslike leaves, its ½–2' fleshy stem, and its ½" white flowers. In all 3 species, the white flowers have a bit of a greenish look because of the green or yellow-green glands at the base of the 6 tepals. Sand Corm has a broadly cylindrical inflorescence dense with flowers. The stamens are a little longer than the tepals and usually stick almost straight up out of the flower bowl, displaying the colorful anthers with a flourish. As with all *Zigadenus* species, Sand Corm is *poisonous* to livestock and to humans.

Flowering Season: March–June.

Habitat/Range: Dry slopes, openings in the sagebrush steppe and the montane, 4,500–9,000', throughout the Great Basin except central Nevada, e.g., Charles Sheldon National Wildlife Refuge, Great Basin National Park.

Comments: *Zigadenus* (also spelled *Zygadenus*) means "yoke gland" in reference to the greenish yellow glands arranged in pairs at the base of the tepals. *Paniculatus* means "panicled" in reference to the branching inflorescence.

221

DEATH CAMAS
Zigadenus venenosus
Lily Family (Liliaceae)

Description: *Z. venenosus* may be the most spectacular of the 3 Great Basin species of *Zigadenus,* for its ½–2½' fleshy stem is stout and bears a densely flowered, conical raceme of flowers that can be up to 8" long. With their 6 creamy white tepals, green ovaries, yellow-green glands, and often sparkling nectar, the flowers have a lush, edible look, but don't even think about eating any part of this plant. As the species name indicates, this plant (as all *Zigadenus* species) is extremely *poisonous.* In fact, *Z. venenosus* is responsible for a great many sheep deaths as its leaves are easily confused (by sheep and herders alike) with other, nontoxic, grasslike plants. The anthers protrude out of the flowers but don't really stand out as they are the same creamy white as the tepals.

Flowering Season: April–July.

Habitat/Range: Creekbanks, damp meadows, openings in the sagebrush steppe and the montane, to 8,000', throughout the Great Basin except central and eastern Nevada, e.g., Peavine Mountain, Steens Mountain.

Comments: *Zigadenus (Z. paniculatus). Venenosus* means "very poisonous."

BUCKBEAN
Menyanthes trifoliata
Buckbean Family (Menyanthaceae)

Description: Where you see one Buckbean, you are likely to see many—and what an unusual and fascinating sight it is, especially since you'll probably be standing at least ankle-deep in water or very spongy ground at the time! Buckbean thrives in bogs or shallow water, so you will have to "take the plunge" to get close to this beauty. As you approach a plant, you'll see that the ½–1½' stem ends in a raceme of many of the bright white flowers. Then you'll see the intrigue—each ½–1", star-shaped flower is covered with erect, threadlike, white hairs lining the 5 petals. And in startling contrast, the 5 stamens on the edge of the flower throat rising above the hairs are black, often covered with golden pollen, while the 2-parted stigma in the center of the throat is fleshy and greenish yellow. As the species name indicates, the broad, basal leaves have 3 leaflets.

Flowering Season: May–August.

Habitat/Range: Bogs, lake edges, shallow ponds in the montane, 6,500–9,000', in eastern Nevada, e.g., Ruby Mountains.

Comments: *Menyanthes* means "month flower," probably in reference to the approximate blooming time. *Trifoliata* means "3-leaved."

BROWN-EYED EVENING PRIMROSE
Camissonia claviformis
Evening Primrose Family (Onagraceae)

Description: Although all the evening primroses bloom for only one "day," some open in the late afternoon or early evening and bloom for one night, while others open in the morning and wilt before nightfall. Most *Oenothera* species are night blooming, while most *Camissonia* species are day blooming, but Brown-Eyed Evening Primrose is one of the unusual *Camissonia* species that is open mostly during the hours of darkness. The ½–1", white (sometimes yellow), 4-petaled flowers are distinguished by a maroon, red, or brown eye in their center. The protruding anthers are a creamy yellow, and the globelike stigma (which distinguishes the *Camissonia* genus from the *Oenothera* genus) is cream or greenish. The flowers are thickly clustered, especially in bud when they nod tightly together. The seedpod, as the species name indicates, forms a thick, ascending cylinder.

Flowering Season: May–July.

Habitat/Range: Sandy or rocky flats and slopes in the desert shrub and the sagebrush steppe, to 6,500', throughout the Great Basin, e.g., White Mountains, Steens Mountain.

Comments: L. A. von Chamisso was a French-born German botanist of the late 18th and early 19th centuries. *Claviformis* means "club shaped" in reference to the fruit.

NEVADA EVENING PRIMROSE
Camissonia nevadensis
Evening Primrose Family (Onagraceae)

Description: Nevada Evening Primrose is easily recognized as a species of *Camissonia* by its 4 separate, diamond-shaped petals, its reflexed sepals, and its globular stigma. True to its family name, but atypical for its genus, this plant is vespertine (i.e., the flower opens in late afternoon or evening and wilts by the following morning). The ½–¾" white flowers resemble those of several species of *Camissonia,* but its growth form is quite distinctive. Several (often reddish) stems radiate out along the ground from a central taproot, and then curve up at the tips to create a short spike (only a couple inches high) that bears a cluster of flowers and narrow leaves. Often these flower and leaf clusters will be quite separate, looking a bit like floral footsteps sneaking cross the flats.

Flowering Season: April–May.

Habitat/Range: Sandy, gravelly, or clayey (often alkaline) flats in the desert shrub and the sagebrush steppe, 4,000–6,500', in western Nevada, e.g., Virginia Range, Pyramid Lake.

Comments: *Camissonia (C. claviformis). Nevadensis* means "of Nevada."

DIFFUSE GAYOPHYTUM

Gayophytum diffusum
Evening-Primrose Family (Onagraceae)

Description: With its tiny (⅛–¼"), white flowers and its slender stems, Diffuse Gayophytum could easily be overlooked; however, when you do notice one plant, you are likely to see many, for they usually grow in large masses in dry openings in the woods. And it is well worth finding this plant, for it has a delicate, graceful appearance and intriguing flowers. The slender, 4–20", reddish, branching stems are a perfect complement for the linear, bright green, often red-margined leaves. The tiny, white flowers with their 4 petals in a cross open in the morning and wither red by evening. Since the flowers are also red in bud, their brief life cycle creates a certain satisfying sense of coming full circle.

Flowering Season: May–September.

Habitat/Range: Sandy flats and slopes, openings in the sagebrush steppe and the montane, to 10,000', throughout the Great Basin, e.g., Peavine Mountain, Deep Creek Mountains.

Comments: Claude Gay was a 19th-century French botanist. *Diffusum* means "spread out" in reference to the delicate, branching stems.

TUFTED EVENING PRIMROSE
Oenothera caespitosa
Evening Primrose Family (Onagraceae)

Description: Of all the showy, white evening primroses in the Great Basin, Tufted Evening Primrose is certainly one of the most spectacular—its flowers are huge (up to 4½" across) and usually lie on or close to the ground (as the species name suggests, the plant has a short, sprawling stem). Even from a speeding car, you will probably spot these flowers painting the ground with large, bright white splotches often tinged with pink or rose (the wilted blossoms). As with most *Oenothera* species, the blooms open at dusk and wilt the following morning. To attract night pollinators (moths), these night-blooming flowers have nectar and are strongly and deliciously fragrant. Their pollen is profuse and sticky-stringy to facilitate being carried by the moths (or sometimes by prowling wildflower lovers, inset photo). There are numerous varieties of this species with leaves of varying shapes (but usually toothed) and various surfaces (i.e., hairy or smooth). The large, reddish sepals reflex when the flowers open.

Flowering Season: April–August.

Habitat/Range: Sandy or gravelly flats, along roads in desert shrub, the sagebrush steppe, and the montane, to 10,500', throughout the Great Basin, e.g., Peavine Mountain, Great Basin National Park.

Comments: *Oenothera (O. deltoides). Caespitosa* means "tufted" or "prostrate." Also called Sand-Lily and Fragrant Evening Primrose.

BIRDCAGE EVENING PRIMROSE
Oenothera deltoides
Evening Primrose Family (Onagraceae)

Description: The evening primroses (genera *Oenothera* and *Camissonia*) are among the Great Basin's most spectacular and fascinating flowers, treasured all the more for their brief bloom. Birdcage Evening Primrose is especially beautiful and intriguing, both for its massive flower displays (often covering many square yards of sandy flats or dunes) and for the bizarre shape of old plants with outer stems that curve inward to form baskets or cages (inset photo). The stout, pithy plant stem (up to 2' tall) is covered with whitish "bark" that eventually exfoliates. The leaves are long, narrow, and pointed and are often toothed. The 4-petaled, 1½–2½" flowers are bright white with slightly yellow centers. The crinkly anthers and long, slender, 4-parted stigma are creamy yellow. As with many *Oenothera* species, the flowers of Birdcage Evening Primrose open in late afternoon or evening and fade pink or lavender in the morning. Also like most *Oenothera* species, they are deliciously fragrant.

Flowering Season: April–June.

Habitat/Range: Sandy flats, dunes in the desert shrub and sagebrush steppe, to 5,000', in western Nevada, southern Oregon, and western Utah, e.g., Pyramid Lake, Steens Mountain.

Comments: *Oenothera* means "wine scented." *Deltoides* means "triangular," in reference to the diamond-shaped leaves. Also called Dune Primrose, Devil's Lantern, Basket Evening Primrose, and Lion-in-a-Cage.

WHITE REIN-ORCHID
Platanthera leucostachys
Orchid Family (Orchidaceae)

Description: White Rein-Orchid is a much more conspicuous plant than its close relative, Green Bog Orchid *(P. sparsiflora)*, primarily because of the color of its flowers (bright white), but also because of its height (to over 3') and its long (up to 15"), densely flowered inflorescence. The upper sepal and upper 2 petals form a hood over the reproductive parts, the lower 2 sepals extend out as wings, and the lower petal forms a lip that broadens at the base (the meaning of the former species name *dilatata*) and extends into a gracefully curving spur, which can be up to twice as long as the lip. The narrow, parallel-veined leaves clasp the stem and alternate up it. The leaves on the lower half of the stem are much larger and more profuse than those higher up.

Flowering Season: June–August.

Habitat/Range: Wet meadows, streambanks, bogs in the montane and the alpine, 6,000–11,500', throughout the Great Basin, e.g., Peavine Mountain, Ruby Mountains.

Comments: *Platanthera* means "wide anther." *Leucostachys* means "white ear of corn" in reference to the densely flowered raceme. Formerly known as *Habenaria dilatata*. Also called Sierra Rein-Orchid.

PRICKLY POPPY
Argemone munita
Poppy Family (Papaveraceae)

Description: Of all the showy flowers of the Great Basin that tend to grow along roads, Prickly Poppy may be the most common and widespread. Along practically any road—frequented or deserted—you have a good chance of finding this ubiquitous plant, often with very little else blooming around it. And what a wonderful flower to be so common! Its 6 (sometimes 4) crepe-papery, snowy white petals form a bowl that can be 3" across; its clump of 150–200 stamens is a dazzling orange or yellow; and the pistil is topped by a globular, maroon stigma that displays itself proudly above the surrounding stamens. The 2–5' plant stem, the lobed leaves, and the calyx are all covered with silvery or brown prickles. These spines and the plant's poisonous alkaloids are strong deterrents to grazing herbivores.

Flowering Season: March–August.

Habitat/Range: Sandy or gravelly flats in the desert shrub, the sagebrush steppe, and the montane, to 9,000', throughout the Great Basin, e.g., Washoe Valley, Great Basin National Park.

Comments: *Argemone* means "cataract of the eye," an affliction that some species purportedly can remedy. *Munita* means "armed" in reference to the spines.

STEER'S HEAD
Dicentra uniflora
Poppy Family (Papaveraceae)

Description: Count yourself fortunate if you get to see the flowers of Steer's Head, for the plant is uncommon in the Great Basin and is difficult to find (for several reasons) even in places where it does occur. First, the plant is an early bloomer, so you'll have to be out looking for it before much else is blooming. Second, the lacy leaves are usually a bit apart from the flowers, growing on their own separate stem. Third, the flowers are small (½"), solitary, and close to the ground (at the tips of 1–3" stems) and their pink-tinged white color blends easily into their gravelly habitat. But despite all this, Steer's Head is well worth seeking, for (as the common name suggests) its flowers are fascinating, eerily resembling the bleached skull of a cow. The inner 2 petals of the 4 form the tapering snout, while the outer 2 curve back to form the horns. Although a flower of Steer's Head may appear to signal the end for some unfortunate miniature cow, it actually signals the beginning of another flower season—a good sign indeed!

Flowering Season: April–June.

Habitat/Range: Gravelly flats and slopes in the montane, 6,500–9,000', in western and northeastern Nevada, southern Oregon, western Utah, e.g., Santa Rosa Range, Steens Mountain.

Comments: *Dicentra* means "twice spurred" in reference to the outer petals. *Uniflora* means "single flower."

FRINGED GRASS-OF-PARNASSUS
Parnassia fimbriata
Grass-of-Parnassus Family (Parnassiaceae)

Description: Fringed Grass-of-Parnassus is as dramatic and exotic looking as its name, for its ½–1" flower has delicate, white, yellow-tipped threads fringing the 5 large petals. Each slender, ½–2' stem bears only one of these wonderful flowers at its tip, although usually many plants grow together, creating a small Grass-of-Parnassus "forest." The leaves are mostly basal and heart shaped; sometimes there is one additional leaf clasping the stem at or above its midpoint. This species shares many characteristics with members of the Saxifrage Family, of which it was considered to be a part until recently placed in its own family.

Flowering Season: June–October.

Habitat/Range: Wet meadows, streambanks, often in rocks in the montane, 6,000–11,000', in central and eastern Nevada, e.g., Toiyabe Range, Ruby Mountains.

Comments: *Parnassia* refers to Mt. Parnassus in Greece, mistakenly thought by an early Greek naturalist to be the home of a *Parnassia* species. *Fimbriata* means "fringed" in reference to the petals.

BALL-HEAD GILIA
Ipomopsis congesta
Phlox Family (Polemoniaceae)

Description: Although an individual flower of Ball-Head Gilia (with its 5 white petal lobes flaring out of the flower tube) is easily recognizable as a member of the Phlox Family, the small size of the flowers and the tight, spherical flower heads can easily throw you off. The tiny (⅛–¼" across) flowers are crammed into the flower heads, creating a bit of a jumbly, overlapping mess. The petals are dirty white, sometimes with purple flecks. The flower tubes are difficult to see as they barely protrude out of the sepals. Most of the leaves of this dwarf plant form a low mat above which rise 4–8", often red stems. You can find Ball-Head Gilia occasionally among sagebrush at lower elevations, but sometimes on rocky or gravelly exposed flats near or above timberline you will find great gardens of this plant almost evenly spaced over the rocky terrain.

Flowering Season: June–August.

Habitat/Range: Sandy, gravelly, or rocky places in the sagebrush steppe, the montane, and the alpine, to 12,000', throughout the Great Basin, e.g., White Mountains, Steens Mountain.

Comments: *Ipomopsis* means "striking appearance." *Congesta* means "congested" in reference to the densely flowered flower heads. Sometimes known as *Gilia congesta*.

PRICKLY PHLOX
Leptodactylon pungens
Phlox Family (Polemoniaceae)

Description: Prickly Phlox is a bit like a taller, shrubby version of Spreading Phlox *(P. diffusa)*. Both plants grow in rocky areas in the mountains, both have prickly, needlelike leaves, and both have white, tubular flowers. However, there are some very noticeable differences between these two fragrant-flowered members of the Phlox Family. First, as mentioned, Prickly Phlox is a shrub that can reach 2–3' tall, while Spreading Phlox forms a low cushion or mat. Second, the flowers of Prickly Phlox have longer tubes and rarely fully open, so they look more like spiraling funnels than the flat pinwheels of Spreading Phlox. Third, although Spreading Phlox can have white, pink, or lavender flowers, the flowers of Prickly Phlox are almost always white with some pink or pale lavender wash on the outside of the petals. Lastly, Prickly Phlox not only grows in rocky areas above timberline, but extends all the way down to the desert shrub—an amazing elevational range.

Flowering Season: May–August.

Habitat/Range: Sandy or rocky slopes, rock ledges, gravelly flats in the desert shrub, the sagebrush steppe, the montane, and the alpine, to 13,000', throughout the Great Basin, e.g., Fly Canyon, Great Basin National Park.

Comments: *Leptodactylon* means "slender finger" in reference to the leaf segments. *Pungens* means "sharp pointed" also in reference to the leaves. Also called Granite Gilia.

NUTTALL'S LINANTHUS
Linanthrastrum nuttallii
Phlox Family (Polemoniaceae)

Description: In the *Phlox* genus and in several other genera in the Phlox Family, there are many species of low, mound-forming or cushion-forming plants with stiff, linear leaves and white (to pink or lavender), tubular flowers. Nuttall's Linanthus is an interesting example of this type of plant, which has been placed in its own genus *(Linanthrastrum)* because its leaves are different than those of its fellow Phlox family genera (they are stiffer than *Linanthus* species but softer than *Leptodactylon* species). It is a striking plant with extensive, densely flowered mats that bring bright color to the rocks and forest openings that they carpet. The 5 (sometimes 6) white petals are narrower than those of many of its close relatives. The bright yellow anthers protrude slightly from the yellow flower tube. The leaves consist of 5–9 linear segments that are in whorls around the stem.

Flowering Season: June–August.

Habitat/Range: Rocky places, open slopes in the sagebrush steppe and the montane, to 11,000', throughout the Great Basin, e.g., White Mountains, Ruby Mountains.

Comments: *Linanthrastrum* means "bearing a partial resemblance to *Linanthus*," which is another genus in the Phlox Family. *Linanthus* means "flax flower." Thomas Nuttall was a distinguished, 19th-century, English-born naturalist. Also known as *Linanthus nuttallii*.

SLENDER PHLOX
Microsteris gracilis
Phlox Family (Polemoniaceae)

Description: Although some botanists consider this tiny-flowered plant a species of *Phlox*, most separate it into its own genus *Microsteris,* of which it is the only species. The slender, 2–12" stem can be unbranched or much-branched and bears opposite pairs of ½–1", narrow leaves. The stem is often sparsely sticky-hairy. The ½" flower tube, though short, is long compared to the width of the ⅛–¼" flower, although this may not be immediately apparent since the long, fingerlike, hairy sepals conceal almost all of the tube. The 5 white or bright pink petal lobes are slightly notched at the tips, creating a bit of a heart shape. These tiny flowers often hide in the grass, but once you see one, you usually will see many.

Flowering Season: March–July.

Habitat/Range: Grassy meadows in the sagebrush steppe and the montane, to 8,000', throughout the Great Basin, e.g., Charles Sheldon National Wildlife Refuge, Steens Mountain.

Comments: *Microsteris* means "small support," presumably in reference to the plant's small size. *Gracilis* means "slender." Sometimes known as *Phlox gracilis.*

COMPACT PHLOX
Phlox condensata
Phlox Family (Polemoniaceae)

Description: The flowers of Compact Phlox are quite similar to those of Spreading Phlox *(P. diffusa)* with which it sometimes grows, but the growth form of these two species is decidedly different. Both plants have pinwheel-like, white, pink, or lavender, 5-petaled flowers that often grow so dense on the plant that they completely hide the leaves, though the ¼–½" flowers of Compact Phlox are a bit smaller than those of Spreading Phlox. While Spreading Phlox forms a relatively loose, low mound, Compact Phlox forms an incredibly tight, dense cushion that hugs the rocks on which it grows. These amazing cushions create a "fortress" that other plants may have great difficulty competing with, and a shelter from the cold and wind of the alpine environment for some insects.

Flowering Season: July–August.

Habitat/Range: Rocky slopes and ridges in the montane and the alpine, 6,000–12,000', in eastern California, Nevada, e.g., Toiyabe Range, Ruby Mountains.

Comments: *Phlox (P. hoodii). Condensata* means "compacted."

SPREADING PHLOX
Phlox diffusa
Phlox Family (Polemoniaceae)

Description: Spreading Phlox is one of the several prickly, mat-forming *Phlox* species that light up dry, sandy or rocky areas in the Great Basin. Like Cushion Phlox *(P. hoodii)*, its ½–¾", white, pink, or lavender flowers can grow so dense on the mat that it's difficult to see the leaves. The 5-petaled flowers of these two *Phlox* species are nearly identical (though the petals of Spreading Phlox are a little less rounded and more diamond-shaped), but the leaves of Spreading Phlox are not as stiff or as hairy as those of Cushion Phlox (though they are still needlelike and sharp tipped). Also the elevational range of Spreading Phlox is considerably broader than that of Cushion Phlox, occurring from sagebrush flats to rocky ridges above timberline. Spreading Phlox is an early spring bloomer no matter where it's growing, welcoming spring in March or April in lower elevations and in July or August above timberline.

Flowering Season: March–August.

Habitat/Range: Dry, sandy or rocky places in the sagebrush steppe, the montane, and the alpine, 6,000–13,500', in western and northwestern Nevada, eastern California, southern Oregon, e.g., White Mountains, Charles Sheldon National Wildlife Refuge.

Comments: *Phlox (P. hoodii)*. *Diffusa* means "spreading."

CUSHION PHLOX
Phlox hoodii
Phlox Family (Polemoniaceae)

Description: The Great Basin has numerous species of *Phlox*, many of which form low mounds or cushions with needlelike leaves and white or pink or lavender flowers. Many of these species reach up into the high mountains, sometimes even above timberline. *Phlox hoodii,* on the other hand, is the most common dwarf phlox of the sagebrush steppe in the Great Basin, rarely occurring above 8,500'. Cushion Phlox forms a mat or low cushion that often is so dense with the overlapping ½–¾" flowers that you have a difficult time seeing the leaves. The pinwheel flowers are bright white or pink-purple with yellow throats and yellow anthers sunk into the flower tube. The tiny, spine-tipped leaves are usually sticky-hairy.

Flowering Season: April–June.

Habitat/Range: Dry, sandy or gravelly places in the sagebrush steppe, 4,500–8,500', throughout the Great Basin, e.g., Sweetwater Mountains, Deep Creek Mountains.

Comments: *Phlox* means "flame" in reference to the brightly colored flowers of some species. It is not certain who Hood was. Also called Carpet Phlox.

LONG-LEAF PHLOX
Phlox longifolia
Phlox Family (Polemoniaceae)

Description: One of the numerous *Phlox* species with white or pink flowers, Long-Leaf Phlox does not have the cushion or mat growth form or the tiny, prickly leaves of many of its kin. Rather it has 4–16" stems that often grow up through surrounding shrubs and has narrow (but not needlelike), long (1–4"), pointed, sticky-hairy leaves. The 5 petals of the ½–1½" flowers are somewhat clawed (i.e., narrowest at the base) and are sometimes a bit heart shaped. The flowers are sweetly scented and can be pure white, pure pink, or some of each color. The yellow anthers protrude slightly out of the flower tube. The sepals are almost as long as the flower tube and conceal most of it.

Flowering Season: April–July.

Habitat/Range: Dry, sandy or rocky places in the sagebrush steppe and the montane, to 8,000', throughout the Great Basin, e.g., Peavine Mountain, Great Basin National Park.

Comments: *Phlox (P. hoodii). Longifolia* means "long leaf." Considered by some botanists to be the same as *P. stansburyi*.

233

ONION-HEAD BUCKWHEAT
Eriogonum latens
Buckwheat Family (Polygonaceae)

Description: Although many buckwheats have large, more-or-less spherical clusters of tiny flowers at the tips of leafless or nearly leafless stems (i.e., scapes), the clusters (heads) of Onion-Head Buckwheat are unusually large and showy. At the tip of each smooth, 4–20" scape is a ball-like head of creamy white or pale yellow flowers that can be up to 2" wide. Each flower has 6 petal-like sepals. The stamens, with their tiny, yellow or cream anthers, protrude from the flowers, creating a fuzzy look. Especially above timberline, where most plants and flowers tend to be rather small, the beefy, fuzzy flower heads of Onion-Head Buckwheat can be quite striking and even startling. The basal leaves are large, round, leathery, and deep green, often forming a mat 1' or more in diameter.

Flowering Season: June–August.

Habitat/Range: Talus slopes, rocky flats in the montane and the alpine, 8,000–12,000', in eastern California, western Nevada, e.g., White Mountains.

Comments: *Eriogonum (E. spergulinum). Latens* means "hiding."

NUDE BUCKWHEAT
Eriogonum nudum
Buckwheat Family (Polygonaceae)

Description: For buckwheats, it's not unusual to be "nude"—many species have leafless stems rising above basal leaves. However, Nude Buckwheat may look more naked than most, for it is taller than most of its kin (up to 5'), it has no leaflike bracts under the flower heads or anywhere along the stems, and its roundish flower heads tend to be rather small (½" across). Though its tiny flowers are a somewhat dull white, this is nonetheless a showy plant, for the reddish anthers add a sprinkle of color, and the many-branched stems add architectural interest. The large, broad, basal leaves are dark green and have long petioles.

Flowering Season: June–September.

Habitat/Range: Dry slopes and flats in the sagebrush steppe and the montane, 6,000–8,000', in eastern California, western Nevada, e.g., Peavine Mountain. This species occurs mostly in the Sierra Nevada.

Comments: *Eriogonum (E. spergulium). Nudum* means "nude" in reference to the leafless stems.

ALTERED-ANDESITE BUCKWHEAT
Eriogonum robustum
Buckwheat Family (Polygonaceae)

Description: Altered-Andesite Buckwheat, though a Nevada endemic that grows only in the specialized environment of altered andesite soils, is in many other ways a typical *Eriogonum* species. It is a low plant with oval, basal leaves that form a thick rosette. Often several plants grow together, creating a mound more than a foot in diameter. Rising above the basal leaves are stout, 2–8" stems bearing densely flowered umbels of white, creamy, greenish or rose, papery flowers, each with 6 petal-like sepals. Beneath the flower umbels are narrow, leaflike bracts. It is unusual, however, not only for its habitat, but also for its especially large leaves (the blades are 1–3" long and almost as wide), which are densely covered with matted, gray hairs. It is sometimes considered to be a variety of *E. lobbii*, so it is not surprising that it looks very much like a White-Flowered Lobb's Buckwheat (but with larger leaves and with erect, rather than prostrate, flower heads).

Flowering Season: May–July.

Habitat/Range: Dry, altered-andesite soils in the sagebrush steppe, to 7,500', in western Nevada, e.g., Virginia Range.

Comments: *Eriogonum (E. spergulium). Robustum* means "robust" in reference to the large, showy plant. Sometimes known as *E. lobbii* var. *robustum.*

SPURRY BUCKWHEAT
Eriogonum spergulinum
Buckwheat Family (Polygonaceae)

Description: Spurry Buckwheat is a good illustration of how important it is to look at an individual flower in order to identify a plant. Most buckwheat species have spherical or cylindrical clusters of flowers at the tips of or in the axils of fairly stout stems, which rise above broad, mostly basal leaves. Spurry Buckwheat is nothing like this! Its 2–16" stem is extremely slender with many branches, at the tips of which are tiny (⅛") individual flowers. The stem leaves (and some basal leaves) are short and needlelike. The entire plant has a fragile, wispy look. Even though the plant may not look like a typical buckwheat, the flowers do—6, crepe-papery sepals (white) with red midveins. The threadlike stems are usually reddish as well.

Flowering Season: June–September.

Habitat/Range: Sandy or gravelly flats, washes in the montane, 5,000–9,200', in eastern California, western and northwestern Nevada, southern Oregon, e.g., Wassuk Range.

Comments: *Eriogonum* means "wooly knees." *Spergulinum* means "scatter net," probably in reference to the network of branching, wiry stems on each plant.

WESTERN BISTORT
Polygonum bistortoides
Buckwheat Family (Polygonaceae)

Description: Although the individual flowers of bistort, like those of most buckwheats, are quite small (¼"), they form dense, thumblike clusters that can bring quite a bit of brightness to wet, grassy mountain meadows. The ½–2' plants grow from rhizomes so tend to form extensive stands of bright white (sometimes pinkish) flower heads that can be seen from a long away off. Despite their long-range visibility, however, these plants may announce their presence to your nose before your eyes. Depending on how sensitive your nose is and how you feel about the aroma of dirty laundry, you may notice a faint sweet fragrance sprinkling the air or a heavy, sickly, dirty-socks aroma oppressing it! Each tiny flower has 5 petal-like sepals.

Flowering Season: May–August.

Habitat/Range: Wet meadows, streambanks in the montane, 7,000–10,000', throughout the Great Basin, e.g., Steens Mountain, Ruby Mountains.

Comments: *Polygonum* means "many knees" in reference to the swollen nodes of some species. *Bistortoides* means "resembling *Bistorta*," a closely related genus in the Buckwheat Family. Also called Dirty Socks.

ALPINE KNOTWEED
Polygonum phytolaccifolium
Buckwheat Family (Polygonaceae)

Description: For having such tiny (⅛–¼") flowers, Alpine Knotweed is a surprisingly large and showy plant. It grows up to 8' tall, and its stout stem bears elongated panicles of up to 1' of the creamy, white flowers. It often grows in large clusters near lakes or streams, where it can add quite a mass of white to what is likely to be a multihued garden of many robust plants. Alpine Knotweed is by far the tallest of the more than 20 *Polygonum* species in the Great Basin. Befitting a large plant growing in damp or wet areas, its leaves are large (4–8" long and about 2" wide) and showy. As with all Buckwheat Family members, there are no true petals; in this species the perianth consists of 5 petal-like sepals.

Flowering Season: June–August.

Habitat/Range: Moist meadows, talus slopes in the montane, 7,000–10,000', in eastern Nevada, e.g., Ruby Mountains.

Comments: *Polygonum (P. bistortoides). Phytolaccifolium* means "waxy leaf." Also called Mountain Lace.

PYGMY LEWISIA
Lewisia pygmaea
Purslane Family (Portulacaceae)

Description: Pygmy Lewisia is one of those plants that is almost as interesting and beautiful without its blooms as with them. Its tight rosette of narrow, overlapping, fleshy, up-curving leaves looks kind of like a sea anemone transported to the rocky terrain near and above timberline. Then add the wonderful flowers, and you really have a treat! Set in among the leaves are very short (1–2"), radiating stems, each bearing only 1 small flower with 6–9 white or pink, translucent petals. Look carefully at the calyx—it is a beautiful deep maroon color with jagged edges.

Flowering Season: July–September.

Habitat/Range: Rocky flats and ridges in seep areas (often near snow melt) in the montane and the alpine, 8,000–14,000', throughout the Great Basin, e.g., Wassuk Range, Deep Creek Mountains.

Comments: Meriwether Lewis was coleader of the famous Lewis and Clark Expedition. *Pygmaea* means "dwarfed."

BITTERROOT
Lewisia rediviva
Purslane Family (Portulacaceae)

Description: Although widespread through the mountains of the American West, it is always a joy and a bit of a surprise to come across Bitterroot, for its spectacular flowers are 2–3" across and often occur in large numbers on barren rocky flats or on dry sandy patches interspersed with sagebrush. The color of the numerous (10–19) petals varies from white to pale or intense pink. The 30–50 stamens are tipped with delicate, pink, arrowshaped anthers and surround a central cluster of 6–8 creamy, wormlike stigmas. Unlike most members of the Purslane Family, which have only 2 green sepals, Bitterroot has 6–8 petal-like sepals. These gorgeous flowers close at night, opening again by midmorning (on sunny days).

Flowering Season: May–July.

Habitat/Range: Gravelly or rocky slopes, flats, and ridges in the sagebrush steppe and the montane, to 10,000', throughout the Great Basin, e.g., Peavine Mountain, Steens Mountain.

Comments: *Lewisia (L. pygmaea). Rediviva* means "brought to life," perhaps in reference to its medicinal qualities or perhaps to the reviving of the original, dried specimen from the Lewis Herbarium (it was later successfully grown in Pennsylvania).

TOAD LILY
Montia chamissoi
Purslane Family (Portulacaceae)

Description: On wet, springy, grassy banks of creeks and seeps and in wet, grassy meadows, you will often find masses of Toad Lily, the shiny white (sometimes pale pink), ¼–½" flowers sprinkled atop a thick mat of small, lush green, egg-shaped leaves. The glistening white, 5-petaled flowers have a yellow-green eye at their center from which project the delicate, white filaments with their tiny pink anthers. As with most members of the Purslane Family, the petals are cupped by 2 fleshy sepals. The mat of flowers and leaves is the result of the stems running along the ground and rooting and sprouting every so often. Because of these runners, you are very unlikely to ever find a single Toad Lily flower by itself or even with only a few others.

Flowering Season: June–August.

Habitat/Range: Wet meadows, streambanks, seeps in the sagebrush steppe and the montane, 6,500–10,000', throughout the Great Basin, e.g., Peavine Mountain, Charles Sheldon National Wildlife Refuge.

Comments: Giuseppe Montia was an 18th-century Italian botanist. Chamissoi *(Camissonia claviformis)*.

MARSH MARIGOLD
Caltha leptosepala
Buttercup Family (Ranunculaceae)

Description: Marsh Marigold has a special place in the heart of most wildflower lovers, for it is one of the first spring bloomers (often with buttercups), decorating mountain streambanks and boggy patches of ground just free from snow with their large, cheery, white blossoms. The 3–15" plants have 1 or a few leafless stems, each of which has a solitary ½–1½" flower perched at its tip. The flower consists of 5–11, bright white, tongue-shaped, petal-like sepals radiating out from a cluster of many yellow reproductive parts. The lush, broad (to 3"), kidney-shaped, basal leaves are each at the end of a petiole that can be up to 10" long. In summer, when most other plants are blooming, all that will be left of Marsh Marigold blooms will be a dense, thimblelike cluster of beaked, yellowish green fruits.

Flowering Season: May–July.

Habitat/Range: Seeps, streambanks, marshy meadows in the montane, 6,000–10,000', throughout the Great Basin, e.g., Ruby Mountains.

Comments: *Caltha* means "bowl shaped" in reference to the flowers. *Leptosepala* means "slender sepals."

AQUATIC BUTTERCUP
Ranunculus aquatilis
Buttercup Family (Ranunculaceae)

Description: When you think of a buttercup, you probably think of some delightfully bright yellow flower growing in a damp, grassy meadow or along a creek. Aquatic Buttercup would probably be a surprise, then, for its delicate, ¼–½" flowers have bright white petals and the plant, as its name indicates, grows in ponds, marshes, and creeks. The stems, submerged or floating, are much-branched, forming a complex network. The threadlike leaves are usually submerged just below the surface, so the branches and leaves together can form quite a thick mat, clogging the waters. The graceful flowers usually rise several inches above the surface on long, slender pedicels. Many of the flowers will have 5 petals, but they can range from 4–10.

Flowering Season: June–August.

Habitat/Range: Ponds, ditches, creeks in the sagebrush steppe, to 6,500', throughout the Great Basin, e.g., Charles Sheldon National Wildlife Refuge.

Comments: *Ranunculus (R. alismifolius). Aquatilis* means "aquatic."

TOBACCO BRUSH
Ceanothus velutinus
Buckthorn Family (Rhamnaceae)

Description: Dry, hot slopes in the Great Basin's sagebrush steppe and montane zones are often covered with "chapparal" vegetation—evergreen shrubs that depend on fire to survive and reproduce. Fire allows the seeds to germinate and burns out competitors (whereas the chapparal plants have root crowns that allow them to resprout quickly after the above-ground parts are burned). Various species of *Ceanothus* and *Arctostaphlos* (*A. nevadensis* and *A. patula*) are the main components of this chapparal vegetation. Tobacco Brush is a common member of this community, creating almost impenetrable thickets, especially on south-facing slopes and especially where fire or logging has created treeless openings. This 2–5' shrub bears broad, 1–3", oval leaves that are shiny on the upper surface and velvety on the undersurface. They contain a highly flammable oil that aids fire and that exudes a wonderful, spicy, cinnamon-like fragrance, especially on sunny days. The tiny (⅛–¼"), 5-petaled, white flowers form dense, terminal clusters.

Flowering Season: June–July.

Habitat/Range: Dry, open slopes in the sagebrush steppe and the montane, 5,000–11,000', throughout the Great Basin, e.g., Steens Mountain, Ruby Mountains.

Comments: *Ceanothus* was an ancient Greek name for "thorny plant" in reference to the thorns on many *Ceanothus* species (though not *C. velutinus*). *Velutinus* means "velvety" in reference to the undersides of the leaves.

UTAH SERVICEBERRY
Amelanchier utahensis
Rose Family (Rosaceae)

Description: One of the several white-flowered shrubs of the Rose Family that grows in the Great Basin, serviceberry is easily recognized by its narrow, somewhat twisted, bright white petals. Utah Serviceberry is a 3–15' shrub with somewhat rough, gray stems (reddish when young) and broad, serrated, shiny green (sometimes finely hairy) leaves. The plant is thick with both leaves and flowers that comingle in seemingly almost equal numbers. The ½–¾" flowers have 5 narrow, widely separated petals with a cluster of 15–20 stamens with white filaments and pale yellow anthers. Usually at least one or two of the petals twist a bit as they flare out of the flower tube.

Flowering Season: April–June.

Habitat/Range: Sandy or rocky slopes, canyons in the sagebrush steppe and the montane, to 10,000', throughout the Great Basin, e.g., Peavine Mountain, Deep Creek Mountains.

Comments: *Amelanchier* is derived from the French common name. *Utahensis* means "of Utah." Sometimes one variety is known as *A. pallida*.

BUSH OCEANSPRAY
Holodiscus dumosus
Rose Family (Rosaceae)

Description: In late summer when many of the mountain flowers are at least beginning to fade and wither, Bush Oceanspray comes into its own, adorning rocky slopes and rock ledges with its cheery plumes of beautiful, creamy flowers. This 1–3' shrub is thick with small, broad, serrated leaves and plumes of the ¼", 5-petaled flowers, with many, long-protruding reproductive parts that create a fuzzy, frothy look. The reddish stems of the current year contrast sharply with the gray stems of previous years.

Flowering Season: June–August.

Habitat/Range: Rocky slopes, ledges, forest openings in the montane, 5,000–11,500', throughout the Great Basin, e.g., Steens Mountain, Great Basin National Park.

Comments: *Holodiscus* means "whole disk" in reference to the unlobed disk surrounding the ovary. *Dumosus* means "shrubby." Also known as *H. microphylla*. Also called Rock-Spray.

STICKY CINQUEFOIL
Potentilla glandulosa
Rose Family (Rosaceae)

Description: Of the several cinquefoils you can find commonly in the Great Basin, Sticky Cinquefoil is one of the few with flowers that are not bright yellow. Instead, its ¼–¾" flowers are creamy white or sometimes pale yellow. The ½–2' stems bear several pinnately divided leaves with 2–4 pairs of small, opposite leaflets and one larger terminal one. Despite the common name, the leaves are only sometimes glandular-sticky, though the stems and sepals are usually so. All the leaflets are toothed. The 5 rounded petals are about the same length as the green, triangular sepals. The 25–30 stamens have small, bright yellow anthers.

Flowering Season: June–August.

Habitat/Range: Grassy meadows, forest openings in the montane, 6,500–10,000', throughout the Great Basin, e.g., Steens Mountain, Great Basin National Park.

Comments: *Potentilla* means "potent" in reference to medicinal qualities. *Glandulosa* means "glandular" in reference to the sometimes sticky stem.

BITTER CHERRY
Prunus emarginata
Rose Family (Rosaceae)

Description: Often forming difficult-to-penetrate thickets among aspens along mountain creeks, Bitter Cherry is a gray-stemmed (reddish in youth) shrub or small tree that can reach 20' tall but more often is 6–10'. Its ½–1½" oval leaves are finely toothed and grow in clusters of several in short petioles off the smooth, slender stems. The white, 5-petaled flowers also form clusters (of 3–12 flowers) on short lateral shoots. The ½" flowers have a fuzzy look to them because of the clump of over 20 long, protruding stamens. The tiny anthers are yellow. The flowers have a warm, sweet fragrance. The small, round fruits are a delicious red, but aren't quite so delicious tasting—they are pulpy and bitter.

Flowering Season: May–July.

Habitat/Range: Rocky slopes, along streams, in the sagebrush steppe and the montane, 5,000–9,000', throughout the Great Basin, e.g., Peavine Mountain, Steens Mountain.

Comments: *Prunus* is the ancient Latin name for plum. *Emarginata* means "with a shallow notch at the tip" in reference to the leaves.

WESTERN CHOKECHERRY
Prunus virginiana
Rose Family (Rosaceae)

Description: Western Chokecherry is quite similar to its fellow *Prunus* species Bitter Cherry *(P. emarginata)*—it is a shrub or small tree with clusters of ½", white, 5-petaled flowers with the fuzzy look (due to many protruding reproductive parts) typical of the Rose Family. Also, as the two common names suggest, the berries of both species have a rather similar effect on anyone who tries to eat them! However, Chokecherry is easily distinguished from Bitter Cherry primarily by its distinctive, long (2–6"), cylindrical racemes that droop off the ends of slender stems. These racemes have a delightfully tidy appearance, as the numerous (often 50 or more) flowers are tightly and evenly packed, forming a remarkably smooth-edged cylinder—very much like a trimmed hedge. The broad leaves are shiny green and smooth edged.

Flowering Season: May–July.

Habitat/Range: Streambanks, canyon bottoms, along roads in the sagebrush steppe and the montane, 4,800–10,000', throughout the Great Basin, e.g., Charles Sheldon National Wildlife Refuge.

Comments: *Prunus (P. emarginata). Virginiana* means "of Virginia."

CLIFF ROSE
Purshia stansburiana
Rose Family (Rosaceae)

Description: Imagine a 10' tall shrub so heavy with flowers that you can hardly see the stems or even the leaves! Cliff Rose can be so densely covered with its ½–1", creamy white or pale yellow, 5-petaled flowers that it seems to be just a wall of blossoms. And what wonderful blossoms they are! As with most *Purshia* species, the flowers are deliciously fragrant; as with all members of the Rose Family, they have masses of reproductive parts—in this case a warm yellow color. The styles elongate into long, feathery, reddish strands that extend dramatically beyond the petals. A bush thick with blossoms and fruits is a sight and fragrance not soon to be forgotten!

Flowering Season: May–August.

Habitat/Range: Dry slopes, canyons, washes in the desert shrub and the sagebrush steppe, to 9,000', throughout the Great Basin except in the extreme north, e.g., White Mountains, Great Basin National Park.

Comments: Frederick Pursh was a German-born, 19th-century botanical explorer. Captain Howard Stansbury led a U.S. government survey of the Great Salt Lake in 1850. Formerly known as *Cowania mexicana*.

NORTHERN BEDSTRAW
Galium boreale
Bedstraw Family (Rubiaceae)

Description: Bedstraw flowers are usually very small and an inconspicuous greenish white, so the genus is probably most easily identified by its distinctive whorls of 4 or more narrow leaves and its 4-angled stems. Northern Bedstraw is typical of the genus with its square, 1–2' stem along which are spaced numerous whorls of 4 narrow leaves; however, the leaves are unusual in being rather leathery and in having 2 or 3 pronounced veins. The flowers of this species are also unusual for the genus, for they are bright white and occur in a showy, much-branched, much-flowered inflorescence. As with most *Galium* species, the flowers of Northern Bedstraw usually have 4 petals, but not infrequently have 5.

Flowering Season: May–August.

Habitat/Range: Damp meadows, forest openings in the montane, to 9,000', in eastern Nevada, southern Oregon, e.g., Ruby Mountains.

Comments: *Galium* means "milk" in reference to the use of some species in curdling. *Boreale* means "northern."

BASTARD TOADFLAX
Comandra umbellata
Sandalwood Family (Santalaceae)

Description: Although this 4–12" plant does have green leaves, it is a root parasite (maybe this has something to do with the epithet in the common name!), frequently feeding on sagebrush and pine trees. Its ½–1½", linear, pointed, gray-green leaves are thick and are glabrous or covered with a powdery film. The ¼–½" star-shaped flowers have 4–6 (usually 5) pointed, white, petal-like sepals (there are no true petals). The fruits are ¼–½", rather dry, bluish (purplish or brown), round berries. The plant serves as an alternate host for the common comandra blister rust, which can be very destructive to pine trees.

Flowering Season: April–July.

Habitat/Range: Dry, sandy places in the sagebrush steppe and the montane, to 10,000', in central and eastern Nevada, western Utah, southern Oregon, e.g., Steens Mountain, Great Basin National Park.

Comments: *Comandra* means "hair man" in reference to the tuft of hair at the base of each stamen. *Umbellata* refers to "umbel."

247

ROUND-LEAF ALUMROOT
Heuchera cylindrica
Saxifrage Family (Saxifragaceae)

Description: It's a delight to come across Round-Leaf Alumroot decorating a rock ledge or talus slope with its lush leaves and perky spikes of flowers. The rather fleshy, deep green, lobed leaves usually form mats that follow the contours of the ground. Above these leaves rise several ½–2' leafless stems bearing densely flowered spikes of small, cuplike, white (often pinkish) flowers. The small "cups" are formed by 5 petal-like sepals; there are no true petals. The stamens are shorter than the sepals, so are contained within the "cups."

Flowering Season: May–September.

Habitat/Range: Rock crevices, ledges, talus slopes in the montane, 6,000–10,000', in northern and eastern Nevada, southern Oregon, e.g., Steens Mountain, Ruby Mountains.

Comments: *Heuchera (H. rubescens). Cylindrica* means "cylindrical" in reference to the spikes of flowers. Also called Mat Alumroot.

PINK ALUMROOT
Heuchera rubescens
Saxifrage Family (Saxifragaceae)

Description: Pink Alumroot is in many ways a typical member of the Saxifrage Family with its 1–2", round, scalloped, basal leaves, its leafless stems, and its small (½"), delicate, white flowers. It is, however, even wispier than most of its kin, its slender, 6–12" stems dancing in the slightest breeze, taking the clusters of tiny flowers on a wild ride. The plants usually grow in dense masses on rock ledges and in crevices, so when they start shaking in the wind, it may seem like the whole rock face is moving. Although the 5 petals are bright white, the sepals are pink or rose, so the overall impression of the flowers is pink—clouds of shimmering pink.

Flowering Season: June–August.

Habitat/Range: Rock ledges, crevices in rock cliffs in the montane, to 11,000', throughout the Great Basin, e.g., White Mountains, Great Basin National Park.

Comments: Johann von Heucher was an 18th-century German professor of medicine. *Rubescens* means "becoming red."

SLENDER WOODLAND STAR
Lithophragma tenellum
Saxifrage Family (Saxifragaceae)

Description: Woodland Star is a wonderful name for this plant, for the 5 petals of the ½" white flowers are each delicately palmately lobed into 5–7 parts, creating a flower with many narrow, radiating "rays." And since the racemes of Slender Woodland Star have 3–12 flowers, a single plant can seem like a miniconstellation of stars! The leaves are glandular-hairy (either sparsely or densely so) and are, as with all *Lithophragma* species, deeply palmately lobed. Unlike some species', the leaf axils of Slender Woodland Star do not have bulbils—the small, spherical reproductive structures that fall to the ground and sprout.

Flowering Season: April–August.

Habitat/Range: Dry scrub, openings in the sagebrush steppe and the montane, to 10,500', throughout the Great Basin, e.g., Steens Mountain, Great Basin National Park.

Comments: *Lithophragma* means "rock hedge" in reference to the rocky habitats of many species. *Tenellum* means "delicate."

PEAK SAXIFRAGE
Saxifraga nidifica
Saxifrage Family (Saxifragaceae)

Description: Peak Saxifrage is very much like many other *Saxifraga* species with slender, branching, slightly glandular stems, basal leaves, and tiny, white flowers. The 8–16" stem rises above broad, deltoid leaves that are flat on the ground and, unlike those of many other saxifrages, are smooth (not toothed) on the edges. The branching inflorescence has up to 75 flowers that occur in numerous many-flowered clusters. As with all the species of this genus, the split ovary swells into two arching beaks in fruit. The 10 stamens radiate out over and between the 5 petals, creating a bit of a fuzzy look.

Flowering Season: May–July.

Habitat/Range: Streambanks, seep areas in rocky places in the montane and the alpine, to 11,000', in northeastern and eastern Nevada, southern Oregon, e.g., Santa Rosa Range, Steens Mountain.

Comments: *Saxifraga (S. oregana). Nidifica* means "of a nest."

249

BROOK SAXIFRAGE
Saxifraga odontoloma
Saxifrage Family (Saxifragaceae)

Description: Although the flowers of Brook Saxifrage are very similar to those of Bog Saxifrage *(S. oregana)* and are typical of all *Saxifraga* species—small, white, 5-petaled with a 2-beaked pistil and 10 reddish anthers—Brook Saxifrage creates an impression almost diametrically opposed to that of Bog Saxifrage. Whereas the thick, fleshy, unbranched stems with the densely flowered racemes of Bog Saxifrage give it a solid, almost chunky appearance, the slender, ½–2', branching stems with the loose, open panicles of flowers of Brook Saxifrage give it a delicate, almost wispy appearance. Its basal leaves are round or kidney shaped and are beautifully scalloped. The 5 separate petals are roundish, their bright white color providing a wonderful background for the reddish anthers and the red styles. Often when you find this plant along a fast-moving creek, the breeze initiated by the rushing water will be enough to set the flowers dancing on their slender pedicels.

Flowering Season: May–September.

Habitat/Range: Streambanks, wet meadows in the montane, 5,500–10,000', throughout the Great Basin, e.g., Ruby Mountains, Deep Creek Mountains.

Comments: *Saxifraga (S. oregana). Odontoloma* means "toothed" in reference to the leaves.

BOG SAXIFRAGE
Saxifraga oregana
Saxifrage Family (Saxifragaceae)

Description: The delicate, ¼" flowers of Bog Saxifrage look almost out of place branching off the thick, fleshy, leafless stalk. These glandular-sticky stalks can reach more than 3' tall and frequently create vast "forests" in a bog or marshy meadow. The 3–10" basal, ovate leaves are smooth edged or have fine serrations. Despite their small flowers, Bog Saxifrage plants are very showy in bloom and in seed. In bloom the 5 widely spaced, bright white petals radiate out of the green hypanthium (central disk). The 10 filaments with their orange or red anthers also radiate from the periphery of the disk, 5 of them positioned over a petal, while the other 5 lie between petals. The green pistil is obviously 2-beaked. In seed the beaks become even more prominent, turning to a deep red-purple.

Flowering Season: April–August.

Habitat/Range: Wet meadows, bogs, streambanks in the montane, 6,000–9,000', in eastern California, northwestern and western Nevada, western Utah, e.g., Sweetwater Mountains, Pine Forest Range.

Comments: *Saxifraga* means "stone breaker" in reference to the rocky habitat of some species and probably also to the historical use of some species to dissolve gallstones. *Oregana* means "of Oregon."

HOT-ROCK PENSTEMON
Penstemon deustus
Snapdragon Family (Scrophulariaceae)

Description: There are scores and scores of *Penstemon* species that occur in the Great Basin, most of which are some shade of red, pink, purple, or blue. We are blessed to have so many species, for these long-tubular flowers are some of the most delightful and colorful members of the Western flora. Hot-Rock Penstemon is a bit of a rarity for a Great Basin penstemon, for it is none of the usual colors. Instead, its rather small (½–¾") trumpetlike flowers are a creamy white with brownish or red-purple nectar guidelines inside the throat. Also unusual is the upper lip of the tube (the upper 2 petals), which is much shorter than the lower lip (the lower 3 petals) and often appears to be shriveled or burnt (brown). The 4–16" stem, the toothed oval or spatula-shaped leaves, and the sepals are usually glandular and sticky to the touch.

Flowering Season: May–July.

Habitat/Range: Dry, rocky slopes in the sagebrush steppe and the montane, to 10,000', throughout the Great Basin, e.g., Steens Mountain, Toiyabe Range.

Comments: *Penstemon* means "5 stamen" in reference to the infertile 5th stamen (i.e., without anther). *Deustus* means "burnt" in reference to the often shriveled upper lip of the flower.

DWARF CHAMAESARACHA
Chamaesaracha nana
Nightshade Family (Solanaceae)

Description: Dwarf Chamaesaracha looks a bit like an extremely miniaturized version of Sacred Datura *(Datura wrightii).* In both plants, white flowers with 5 fused petals rest on a bed of broad, more-or-less triangular leaves. However, though both these plants share this Nightshade (or Potato) Family look, they are also easily distinguished. While datura is a 1–3' plant with huge, trumpetlike flowers, chamaesaracha is a ground-hugging plant with a stem that rarely exceeds 8" tall and flowers that are 1–1½" saucers or shallow bowls, which are yellowish green at their center. The flowers of chamaesaracha occur at the ends of ½–1" pedicels that branch out of the leaf axils, so sometimes the flowers are partly obscured by the leaves.

Flowering Season: May–July.

Habitat/Range: Sandy or rocky places, openings in the sagebrush steppe and montane, 6,000–9,000', in northwestern Nevada, e.g., Charles Sheldon National Wildlife Refuge.

Comments: *Chamae* means "on the ground" in reference to its ground-hugging growth form. *Saracha* is another genus in the Nightshade Family named after Isidore Saracha, a Spanish monk. *Nana* means "dwarf." Sometimes known as *Leucophysalis nana.*

SACRED DATURA
Datura wrightii
Nightshade Family (Solanaceae)

Description: Sacred Datura is an intriguing and even astonishing plant. Its 5-petaled, funnel-shaped flowers are enormous for wildflowers (up to 8" long and as much as 4" across), and their bright white corolla contrasts dramatically with the plant's large (to 10"), egg-shaped or triangular, dark green leaves. Before the flowers open, they are long, narrow, usually purplish-tinged torpedoes. To see one of these 1–3' plants, thick with unopened and opened flowers against their background of dark green leaves, is a stunning and magical sight. It probably won't surprise you to learn that the plant has numerous rather romantic common names (see the Comment section). Most of these refer not only to the amazing flowers but also to the plant's toxic (sometimes hallucinogenic) properties, which were used in Native American rituals (under very controlled and prescribed circumstances).

Flowering Season: April–August.

Habitat/Range: Sandy flats, washes, disturbed places in the desert shrub and the sagebrush steppe, to 5,000', in central Nevada, e.g., around Fallon. This species occurs mostly in the Mojave Desert.

Comments: *Datura* is the ancient Hindu name. Charles Wright was a 19th-century Texas plant collector. Also called Jimson-Weed, Thorn-Apple, Moon Flower, and Angel's Trumpet.

WHITE PLECTRITIS
Plectritis macrocera
Valerian Family (Valerianaceae)

Description: Although the clustered flowers of White Plectritis are very small, they have a distinctive look to them that just cries out "plectritis!" Only after examining one of these tiny white (or pale pink) flowers carefully will you discover what this identifying feature is—its spurred flower tube. Even with a cursory glance at this plant, you might suspect the Valerian Family, however, for the leaves occur in a few opposite pairs and the flowers create dense clusters with a decidedly fuzzy look due to the slender, long-protruding reproductive parts. White Plectritis has only 3 stamens. The plant ranges from only a few inches to 2' tall.

Flowering Season: April–May.

Habitat/Range: Streambanks, moist openings in the sagebrush steppe, to 6,000', throughout the Great Basin, e.g., Carson Valley, Soldier Meadow.

Comments: *Plectritis* means "spurred" in reference to the base of the flower tube. *Macrocera* means "long horned" also in reference to this spur. Also called White Corn Salad.

MACLOSKEY'S VIOLET
Viola macloskeyi
Violet Family (Violaceae)

Description: Though Macloskey's Violet rises 1–5" above the ground on what appears to be a leafless stem, technically the plant is stemless as the flower hangs from the tip of an arching sprout from an underground runner (i.e., rhizome). This rhizome typically bears many sprouts, so when you find one of these lovely, white flowers, you will usually find many. Often you will discover patches of grassy meadows or muddy depressions (that once were shallow ponds) liberally sprinkled with these sparkling beauties. Though not violet or blue or purple, the ¾–1¼" flowers of Macloskey's Violet are striking with their 5 bright white petals, the lower 3 of which have distinctive purple veins. The lush, smooth, 1–2½", deep green leaves are round or heart shaped.

Flowering Season: June–August.

Habitat/Range: Wet meadows, streambanks, bogs, muddy depressions in the montane, 6,000–10,000', in eastern Nevada, e.g., Ruby Mountains.

Comments: *Viola* is the ancient Latin name. George Macloskey was a natural history professor at Princeton.

GREEN AND BROWN FLOWERS

This section includes flowers that are predominantly brown, green, or gray. Some flowers included here also tend toward yellow, lavender, or pale purple. Check those sections if you don't find what you are looking for here.

THICK-STEM WILD CABBAGE
Caulanthus crassicaulis
Mustard Family (Brassicaceae)

Description: Probably the most conspicuous part of this strange plant is its 1–3', inflated, pale green, tapering, candlelike stem. Most of the leaves are in a basal rosette and are pinnately lobed or cut somewhat like dandelion leaves. With only a few, small stem leaves, most of this remarkable stem is open for the ½–¾", brownish or purple, 4-petaled flowers. The fruits are much more attention grabbing than the flowers, becoming 2–5", erect or ascending, cylindrical pods.

Flowering Season: May–June.

Habitat/Range: Sandy or gravelly flats and slopes in the sagebrush steppe and the montane, 5,000–8,000', throughout the Great Basin, e.g. Steens Mountain, Great Basin National Park.

Comments: *Caulanthus* means "stem flower" from the use of some species as cauliflower-like vegetables. *Crassicaulis* means "thick stemmed."

HEART-LEAF TWISTFLOWER
Streptanthus cordatus
Mustard Family (Brassicaceae)

Description: Bearing some resemblance to its fellow Mustard Family member Thick-Stem Wild Cabbage *(Caulanthus crassicaulis)* with its tall (to 3½'), stout, pale green, smooth stem and its brown-purple, 4-petaled flowers, Heart-Leaf Twistflower is nonetheless easily distinguished from this *Caulanthus* species by its leaves. As the species and common names suggest, the leaves of Heart-Leaf Twistflower are broad and somewhat heart shaped. The leaves are mostly basal, but there are some stem leaves, which clasp or even completely surround the stem. The slender, mostly straight, 2–4" seedpods are erect or ascending. The twisting petals flare out of a vaselike, brown-purple calyx.

Flowering Season: May–June.

Habitat/Range: Dry, stony or gravelly slopes in the sagebrush steppe and the montane, 5,000–10,000', throughout the Great Basin, e.g. Peavine Mountain, Great Basin National Park.

Comments: *Streptanthus* means "twisted flower." *Cordatus* means "heart shaped" in reference to the leaves.

PURPLE FRITILLARY

Fritillaria atropurpurea
Lily Family (Liliaceae)

Description: Typical of fritillaries, the flowers of purple fritillary are fascinating for their color and design. From the branching, ½–2' stems nod a few or several ½–¾", starlike (six-pointed) flowers. As with most members of the Lily Family, all 6 perianth parts (3 sepals and 3 petals) are alike and so are called tepals. In Purple Fritillary the tepals are narrow and pointed and purplish brown with greenish yellow or white mottling. The large, thick anthers and the 3-branched stigma are yellowish. These multicolored flowers hang nearly upside down and can be flat or somewhat curled up. The lower stem is leafless, while the upper stem has several whorls or near-whorls of long, blue-green, grasslike leaves and/or several alternating individual leaves. Despite the unusually colored flowers, Purple Fritillary is sometimes surprisingly difficult to see, effectively camouflaged among its sagebrush neighbors.

Flowering Season: April–July.

Habitat/Range: Dry, gravelly or grassy slopes and flats, canyons in the sagebrush steppe and the montane, 5,500–9,000', throughout the Great Basin, e.g. Charles Sheldon National Wildlife Refuge.

Comments: *Fritillaria* means "dice box" of uncertain significance. *Atropurpurea* means "dark purple" in reference to some of the coloration of the tepals.

GREEN BOG ORCHID
Platanthera sparsiflora
Orchid Family (Orchidaceae)

Description: Although Green Bog Orchid can grow to 2' tall, it is often overlooked among its showier, wet-meadow neighbors. In an environment dominated by green (thick grass, stout plant stems, and broad, lush leaves) and by large, brightly colored flowers, the ½", greenish flowers of Bog Orchid can easily be lost. However, what these flowers may lack in drama and showiness, they make up for in delicacy and intricacy, so you might want to take the time to seek them out. The 10–30 flowers are distributed loosely along the 6–16" raceme. As in almost all orchids, the flowers consist of 3 sepals and 3 petals, all but one of which are quite similar. In Green Bog Orchid the upper 2 petals and the upper sepal form a hood that canopies the reproductive parts. The other 2 sepals form wings that extend vertically. The lower petal forms a narrow, hanging lip with a narrower, cylindrical spur hanging behind it. Whereas the similar Rein Orchid *(P. leucostachys)* has a very long spur, Green Bog Orchid has a spur that is about the same length as the lip. The narrow, parallel-veined leaves clasp and alternate up the stem, being more profuse and much larger on the stem's lower half.

Flowering Season: June–July.

Habitat/Range: Wet meadows, bogs, streambanks, seeps in the sagebrush steppe and the montane, to 10,000', throughout the Great Basin, e.g. White Mountains, Ruby Mountains.

Comments: *Platanthera (P. leucostachys). Sparsiflora* means "few flowered." Also called Sparsely Flowered Orchid.

WESTERN PEONY
Paeonia brownii
Peony Family (Paeoniaceae)

Description: The startling, 1½–2" flowers of Western Peony are even more startling for their early appearance—it is not unusual to find peony in bloom in montane forest openings in May when most other mountain plants have only just begun to think about blooming. With its 5–10, red-maroon or brown, disklike flowers hanging parallel to the ground (often only a few inches above it), these amazing flowers look a bit like flying saucers coming in for a landing. The dense clump of bright yellow stamens could be the retrorockets fired up to slow the descent. Within only a couple weeks, the petals and stamens will fall off as the 2–5 pistils swell into astonishing 2–4", sausagelike fruits, the weight of which pull the entire plant almost to the ground. The large, fleshy leaves are deeply lobed.

Flowering Season: May–June.

Habitat/Range: Dry flats and slopes, openings in the sagebrush steppe and the montane, 5,000–8,000', throughout the Great Basin, e.g. Peavine Mountain, Toiyabe Range.

Comments: Paeon was the physician to the gods in Greek mythology. Robert Brown was a 19th-century keeper of botany at the British Museum.

FENDLER'S MEADOW-RUE
Thalictrum fendleri
Buttercup Family (Ranunculaceae)

Description: Especially for its height (up to 5'), Fendler's Meadow-Rue is a remarkably delicate and fragile-looking plant with thin, deeply divided and scalloped leaves and racemes of tiny, greenish white flowers. You won't have to look too closely to realize that this Meadow-Rue has separate male and female plants, for some plants have delicately dangling, tassel-like flowers, while others have erect, somewhat bristly looking flowers. The former, the male, have scores of brownish yellow stamens hanging from a tiny sepal. In the latter, the female, the white, erect structures are the pistils. Because neither type of plant has petals, you would be correct to suspect that Fendler's Meadow-Rue is wind pollinated.

Flowering Season: June–August.

Habitat/Range: Damp, grassy openings in the sagebrush steppe and the montane, to 10,000', throughout the Great Basin, e.g. Steens Mountain, Great Basin National Park.

Comments: *Thalictrum* means "plant with divided leaves." Augustus Fendler was a 19th-century American plant collector.

STINGING NETTLE
Urtica dioica
Nettle Family (Urticaceae)

Description: Stinging Nettle does just that, so it's an important plant to be able to recognize and avoid. Its 3–7', stout stem is thick with opposite pairs of large, broad, distinctively toothed, velvety leaves. Cascading down from the leaf axils are stringy plumes of tiny, greenish white or brownish, 4-petaled or 5-petaled flowers. If you touch a leaf, the finely pointed, barbed hairs can pierce your skin and inject formic acid. You will probably be thinking of this plant and your encounter with it for several hours as the burn will take that long to subside. Unfortunately, even if you know what Stinging Nettle looks like, you may not always be able to avoid it, for it often clusters around trees, hidden among other tall plants (I speak from painful, firsthand experience).

Flowering Season: June–August.

Habitat/Range: Damp soil, around trees, roadside ditches, seeps in the sagebrush steppe and the montane, to 6,000', throughout the Great Basin, e.g. Santa Rosa Range.

Comments: *Urtica* means "to burn," the origin of which you will understand if you touch this plant. *Dioica* means "dioecious" in reference to the separate male and female plants.

GLOSSARY

anther: the pollen-producing tip of the male sex part of the flower.

axil: the angle between the leaf and the stem.

banner: the upper petals in flowers of the Pea Family.

basal leaves: leaves located at the base of a plant as opposed to up the plant stem.

biloped (or bilobed): divided into two, having two lobes.

bracts: leaf-like structures performing a different function from a leaf, such as the colorful bracts in the inflorescence of paintbrushes and owl's-clovers that attract pollinators.

calyx (calyces): collective term for the sepals.

caudex: a vertical stem at or beneath ground level.

chapparal: a plant or a community of plants comprised of evergreen shrubs that are adapted to fire, i.e., depend on fire for seed germination and plant survival.

clawed: where the limb is narrower than the tip.

corolla: collective term for the petals.

cushion plant: an herbaceous perennial plant forming a dense, rounded mass of short stems and many leaves.

cyme: a flat-topped or round-topped flower cluster in which the flowers on the inner (upper) branches bloom first.

decumbent: mostly lying flat on the ground but with tips curving up.

deltoid: triangular, often in reference to a leaf.

disk flowers: in the Composite Family, the small, tubular flowers that make up the "button" in the center of the flower head.

elliptic: in the shape of an ellipse, i.e., a flattened circle.

filament: in the male reproductive part (the stamen) the stalk that bears the anther at its tip.

flower head: a dense cluster of several flowers, often appearing to be a single blossom.

glandular: bearing glands that usually secrete a sticky liquid.

inferior ovary: an ovary situated beneath the point where the petals attach.

inflorescence: an entire cluster of flowers and associated structures such as bracts and pedicels.

involucre: a set of bracts beneath an inflorescence, as in the set of phyllaries under the flowerhead in the Composite Family.

keel: the inner two petals cradling the reproductive parts in flowers of the Pea Family, somewhat resembling the keel of a boat.

linear: often in reference to leaves, elongate and narrow with parallel sides, needle-like.

mat: a plant with densely interwoven and ground-hugging growth.

monocot: the smaller main group of flowering plants generally with flower parts in threes and parallel-veined leaves.

nectar guides: marking on the petals that are visible to pollinators and help direct then to the nectar in the corolla.

nectary: a gland that secretes nectar, usually associated with a flower.

oblanceolate: narrowly elongate with the widest portion above the middle, usually in reference to a leaf.

ovate: egg-shaped with the widest part near the base, usually referring to a leaf.

palmately compound: describes a compound structure in which the parts (often the leaflets of a leaf) radiate from a common point, rather like the fingers of a hand.

palmately lobed: similar to palmately compound except the divisions do not extend all the way to the base, so there are not separate segments; rather, there is one structure (usually a leaf) with indentations on the margin.

panicle: an inflorescence in which the pedicels are attached to a branching plant stem.

parasite: an organism that feeds on another organism for its nutrients.

pedicel: the stalk of an individual flower.

peduncle: the stalk of an entire inflorescence.

perianth: collective term for the calyx and corolla.

petiole: a leaf stalk.

phyllaries: the narrow, usually green bracts forming the cup under the flower head in the Composite Family.

pinnately compound: describes a compound structure in which the parts (often leaflets of a leaf) branch off the main axis, rather like a feather.

pinnately lobed: similar to pinnately compound, except the divisions do not extend all the way to the base, so there are not separate segments; rather, there is one structure (usually a leaf) with indentations on the margin.

pistil: the female reproductive structure consisting of ovary, style, and stigma.

prostrate: flat on the ground.

raceme: an inflorescence in which the pedicels are attached to an unbranched plant stem.

ray flowers: in the Composite Family, the wide-flaring flowers that radiate from the central "button."

reflexed: abruptly bent or curved downward or backward.

rhizome: an underground, often elongated, horizontal stem connecting numerous plant stems.

rosette: a crowded whorl of basal leaves.

saprophyte: a plant that lives on dead organic matter, neither a parasite nor a photosynthesizer.

scape: a leafless peduncle that arises from ground level.

sepal: the usually green, but sometimes showy, flower parts beneath the petals, forming the outer protective layer in the bud.

sessile: without a petiole, peduncle, pedicel, or other kind of stalk.

spike: unbranched inflorescence of sessile flowers.

stamen: the male reproductive part of the flower composed of the filament and the anther.

staminode: sterile stamen.

stigma: the pollen-receiving tip of the female reproductive part.

stipule: appendage at the base of a petiole, often leaf-like or scale-like.

style: the stalk of the female reproductive part, connecting the ovary and the stigma.

subshrub: a plant with the lower stems woody, the upper stems and twigs not woody or less so, and dying back seasonally.

succulent: fleshy and juicy.

tendril: a slender, coiling structure (usually stem, stipule, or leaf tip) by which a climbing plant becomes attached to its support.

tepal: one of the petals or sepals in flowers whose sepals look just like the petals.

twice-pinnate: usually in reference to a pinnately compound leaf in which the pinnate leaflets are further divided into smaller, pinnate leaflets.

umbel: an inflorescence in which all of the pedicels radiate from a common point on the plant stem.

vernal pool: a pool of water on a hard, impermeable floor that persists through part or all of the spring, disappearing not by drainage but by evaporation.

whorl: a group of three or more structures of the same kind (often leaves or flowers) that radiate, ring-like, from the same point on the stem.

wings: the two lateral petals in flowers of the Pea Family, usually cradling the keel.

REFERENCES

Blackwell, Laird R. *Wildflowers of the Eastern Sierra and Adjoining Mojave Desert and Great Basin,* Lone Pine Publishing, Edmonton, Alberta, Canada, 2002.

Coombes, Allen J. *Dictionary of Plant Names,* Timber Press, Portland, Oregon, 1994.

Cronquist, Arthur, Arthur Holmgren, Noel Holmgren, Pat Holmgren, and James Reveal. *Intermountain Flora: Vascular Plants of the Intermountain West,* New York Botanical Gardens, New York.

Vol. I: Geological and Botanical History, 1972.

Vol. IIIa: Subclass Rosidae (except Fabales), 1977.

Vol. IIIb: Fabales, 1989.

Vol. IV: Subclass Asteridae, 1984.

Vol. V: Asterales, 1994.

Vol. VI: The Monocotyledons, 1977.

Hart, John. *Hiking the Great Basin,* Sierra Club Books, San Francisco, 1991.

Hickman, James (ed). *The Jepson Manual: Higher Plants of California,* University of California Press, Berkeley, 1993.

Kartesz, John T. *A Flora of Nevada,* 3 volumes, PhD dissertation, 1988.

Lloyd, R. and Richard Mitchell. *A Flora of the White Mountains,* University of California Press, Berkeley, California, 1973.

Mansfield, Donald. *Flora of Steens Mountain,* Oregon State University Press, Corvallis, Oregon, 2000.

Mozingo, Hugh. *Shrubs of the Great Basin,* University of Nevada Press, Reno, Nevada, 1987.

Nachlinger, Janet, Frederick Peterson, and Margaret Williams. "Vascular Plants of Peavine Mountain." *Mentzelia: the Journal of the Nevada Native Plant Society, 6,* part 2, 1992.

Shaw, Richard. *Annotated Checklists of the Vascular Plants of Great Basin National Park and Adjacent Snake Range,* unpublished.

Stearn, William. *Botanical Latin,* Fitzhenry and Whiteside, Toronto, Ontario, Canada, 1983.

Taylor, Ronald. *Sagebrush Country: a Wildflower Sanctuary,* Mountain Press, Missoula, Montana, 1992.

Trimble, Stephen. *The Sagebrush Ocean,* University of Nevada Press, Reno, Nevada, 1989.

Welsh, S., N. Atwood, L. Higgins, and S. Goodrich. *A Utah Flora,* Great Basin Naturalist Memoirs, #9, Brigham Young University Press, Provo, Utah, 1987.

PLANTS OF STEENS MOUNTAIN (NORTHERN GREAT BASIN)

Achillea millefolium
Aconitum columbianum
Agastache urticifolia
Ageratina occidentalis
Agoseris aurantiaca
Agoseris glauca
Allium bisceptrum
Allium campanulatum
Allium parvum
Amelanchier utahensis
Antennaria media
Antennaria rosea
Apocynum androsaemifolium
Aquilegia formosa
Arabis hoelbellii
Arabis sparsiflora
Arenaria kingii
Argemone munita
Arnica longifolia
Artemisia spinescens
Artemisia tridentata
Asclepias speciosa
Aster scopulorum
Astragalus lentiginosus
Astragalus malacus
Astragalus newberryi
Astragalus purshii
Astragalus whitneyi
Balsamorhiza hookeri
Balsamorhiza sagittata
Barbarea orthoceras
Berberis aquifolium
Blepharipappus scaber
Brickelia grandiflora

Calochortus bruneaunis
Calochortus eurycarpus
Caltha leptosepala
Calyptridium umbellatum
Camassia quamash
Camissonia claviformis
Camissonia pusilla
Camissonia subacaulis
Camissonia tanacetifolia
Cardaria pubescens
Castilleja applegatei
Castilleja linariifolia
Castilleja miniata
Caulanthus crassicaulis
Ceanothus velutinus
Chaenactis douglasii
Chrysothamnus nauseosus
Cicorium intybus
Cicuta douglasii
Cirsium peckii
Cirsium scariosum
Cirsium vulgare
Cleome lutea
Cleome platycarpa
Collinsia parviflora
Collomia grandiflora
Comandra umbellata
Conium maculatum
Convuvulus arvensis
Cornus sericea
Crepis acuminata
Crepis occidentalis
Cryptantha humilis
Cymopterus terebinthus

Delphinium andersonii
Dicentra uniflora
Downingia bacigalupii
Draba verna
Epilobium angustifolium
Epilobium glaberrimum
Epilobium obcordatum
Eriastrum sparsiflorum
Ericameria discoidea
Ericameria suffruticosus
Erigeron aphaenactis
Erigeron compositus
Erigeron filifolius
Erigeron peregrinus
Eriogonum caespitosum
Eriogonum ochrocephalum
Eriogonum strictum
Eriogonum ovalifolium
Eriogonum umbellatum
Eriophyllum lanatum
Erodium cicutarium
Erysimum capitatum
Fritillaria atropurpurea
Galium boreale
Gayophytum diffusum
Geum macrophyllum
Geum triflorum
Grayia spinosa
Grindelia squarrosa
Hackelia micrantha
Hackelia patens
Helianthus annuus
Helianthus cusickii
Heliotropium curassavicum

Heracleum lanatum
Hesperochiron californica
Hesperochrion pumilis
Heuchera cylindrica
Heuchera rubescens
Holodiscus dumosus
Ipomopsis aggregata
Ipomopsis congesta
Iris missouriensis
Ivesia gordonii
Kalmia polifolia
Layia glandulosa
Lepidium perfoliatum
Leptodactylon pungens
Lewisia pygmaea
Lewisa rediviva
Ligusticum grayi
Linanthrastum nuttallii
Linum lewisii
Lithophragma tenellum
Lomatium dissectum
Lomatium nevadense
Lonicera involucrata
Lupinus arbustus
Lupinus argenteus
Lupinus lepidus
Lupinus nevadensis
Lupinus polyphyllus
Machaerantha canescens
Melilotus alba
Melilotus officinale
Mentzelia albicaulis
Mentzelia laevicaulis
Mertensia ciliata
Mertensia oblongifolia
Microsteris gracilis
Mimulus guttatus
Mimulus lewisii
Mimulus nanus

Mimulus primuloides
Mimulus tilingii
Monardella odoratissima
Montia chamissoi
Nama aretiodes
Navarettia breweri
Nuphar lutea
Oenothera caespitosa
Oenothera deltoides
Oenothera elata
Orobanche fasciculata
Orobanche uniflora
Orthocarpus cuspidatus
Orthocarpus hispidus
Osmorhiza occidentalis
Oxyria digyna
Paeonia brownii
Pedicularis attolens
Pedicularis groenlandica
Penstemon davidsonii
Penstemon deustus
Penstemon procerus
Penstemon rydbergii
Penstemon speciosus
Perideridia bolanderi
Phacelia adenophora
Phacelia hastata
Phacelia heterophylla
Phacelia humilis
Phacelia linearis
Phacelia sericea
Phlox hoodii
Phlox longifolia
Phoenicaulis cheiranthoides
Platanthera leucostachys
Plectritis macrocera
Polemonium occidentale
Polemonium pulcherrimum
Polemonium viscosum

Polygonum bistortoides
Porterella carnosula
Potentilla diversifolia
Potentilla fruticosa
Potentilla glandulosa
Potentilla gracilis
Prunus emarginata
Prunus virginiana
Pseudostellaria jamesiana
Purshia tridentata
Ranunculus alismifolius
Ranunculus aquatilis
Ranunculus eschscholtzia
Ribes cereum
Rorippa nasturtium-aquaticum
Rosa woodsii
Salsola tragus
Salvia dorrii
Sambucus mexicana
Sambucus racemosa
Saxifraga nidifica
Saxifraga odontaloma
Saxifraga oregana
Sedum debile
Sedum lanceolatum
Sedum rosea
Senecio fremontii
Senecio integerrimus
Senecio triangularis
Sidalcea oregana
Silene douglasii
Sisymbrium altissimum
Sisyrinchium douglasii
Sisyrinchium idahoense
Smilacina stellata
Solidago canadensis
Solidago missouriensis
Sphaeralcea grossulariifolia
Sphenosciadium capitellatum

Spiranthes romanzoffiana
Stanleya pinnata
Stellaria longipes
Stenotus acaulis
Stephanomeria tenuifolia
Streptanthus cordatus
Swertia radiata
Symphoricarpos rotundifolius
Taraxacum officinale
Tetrydemia glabrata

Tetrydemia spinosa
Thalictrum fendleri
Thelypodium lacinatum
Thermopsis rhombifolia
Tragapogon dubius
Triteleia hyacintha
Urtica dioica
Veratrum californicum
Verbascum thapsus
Veronica americana

Veronica serpyllifolia
Veronica wormskjoldii
Vicia americana
Viola beckwithii
Viola purpurea
Wyethia amplexicaulis
Zigadenus elegans
Zigadenus paniculatus
Zigadenus venenosus

PLANTS OF PEAVINE MOUNTAIN (WESTERN GREAT BASIN)

Achillea lanulosa
Agastache urticifolia
Ageratina occidentale
Agoseris glauca
Allium atrorubens
Allium bisceptrum
Allium campanulatum
Allium parvum
Allium validum
Antennaria rosea
Apocynum androsaemifolium
Aquilegia formosa
Arabis hoelbellii
Arabis sparsiflora
Arctostaphylos nevadensis
Arctostaphylos patula
Argemone munita
Arnica mollis
Artemisia tridentata
Asclepias speciosa
Astragalus andersonii
Astragalus malacus

Astragalus purshii
Astragalus whitneyi
Balsamorhiza hookeri
Balsamorhiza sagittata
Barbarea orthoceras
Blepharipappus scaber
Calochortus bruneaunis
Calochortus leichtlinii
Calyptridium umbellatum
Camassia quamash
Camissonia claviformis
Camissonia nevadensis
Camissonia pusilla
Camissonia subacaulis
Camissonia tanacetifolia
Cardaria pubescens
Castilleja applegatei
Castilleja chromosa
Ceanothus velutinus
Chaenactis douglasii
Chrysothamnus nauseosus
Cicuta douglasii

Cirsium occidentale
Cirsium scariosum
Cirsium vulgare
Cleome lutea
Cleome platycarpa
Collomia grandiflora
Conium maculata
Convolvulus arvensis
Crepis acuminata
Crepis occidentalis
Cymopterus terebinthinus
Delphinium andersonii
Draba verna
Epilobium glaberrimum
Erigeron aphaenactis
Erigeron filifolius
Eriogonum caespitosum
Eriogonum douglasii
Eriogonum lobbii
Eriogonum nudum
Eriogonum ochracephalum
Eriogonum ovalifolium

Eriogonum spergulinium
Eriogonum strictum
Eriogonum umbellatum
Eriophyllum lanatum
Erodium cicutarium
Erysimum captitatum
Eschscholzia californica
Fritillaria atropurpurea
Gayophytum diffusum
Geum macrophyllum
Grindelia squarrosa
Grayia spinosa
Helianthus annuus
Helianthus cusickii
Holodiscus dumosus
Iris missouriensis
Layia glandulosa
Lepidium perfoliatum
Leptodactylon pungens
Lewisia rediviva
Lilium kelleyanum
Linum lewisii
Lithophragma tenellum
Lomatium dissectum
Lomatium nevadense
Lomatium nudicaule
Lupinus argenteus
Lupinus lepidus
Lupinus malacophyllus
Lupinus nevadensis
Madia elegans
Melilotus alba
Melilotus officinale
Mentzelia albicaulis
Mentzelia laevicaulis
Microsteris gracilis
Mimulus guttatus
Mimulus mephiticus

Mimulus nanus
Mimulus primuloides
Monardella odoratissima
Montia chamissoi
Navarretia breweri
Oenothera caespitosa
Oenothera deltoides
Oenothera elata
Opuntia polyacantha
Orobanche fasciculata
Orthocarpus cuspidatus
Orthocarpus tenuis
Osmorhiza occidentalis
Paeonia brownii
Penstemon deustus
Penstemon gracilentus
Penstemon laetus
Penstemon speciosus
Perideridia bolanderi
Phacelia adenophora
Phacelia curvipes
Phacelia hastata
Phacelia heterophylla
Phacelia humilis
Phlox longifolia
Phoenicaulis cheiranthoides
Platanthera leucostachys
Plectritis macrocera
Polygonum bistortoides
Porterella carnosula
Potentilla glandulosa
Potentilla gracilis
Prunella vulgaris
Prunus andersonii
Prunus emarginata
Prunus virginiania
Pterospora andromedea
Purshia tridentata

Ranunculus alismifolius
Ribes cereum
Rorippa nasturtium-aquaticum
Rosa woodsii
Salvia dorrii
Sambucus mexicana
Scrophularia desertorum
Senecio integerrimus
Senecio multilobatus
Sidalcea glaucescens
Sidalcea oregana
Silene bernardina
Silene douglasii
Sisymbrium altissimum
Sisyrinchium idahoense
Smilacina stellata
Sphaeralcea ambigua
Stanleya pinnata
Stellaria longipes
Streptanthus cordatus
Taraxacum officinale
Tetrydemia glabrata
Thalictrum fendleri
Tragopogon dubius
Trifolium andersonii
Triteleia hyacintha
Urtica dioica
Veratrum californica
Viola beckwithii
Viola purpurea
Verbascum thapsus
Veronica americana
Vicia americana
Wyethia mollis
Zigadenus paniculata
Zigadenus venenosus

PLANTS OF THE WHITE MOUNTAINS (SOUTHERN GREAT BASIN)

Achillea millefolium
Aconitum columbianum
Ageratina occidentale
Agoseris aurantiaca
Agoseris glauca
Allium atrorubens
Allium bisceptrum
Amelanchier utahensis
Angelica lineariloba
Antennaria rosea
Aquilegia formosa
Arabis hoelbellii
Arenaria kingii
Argemone munita
Arnica longifolia
Arnica mollis
Artemisia spinescens
Artemisia tridentata
Asclepias speciosa
Aster scopulorum
Astragalus lentiginosus
Astragalus malacus
Astragalus newberryi
Astragalus purshii
Astragalus whitneyi
Barbarea orthocerus
Calochortus bruneaunis
Calochortus kennedyi
Calyptridium umbellatum
Camissonia claviformis
Camissonia pusilla
Castilleja applegatei
Castilleja chromosa

Castilleja lineariifolia
Castilleja miniata
Castilleja nana
Caulanthus crassicaulis
Chaenactis douglasii
Chrysothamnus nauseosus
Cirsium scariosum
Cleome lutea
Collinsia parviflora
Convovulus arvensis
Cornus sericea
Crepis occidentalis
Echinocereus engelmannii
Epilobium angustifolium
Eriastrum sparsiflorum
Ericameria discoides
Ericameria suffruticosus
Erigeron aphaenactis
Erigeron compositus
Eriogonum caespitosum
Eriogonum latens
Eriogonum nudum
Eriogonum ovalifolium
Eriogonum spergulinum
Eriogonum umbellatum
Eriophyllum lanatum
Erodium cicutarium
Fritillaria atropurpurea
Gayophytum diffusum
Gentiana newberryi
Geum macrophyllum
Grayia spinosa
Hackelia patens

Helianthus annuus
Heliotropium curassavicum
Hesperochiron californicus
Heuchera rubescens
Holodiscus dumosus
Hulsea algida
Ipomopsis congesta
Iris missouriensis
Ivesia gordonii
Layia glandulosa
Lepidium fremontii
Leptodactylon pungens
Lewisia pygmaea
Lewisia rediviva
Linanthrastrum nuttallii
Linum lewisii
Lomatium nevadense
Lupinus argenteus
Lupinus breweri
Machaerantha canescens
Melilotus alba
Melilotus officinalis
Mentzelia albicaulis
Mentzelia congesta
Mentzelia laevicaulis
Mertensia ciliata
Mimulus bigelovii
Mimulus guttatus
Mimulus primuloides
Mimulus tilingii
Monardella odoratissima
Montia chamissoi
Nama aretiodes

Navarettia breweri
Oenothera caespitosa
Oenothera elata
Opuntia basilaris
Orobanche fasciculata
Oxyria digyna
Pedicularis attolens
Penstemon floridus
Penstemon speciosus
Phacelia curvipes
Phacelia hastata
Phlox condensata
Phlox diffusa
Phlox hoodii
Phlox stansburiana
Platanthera sparsiflora
Potentilla diversifolia
Potentilla fruticosa
Potentilla gracilis

Prunus andersonii
Prunus virginiana
Purshia stansburiana
Purshia tridentata
Raillardella argentea
Ranunculus alismaefolius
Ranunculus eschscholtzii
Ribes cereum
Rorippa nasturtium-aquaticum
Rosa woodsii
Salsola tragus
Salvia dorrii
Sambucus mexicana
Scrophularia desertortum
Sedum rosea
Senecio integerrimus
Senecio multilobatus
Silene bernardina
Sisymbrium altissima

Sisyrinchion idahoense
Smilacina stellata
Spaeralcea ambigua
Sphenosciadium capitellatum
Stanleya pinnata
Stellaria longipes
Stenotus acaulis
Streptanthus cordatus
Taraxacum officinale
Trifolium kingii
Veratrum californicum
Verbascum thapsus
Veronica americana
Veronica serpyllifolia
Vicia americana
Viola neprophylla
Zygadenus paniculatus

PLANTS OF GREAT BASIN NATIONAL PARK (EASTERN GREAT BASIN)

Achillea millefolium
Aconitum columbianum
Amelanchier utahensis
Antennaria rosea
Aquilegia formosa
Arctostaphylos patula
Arenaria kingii
Argemone munita
Artemisia tridentata
Astragalus lentiginosus
Astragalus whitneyi
Balsamorhiza hookeri

Balsamorhiza sagittata
Berberis aquifolium
Calochortus bruneaunis
Cardamine cordifolia
Castilleja chromosa
Castilleja linariifolia
Castilleja miniata
Castilleja nana
Caulanthus crassicaulis
Chaenactis douglasii
Chrysothamnus nauseosus
Cicuta douglasii

Cleome serrulata
Comandra umbellata
Cornus sericea
Crepis occidentalis
Delphinium andersonii
Dodecatheon jeffreyi
Epilobium angustifolium
Ericameria discoidea
Ericameria suffruticosus
Erigeron compositus
Erodium cicutarium
Eriogonum ovalifolium

Eriogonum umbellatum
Fritillaria atropurpurea
Geum macrophyllum
Geum rossii
Grayia spinosa
Hackelia patens
Helianthus annuus
Heuchera rubescens
Holodiscus dumosus
Ipomopsis aggregata
Ipomopsis congesta
Lepidium perfoliatum
Leptodactylon pungens
Lewisia pygmaea
Linum lewisii
Lithophragma tenellum
Lupinus argenteus
Melilotus officinale
Mentzelia albicaulis
Mentzelia laevicaulis
Mertensia oblongifolia
Microsteris gracilis
Mimulus guttatus
Mimulus lewisii
Mimulus primuloides
Monardella odoratissima
Montia chamissoi

Oenothera caespitosa
Opuntia polyacantha
Penstemon eatonii
Penstemon palmeri
Penstemon procerus
Penstemon rostriflorus
Penstemon speciosus
Phacelia hastata
Phacelia sericea
Phlox longifolia
Platanthera leucostachys
Polemonium viscosum
Polygonum bistortoides
Potentilla fruticosa
Potentilla glandulosa
Potentilla gracilis
Primula parryi
Prunus virginiana
Pseudostellaria jamesiana
Pterospora andromedea
Purshia stansburiana
Purshia tridentata
Ranunculus alismifolius
Ribes cereum
Rosa woodsii
Salvia dorrii
Sambucus mexicana

Sambucus racemosa
Saxifraga odontaloma
Sedum lanceolatum
Senecio integerrimus
Senecio multilobatus
Silene acaulis
Silene douglasii
Sisymbrium altissimum
Smilacina stellata
Solidago canadensis
Sphaeralcea grossulariifolia
Stanleya pinnata
Streptanthus cordatus
Symphoricarpos rotundifolius
Taraxacum officinale
Thalictrum fendleri
Thermopsis rhombifolia
Tragapogon dubius
Urtica dioica
Verbascum thapsus
Veronica americana
Vicia americana
Viola purpurea
Wyethia amplexicaulis
Zigadenus elegans
Zigadenus paniculatus

INDEX

ABOUT THE AUTHOR

Laird R. Blackwell, who received his Ph.D. from Stanford University in 1974, is chair of the Humanities and Social Sciences Department at Sierra Nevada College at Lake Tahoe, where he has taught psychology, literature, and wildflower field courses for more than 20 years. He has written several popular wildflower field guides: *Wildflowers of the Tahoe Sierra* (1997), *Wildflowers of the Sierra Nevada and Central Valley* (1999), *Wildflowers of Mount Rainier* (2000), and *Wildflowers of the Eastern Sierra and Adjoining Mojave Desert and Great Basin* (2002).

Laird and his wife, Melinda—a high school English and Life Skills teacher—live with their German Shepherd Elwood and two cats at about 7500' on the east side of Mount Rose, looking out over the Great Basin and its wonderful flowers.